Al Jolson

You Ain't Heard Nothin' Yet

You Ain't Heard Nothin' Yet

Also by Robert Oberfirst:

Al Jolson

You Ain't Heard Nothin' Yet

ROBERT OBERFIRST

San Diego • New York
A. S. Barnes & Company, Inc.
In London:
The Tantivy Press

Al Jolson, You Ain't Heard Nothin' Yet text copyright ©1980 by
Robert Oberfirst

A. S. Barnes and Co., Inc.

The Tantivy Press
Magdalen House
136-148 Tooley Street
London, SE1 2TT, England

First Paper Edition, 1982
Manufactured in the United States of America
For information write to A. S. Barnes and Company, Inc.,
P.O. Box 3051, San Diego, CA 92038

Library of Congress Cataloging in Publication Data

Oberfirst, Robert.
   Al Jolson, you ain't heard nothin' yet.

   Includes index.
   1. Jolson, Al, d. 1950. 2. Singers — United States — Biography. I. Title.
ML420.J7402   784'.092'4 [B] 80-16736
ISBN 0-498-02589-6

2 3 4 5 6 7 8 9   84 83 82

This book is dedicated to my brother, Thomas I. Oberfirst, a very gentle person who inspired and encouraged me and to William Morris, Jr., as a token of the author's gratitude.

CONTENTS

ACKNOWLEDGMENTS

I am indebted to William Morris, Jr., ex-president of the William Morris Agency, which represented Jolson for many years, for his careful editing of the entire manuscript and for his contribution of factual data concerning the relationship between his father, William Morris, Sr., and Al Jolson; to Maynard F. Bertolet, the country's outstanding private collector of Jolson records and memorabilia, for material in the Discography and Radiography; to the public libraries of New York, San Francisco, Philadelphia, Los Angeles, the library of the Academy of Motion Picture Arts and Sciences in Los Angeles, and the Museum of Modern Art Department of Film in New York, for making available their files for inspection; special acknowledgment and indebtedness to the late Harry Jolson for access to his private papers and writings about his brother Al Jolson which provided family source material not available elsewhere; and to many others who offered advice, suggestions, and anecdotes of their intimate dealings and personal relationships with Jolson.

R.O

FOREWORD

In the long undocumented past of the theater the words "George Spelvin" were made up to give a name in the program to an actor who was playing an additional role. The bright young bellboy in act one who was programmed under his own name, with a wig, false beard, or mustache could become the aged and infirm night watchman programmed under the name "George Spelvin" in act three, thereby not giving away the management's desire to save on the expense of another actor. It is a tradition that exists today. The name "George Spelvin" in the theater is something like that of Kilroy in the armed services.

This book of the theater has its "George Spelvin," too. In this instance it is the real and lovable Louis (Eppy) Epstein. This is how he was cast for the role: To have named everyone who had been associated with Al Jolson and to have told their relationships would have called for ten volumes. To overcome this the author has given Eppy the roles of many who were close to Al.

The complete story of Eppy's relationship with Al and how much or how little each had given and got from the other must await another telling, but in this book Eppy is to play, along with his own role of never-failing loyalty, the roles of a few—such as Billy Grady, Charles Schwartz, Lou Schreiber, William Perlberg, Morris Stoller, Abe Lastfogel, William Morris, Jr., William Murray, and John Hyde—of the many who were very much a part of Jolson's career. In these associations the indefatigable Jolson drove them at a pace beyond their endurance, but in each and every case their love for Jolie outlived their fortitude.

With the show world steadily moving to its rightful place in the social scheme, it is important that qualities of genius such as Jolson's be analyzed and appreciated. His attributes transcend all laws and possible classification of the theater as divertissement, amusement, entertainment, or worship. If we can find out what made Al Jolson tick—where sane, where not—then we may circumvent the bureaucratic patronage of the show world which is impending. This book goes a long way toward exploring all facets of his life and shows what he was really like.

The story of Al Jolson is the story of show business ... this book gives a good jump off point for exciting conjecture.

William Morris, Jr.

BOOK ONE

Early Years
1886–1900
Russia and Washington Boyhood

1

October 24, 1950, A. M.

A headline in the newspapers: "AL JOLSON, MAMMY SINGER AND KOREAN WAR HERO, DEAD AT 64."

A soldier, somewhere in Korea near the 38th Parallel, receives the news via the communications system while he crouches behind a boulder under enemy shellfire. The G.I. remembers. When Al sang "Sonny Boy," man, that was it.

Old friends on Broadway, newer ones in Hollywood pause in their activities, and remember.

People in London, Paris, Rome, Lisbon, Berlin, Moscow, Tel Aviv, Cairo, Cape Town stop what they're doing, and remember.

That man who sang, laughed, and lived so much . . . dead.

Just one month ago, that September, the graying figure of a man in GI uniform, with his accompanist Harry Akst, had toured the battlefronts in a helicopter. Those eager young faces looked up at him with affection and hung on his every word and note. Their applause at the conclusion of each number was sweet music to Al's ear.

This time with Jolson it was not so much the fact that he had an audience. That counted, of course, but in the main it had become a matter of cheering the boys, to make them feel happy despite their distance from home and loved ones. He made them smile with his cheerful songs; he made them dream of their sweethearts with his sentimental ballads.

But wherever he went, performing on makeshift stages, sometimes with the rain beating down upon his bared head, or with the
shells bursting not too many yards away, he brought his message
with a seemingly inexhaustible energy.

He was like a man possessed. Sixteen days in succession of
daily performances. He could not rest; he did not seek the safer

places. If there was a battalion holding a line against Communist fire, he went there and sang to the G.I.'s. When the officers advised against nearing the enemy, Al's eyes glittered. The hell with 'em. They're not stoppin' Jolie. Get me to the kids.

Sixteen days and a target for enemy bullets, but he delivered his forty-four performances intact. Nobody need know about the cost in pain. Not even Akst, his piano man.

For two hours he conversed with General MacArthur in Tokyo before he said good-bye to the G.I.'s in Korea. The General awarded Al a medallion in recognition of his services. This, then, was the climax of Al's career.

When Jolson finally headed back to the States at the end of September 1950, he was a weary man, but he felt that his mission had been accomplished.

He had promised his wife he would settle down. Besides, he could use a nice long rest. Play with the kids. Tell Erle how beautiful she was.

California-bound on the plane, he opened his eyes after a brief nap and saw the airport strip rise up to meet him. His co-traveler, Harry Akst, nodded, and announced:

Los Angeles, Al.

2

Al knew that Erle would be waiting for him. He had cabled her.

When she was in his arms, he wondered how he could ever have left her.

Her trained eye measured his paleness, the fresh deep lines on his face.

In that first week of October, at his Encino, California, ranch, Al had a field day with his adopted children. Asa, Jr., clung to his daddy as though he'd never let him go. Alicia, under the doctor's care, couldn't help laughing as Al held her in his arms and made funny faces. When alone, Al walked about the ranch, glad he was home.

Erle beamed at him. She reminded him of his promise—that this trip was the last time. He had earned his retirement and she was going to see that he enjoyed it.

She told him they could have loads of fun here. They'd become acquainted with some nice neighbors. Get-togethers, picnics, swimming parties. So much to do and see in California.

Al promised to stay put.

If anybody called him on the phone about an engagement he'd say he was retired—absolutely and positively.

But sometimes the good things in life come when the twilight is already deepening into night.

Al laughed and romped with the children. He kidded around with Erle. But when he was alone there was the shadow of anxiety upon his face. That intermittent ache in the vicinity of his chest— it would go away, but it came back. It interfered with his breathing. But this he kept to himself.

Erle must have no cause for worry.

But he had no idea of how much she really knew.

It was during his hours of sleep that Erle would stay awake through endless anxious moments, keeping her eyes upon him. Something seemed to be bearing down upon him, like an oppressive weight, as he slept. His tossings and sudden starts grew more frequent.

Sometimes he would awaken and sit up, his breath coming in short gasps. Erle would question him. Al would assure her it was a bad dream; a glass of water would fix him up fine.

Erle would greet the mornings with welcoming sighs. It was during the broad daylight hours that Al seemed more like his old self.

With the children they took long drives into the surrounding countryside. They had their little picnics, sometimes with a few select friends, including the durable Louis Epstein.

And then, like the beginning trickle of the source of a stream, Al felt the return of the inevitable urge. The October days began to drag.

It seemed that, sooner or later, the old craving for action would come over him, and he'd grow uneasy. In the third week of October he received a call from Bing Crosby, requesting him to take part in one of Bing's radio programs.

3

Erle listened to Al as he told her the news, that Old Bing needed a helping hand.

Erle assured him that there were hundreds of capable performers who would jump at the chance.

But Al insisted that Bing wanted *him*—Jolie—the old Mammy singer.

Erle pleaded with Al to call Bing back and tell him that Jolie had finally retired. She reminded Al of his promise.

After a brief silence Al looked at Erle and she could read his thoughts like the words on a printed page.

Al paced the floor. He stopped in front of Erle and—though he did not utter a word—his eyes beseeched her. She yielded, whispering, It's all right, Al. Then she insisted, as a condition, that he get a good night's rest. He swore this would be his last performance. After that—well, she'd see—it would be Jolie's farewell to show business. He advised Erle he'd be at the St. Francis Hotel in Frisco. He'd call Harry Akst and Marty Fried, his accompanist and arranger, respectively, and they could go over Al's business. He asked her to listen in. Jolson and Bing Crosby!

In his high glee Al kissed the children. He lifted Alicia up above his head and held her there. A sharp stab of pain almost caused him to drop the child, but he managed to hide this in a sudden maneuver as though it were part of his act. But that didn't fool his wife. She had nurses' eyes that missed nothing—especially where he was concerned.

Next morning, October 23, in the bright sunlight, Al got into his car, leaned out and gave Erle a good-bye kiss. He waved to the kiddies. He started to drive out of the yard. He remembered seeing Erle's dark eyes glistening with tears. Women—God bless them, he thought. They cried at the least little thing. Emotional— they lived by their emotions.

4

That night in his room at the St. Francis Hotel, Al, waiting to do his stint with Bing, was playing cards with Harry Akst, Martin

Fried, and good old Lou Epstein, his retainer. It was a friendly game and, for once, it seemed that Jolson was garnering the pots. This gave him a feeling of elation. Al said he was a lucky dog that night. Epstein told him he was always lucky. All those bombs exploding in his face on his USO tours in World War II and all those Commie bullets in Korea, and here he was—alive and kicking, without a scratch.

Akst and Fried nodded assent. A lucky dog was Al, for sure. And now Al won almost consistently. He could afford to gloat. In the past he had lost too often at cards, as well as at love.

He leaned forward to deal, but the cards remained tight in his hand. He didn't move—for a long moment. His friends looked at him. They could see the beads of perspiration on his forehead, the pain in his eyes.

Fried and Akst suggested that Al rest for a few minutes.

Al dropped the cards on the table, leaned back slowly. He said he was all right. He asked Eppy to deal for him.

Al remained sitting quite still, staring at his friends, his eyes glazed as though he were looking at them through a thickening mist.

Epstein rose. He put his arm about Al, helped him to his feet. He led him to a sofa, and Akst and Fried joined him in making Al comfortable. Al told them not to make such a fuss.

He lay there, flat on his back, his eyes staring up at the ceiling.

His mouth drew back as a bolt of pain shot through his body. He seemed to stiffen and his eyes closed. In a moment his eyes opened again and he looked at Epstein, who was rubbing Al's hands and forehead.

Al's voice, almost inaudible, whispered the words, I'm goin', boys.

Epstein phoned for a doctor. . . .

When the doctor arrived he leaned over Jolson, examining him, giving him an injection. Coronary occlusion, the doctor's diagnosis. Al's eyes opened. He grinned at Epstein, at the doctor. He said, Know somethin', Doc? President Truman had only one hour with General MacArthur but I had two.

The doctor nodded, felt the pulse that had throbbed through all the excitement and thrills that a single lifetime could produce.

There was no response. The doctor looked up at Epstein and whispered, He's gone.

The room was strangely still, as though all the sound had flown out of it. And yet the clock on the bureau ticked loud and clear, counting off the seconds of time which no longer belonged to the man on the couch.

Martin Fried said, I'll wire his brother Harry.

Epstein turned away, stood there by himself in silence.

He knew he had to make one phone call—the worst in his life. He went to the phone, picked it up, told the operator, The Jolson residence in Encino.

In a moment he heard her voice, Yes?

Epstein's own voice faltered. He stammered, It's—it's Al. He—he—

Is he sick?

Epstein's mouth trembled, whispered, He passed away.

A brief quietness. Then Erle's voice, Oh, no—

Epstein replaced the phone in its cradle. He turned to look at his friend lying on the couch in repose at last—after a half century of show business.

And yet he could so easily believe that Al was resting—that any moment he would see his friend rise up, hold up his hands, and call out:

Wait a minute, folks, it's only the beginning and you ain't heard nothin' yet.

5

Al Jolson—whose classic catch-phrase was You Ain't Heard Nothin' Yet.

Al Jolson—Mr. Show Business himself.

Asa Yoelson—the Seventh Cantor.

Critics had spoken of him as an extrovert, an exhibitionist, a master of hokum with a super ego.

If he seemed to be any of these things, still none could deny his sincerity, his honesty of spirit when he delivered his songs to the multitudes that crowded the theaters to hear him.

Toward the end of his career, his peers often described him as a man of unceasing drive and ambition, a human dynamo that, for years, had shown no signs of running down. . . .

*   *   *

He had never felt so weary.

He looked out through the plane window, saw only the rafts of clouds, and between them the blue that was the Pacific Ocean. Outward bound. Korea seemed interminably far, but the plane was his seven-league boots, taking him to "his boys."

Al Jolson—for a long time now a legendary figure to the world in general; to the older generation, a familiar memory; to the youth of the land—what else could he mean to them?—an elderly past master of a form of singing and theatricals that had long since been relegated to the field of "corn." And yet he had to smile now. Corn? Perhaps—but he could now envisage those rapt young faces of the boys who would be listening to him in Korea. . . .

Lulled by the humming of the plane's motors, he remembered so many things—of other days—young days that belonged to age as well as to youth—it was only a matter of a passage in time.

He could go back—yes—back even to that first day of his life in that ancient town of Srednike, Lithuania, in a Czarist Russian empire that had long since vanished. It was a long span from this year of 1950 to the date of his birth, May 26, 1886. He laughed now when he thought of it. His mother had told him the story (which had become a family tradition) that when he was born, his father, Moses Reuben Yoelson, the dedicated sixth cantor in an unbroken line of descent, had immediately declared the infant to be the seventh cantor upon hearing that lusty first vocal outburst.

His mother—he remembered her as always busy with her hands—cooking, sewing, cleaning house, and turning the pages of her *sidder* (prayer book), in the women's gallery of the synagogue.

His father—Al always felt a pang of sadness when he thought of his father—the respectable, dedicated Cantor Yoelson who had tried so hard and so long to make Al his successor to carry on the tradition.

He could piece it all together—his heritage—from what his mother had told him, and from the time he had begun to remember what he had seen. The whole pattern of his career began with his father, Moses Reuben Yoelson, who had applied for a cantorship post to one Asa Cantor, the president of a synagogue in the little town of Keidani, not many *versts* from Kovno. Mr. Cantor could not give him a full cantor's position at once, but hired him as assistant in the synagogue, and so well did young Yoelson perform his duties, chanting certain portions of the services, that the president invited him to his home. Here Yoelson met Mr. Cantor's pretty daughter, Naomi, who liked the young singer at once. Soon a marriage contract was drawn up, one clause of which provided that the newlyweds live in the Cantor household for one year. It was in this house that the first child, Rose, was born. Al's father then moved, taking a position as a full-fledged cantor in the synagogue in the nearby village of Srednike. Here the family lived—as Al could remember—in a three-room log-constructed house with a floor of hard-packed dirt. It was in this house that the rest of the children were born: first his sister Etta, then Hirsch (Harry), then another sister who died in infancy. After that Al himself came into the world and was named Asa after his grandfather.

He remembered that his father, to add to the meager family income, had become a *schochet*, a slaughterer of animals of kosher meat. The Yoelsons moved into better quarters, occupying one half of a large house, with a real wooden floor, owned by one Haym Yossi, a black-bearded, loud-voiced giant of a lumberman, who lived alone in the other half of the house. He received from the Yoelsons thirty-five rubles yearly rental.

Al recalled that he and his brother Harry were compelled to attend *cheder* (Hebrew school) one hour each day, studying the Talmud and Hebrew writing. Also there was an instructor who came to the house and taught them the Russian, German, and English languages. His father had always wanted his children to be "educated." As soon as the boys were able to talk they were given voice lessons by their father.

Because of oppressive conditions in Czarist Russia, his father began to dream of going to America to establish a new life, as so many of his countrymen were beginning to do. In 1891, he put the dream into reality and sailed for America. He wrote to Al's mother that he had found a fine home in the main city of America, Washington, D.C., and had a position as cantor and rabbi in a synagogue.

In the summer of 1894 Yoelson sent the steamer fare for the family to join him in America. Al had never truly realized the hardship his mother had endured in transporting the four brats from Srednike by wagon to Kovno, then bundling them into a train bound for the port on the Baltic. After that they boarded an ancient creaking steamboat that wheezed across the Baltic and the North Sea. He remembered how seasick he had become, as had his poor mother, while Harry had almost passed out.

Then, at last, Liverpool and a ship to America. The boundless expanse of blue-green, white-capped waters of the Atlantic. He remembered his first sight of the Statue of Liberty, with the torch, and the towers of New York. He recalled his father greeting them at the pier, and he was almost like a stranger, they had not seen him for so long. Then the train ride to Washington, and their new home in that fabulous city.

The end of an old life—the beginning of a new.

6

Al couldn't repress a laugh.

What would some of those Broadway critics and cynics have said about Al Jolson, the brash star of so many smash stage productions, the singing sensation of talking pictures and radio, had he chucked everything and actually become his father's successor as the Seventh Yoelson Cantor?

The plane glided steadily on its course toward Korea. The Pacific Ocean seemed without boundary, but at the journey's end he'd find the G.I. kids, waiting for him. . . .

Today—1950—there was a new style of singing, with the aid of an electric microphone that took any whisper of a voice and multiplied its volume until it rivaled the vocal strength of a Caruso or a Pinza. But the singing itself was more of a crooning, and there was no impact, none of that good old showmanship of belting a song across.

He recalled the old Winter Garden days. He remembered cannonading out song after song—those favorite tunes and lyrics that never failed to slay them even unto this very day—the immortal "My Mammy," the stirring "Waiting for the Robert E. Lee," and the nostalgic Gershwin hit, "Swanee."

He remembered now the advice of his friend and manager, Lou Epstein, back in 1940:

You're the champ, Al. Everybody knows that. And like a real champ, you should announce your retirement. Believe me, Al, you've earned it.

He recalled—and he smiled at—his own answer:

Look, pal, Jolie never retires. Don't you remember? You ain't heard nothin' yet.

Al, you're crazy. Take my advice. There is no comeback for an old champ.

But the events that had followed that conversation had contradicted Eppy's advice—overwhelmingly.

This trip to Korea—his wife Erle had been dead set against it. He recalled the tears in her eyes as she had pleaded:

Please, Al, can you stand the trip?

But he couldn't let the boys down.

Good thing he didn't mention the pain that came and went somewhere in the vicinity of his chest. He had steered clear of being too particular about it. Might have spoiled his plans and kept him home.

Erle had pleaded, but he had to go. . . . He smiled now, happily, at the memory of the reception the World War II G.I. kids had given him on the battlefront. . . . He had managed to give them quite a number of performances, at times under shellfire. And their favorite song? He could still hear their eager cry: Al, sing "Sonny Boy!" Maybe his wife had been right. He did feel kind of wobbly now, but he wouldn't have it otherwise. He thought of Erle and the kids back home in Encino. He was sure Erle would understand. She was a good kid, and yes, siree, mighty pretty to come home to. . . .

He closed his tired eyes. That pain in his chest—was it because he had only one lung, the other having been collapsed during a siege of pneumonia after a tour of entertaining the troops in World War II?

It was restful in the plane, gliding through the heights. Five times as fast as a train. Today everything was speed. Life itself was so much faster. Often he had felt out of place in this atomic age. In the old days people lived leisurely. They were not in such a hurry. He could see again that quiet street, his boyhood home, his mother in the kitchen cooking the evening meal; his father, in skull cap, sitting at the dining room table with the Hebrew book in front of him; and Al himself, as a boy, sitting beside his father . . . and patiently learning the Hebrew prayers. . . .

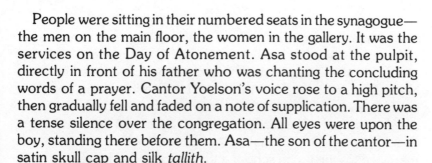

1

People were sitting in their numbered seats in the synagogue—
the men on the main floor, the women in the gallery. It was the
services on the Day of Atonement. Asa stood at the pulpit,
directly in front of his father who was chanting the concluding
words of a prayer. Cantor Yoelson's voice rose to a high pitch,
then gradually fell and faded on a note of supplication. There was
a tense silence over the congregation. All eyes were upon the
boy, standing there before them. Asa—the son of the cantor—in
satin skull cap and silk *tallith*.

Asa could see all those eyes staring at him. Those people, who
had come to hear his father week after week, were now waiting
for Asa to sing to them the sad and beautiful "Kol Nidre." Asa
trembled. This was his father's forte. As for himself, he had never
really wanted to be a cantor, had always felt he was not quite the
right one to sing or chant the Hebrew prayers and hymns to a
congregation. Popular songs in the everyday language of the
people—that was his ambition—to sing to audiences in theaters,
gay songs and sad songs, to make them laugh and to make them
cry. But now he had to oblige his father, he had to satisfy that
devout congregation. His father raised a hand, the signal for him
to begin.

Asa's silvery voice intoned the words of the "Kol Nidre," rising
to a crescendo, and presently the whole temple was filled with the
supplication. The pathos of the hymn reached out and up to the
female contingent in the galleries, and sounds of weeping

increased in intensity. The boy seemed to become an inspired being despite himself. He seemed to be fired by the power of the song, and his father looked upon him in pleased surprise.

When the final notes rose and trembled away in the agelong plea, the congregation remained motionless, the voice of the boy still ringing in their consciousness.

Cantor Yoelson extended his hand and touched the hand of his son.

Then the cantor chanted the next line of prayer.

The congregation rose to respond, in accordance with the Orthodox procedure.

But their eyes were still upon the boy.

2

Asa attended public school in Washington but he was a reluctant student. He would sit at his desk and dream of faraway places, of the excitement in the big American cities like New York, Chicago, and San Francisco. His brother Harry could be content and patient with the status quo, but Asa could not find satisfaction in the classroom, found no attraction in the teacher's droning voice. During that first year in America, however, he managed to sit it out in school and also to study Hebrew with his father.

He attended synagogue regularly on Friday evenings and Saturday mornings. He stood near his father at the pulpit and listened to him chanting from the Torah and, in time, after instructions, Asa joined in the chanting, adding his own young voice at designated moments. Sometimes he had to utter a low hum, or a higher hum; at times he would intone "Amen" or "Adonoi" on signal from his father. The congregation came to regard him as its next cantor. In those days Asa was part of the life of a modest Jewish family. He came to know the landmarks of the nation's capital. Like any boy he had his share of playing marbles in the street, or mumblety-peg, or cowboys and Indians, or Brooklyn steps. And like all boys he learned soon enough that girls were not just playmates, they were soft and nice to touch, and their mouths were nice to kiss. But, to Asa, girls, like other diversions, had to keep to their time and place.

Often he got into fights with other boys. Any time a boy referred to his being a Jew in a derogatory fashion, Asa was in there like a flash, punching away. There were times, also, when he came home sporting a "shiner" to an alarmed mother and a disapproving father.

3

In this new land there were joys, and sorrows, too. When Asa was ten there was the final illness of his mother. She had not been a strong woman and life had been too difficult for her. Mr. Yoelson led Asa into the bedroom and let him look at his mother lying there, still, not moving.

After that, for one year, Asa and Harry recited the "Kaddish"— the prayer for the deceased—three times a day in the synagogue.

Wounds heal, and in time Asa and his older brother, growing up together in Washington, did things as a team. They became very close, selling newspapers to earn money, then using their voice training to increase their income, by singing on street corners. Their boy soprano concerts attracted the attention of pedestrians, people tossed coins to them, and the boys made a discovery—they earned more from this than from their newsboy enterprise.

There was one favorite stage they used, the pavement in front of the Hotel Raleigh, the habitation of government officials.

Here, in the good old summertime, the Congressmen, Supreme Court justices, and sundry politicians would sit on chairs placed on the sidewalk to get the benefit of any cooling breeze. Here, standing in front of them, Asa and Harry would go into their act, singing song after song, some on the frisky side like "Sweet Marie," "The Sidewalks of New York," and "Who Threw the Overalls in Mrs. Murphy's Chowder?" or perhaps songs on the sentimental side to impress the important listeners, like the Stephen Foster numbers, "My Old Kentucky Home," and "Jeannie with the Light Brown Hair," or "Listen to the Mocking Bird," "Come Where My Love Lies Dreaming," and "When You and I Were Young, Maggie." After each performance the boys would pass their hats around and the coins would clink in musical cadence.

During the warm summer days Asa and Harry took a flyer in an ordinary business venture. They had procured for a couple of dollars an old, broken-down wagon which they somehow patched up so that it remained upright on its four wheels. They hired a bony sway-backed horse that matched the wagon. At the wholesale farmers' market they bought watermelons at three and sometimes four for a nickel. These they sold at five cents each, finishing one load and returning to the market to obtain another. Here, too, in their huckstering, they made use of their singing, chanting out a jingle of their own composition:

Wa-a-a-a-ter-melons—
Red to the rind—
Five cents a piece—
An' ya eat 'em all da time!

They would finish their business transactions early so that they could visit the Bijou Theater and watch the matinee burlesque show, their parents never being the wiser. They would also visit the legitimate theater to watch, with bated breath, such masterpieces of the drama as *Uncle Tom's Cabin*, *Ten Nights in a Barroom*, and that perennial heart-wringing tear-jerker, *East Lynne*.

Asa, singing on a street corner for coins, attracted the attention of a raggedly dressed thespian by the name of Hopp, who looked like old Fagin himself stepped out of the pages of Charles Dickens. Asa was to be his Artful Dodger. Hopp gave Asa a five-cent piece and asked the boy to accompany him to a store building that had been converted into a theater of sorts. At the next performance, Asa's clear boy soprano voice became the most attractive part of the show, which was a bizarre conglomeration called hopefully "Rich & Hopp's Big Company of Fun Makers." Hopp tied an old, torn tablecloth about Asa's waist as a sash, in which costume the youngster sang his numbers to an audience of ten or twelve loungers, including a couple of red-nosed imbibers. The company disbanded abruptly when the audience dwindled down to three nickel admissions.

At this time nothing could keep Asa, age twelve, away from the theaters of Washington. His favorite was the Bijou where the burlesque shows fascinated him, not so much the generous display of feminine epidermis on the stage as the baggy-trousered comedians and the smooth singers who graced the show. Asa's favorite spot was a seat in the balcony, not too far from the stage, from which vantage point he could look down into the wings where the various performers awaited their cues. This was the world he craved. In that same theater, when Eddie Leonard, then known as a "coon shouter," sang his song, "I'd Leave My Happy Home for You," he asked the audience to join in with him in the chorus, but not a single voice responded. Perhaps it was a shy audience, but Asa saw no reason why he should refrain. He knew the number. He knew he could do it. He stood up and started to sing in his bell-like boy soprano to a surprised and pleased audience. At the finish Eddie Leonard asked the listeners to give the kid a "great big hand," which they did. This was Asa's first real theater performance.

On another occasion it was Aggie Beeler, burlesque queen, playing at the same Bijou in a show called "The European Sensation." When she sang the chorus of "My Jersey Lily" she motioned the audience to join with her and again no one did but Asa. From his spot on the balcony, he burst forth once more into song. He was a sensation, the audience almost forgetting about old Aggie herself.

Miss Beeler invited Asa backstage into that world he had dreamed about. The partially clothed females crowded about him and he felt uneasy, but Aggie made him feel so much at home that he was convinced to join the troupe on its tour.

That night, while the family slept, Asa stole out of the house and ran away to become a genuine professional "actor."

But Miss Beeler had changed her mind, telling him to come back in five years.

Asa, instead of going home, walked off in the opposite direction and kept on walking. The daily monotonous repetition of fatherly scoldings, the picking on him by his sisters, the eternal Hebrew lessons—all this had exhausted his patience. His father was preparing him for his Bar Mitzvah, now a year away. And now Miss Beeler's rejection. Asa had reached his decision to stay away from home.

He walked to the outskirts of Washington, trying to live down his first keen disappointment.

Soon he felt tired, hungry.

Then he thought of how much his father, his brother, his sisters would be hurt. Dusk came, deepened. He turned around and started back home.

4

At twelve years of age Asa wandered all about the Washington streets, was intrigued by an encampment of the Fifteenth Pennsylvania Volunteers, awaiting transport to Cuba and the Spanish-American battlefront. A jovial officer grinned at him. The boy did not hesitate to tell him his name was Asa Yoelson and he could sing.

Asa needed no invitation. From a retentive memory he sang "The Sidewalks of New York," "Tenting on the Old Camp Ground," and "Carry Me Back to Old Virginny," swinging his arms and raising his voice until it floated over the ranks of the uniformed listeners. They called for an encore, and many more songs before they let him stop, among them "Nelly Bly," "Oh Susannah!," "I Love My Little Honey," and "Hello, Ma Baby."

Asa tried to join the regiment, but the recruiting officer told him to come back in five years. Everybody was telling him to come back in five years.

The officer, however, managed to arrange for Asa to accompany the regiment as mascot. That was the first experience he had of singing to the troops—in the year 1898.

He got as far as Key West.

There the officer wisely shipped him back to Washington, back to his father and the synagogue. As Al Jolson recounted later, his father gave him the most thorough whipping he had ever had—using to full advantage a strip of leather harness to which was attached a sizable buckle. The pleas of Asa's sisters for mercy went unheeded.

3

1

What is the most crucial day in a Jewish boy's life? When he is Bar Mitzvah, of course, on his thirteenth birthday—the day when he supposedly steps out of his childhood and into his manhood. And so it came to be with Asa.

The congregation turned out in full force to hear the cantor's son recite his portion of the Torah. Members and friends of the family were emphatically present. His brother, Harry, grinned at him from a front seat. In the gallery sat his sisters, Rose and Etta. The news spread, "Cantor Yoelson's son Asa is Bar Mitzvah this Saturday," and the synagogue was crowded to the last inch.

Finally the moment had come. In skull cap and *tallith* Asa stood on the dais, before the table on which the Torah scroll lay unrolled. The elders of the synagogue read sections from the scroll. Cantor Yoelson intoned a short prayer, then he gave Asa the signal to begin his recitation. A tense silence settled over the congregation.

In a clear, rising voice Asa began his *maftir*.

As he chanted the words from the Torah his confidence increased and with that his voice grew firmer. Once more inspiration seized him. It was like a flame fanned by a rising wind; his voice filled the synagogue, and the people listened, pleased and moved. Yes, it was agreed, Asa Yoelson would indeed make a good cantor.

2

On Friday, at sundown, the Sabbath officially began. Rose, acting in her mother's place, covered her face with her hands, stood in front of the lighted candles on the dining room table, and said a prayer. Etta helped set the table.

Cantor Yoelson and his sons, Asa and Harry, then came in from the synagogue, took their places at the table, and the cantor offered a prayer of thanksgiving, Asa and Harry punctuating the end of the prayer with an Amen. Then Rose began serving the Friday night dinner: first, the gefilte fish and the mouth-burning *chain* (ground horseradish) as appetizer, then golden chicken soup, followed by the cooked chicken itself. There also was a helping of *lokshen kugel*, and all this was topped off with *flomen comput* (stewed prunes) for dessert.

After the meal another brief prayer of thanksgiving and then Cantor Yoelson nudged Asa to sing "En Kelohenu," a custom on Friday night. Asa had expected this; so, with his father, Etta, Rose, and Harry as an audience, he sang the repetitive verses from beginning to end, careful to keep the orthodox cadence and not to slide off suddenly into what was then known as theater-stage singing. As Harry recalled in his biographical journal, Asa would brush off, as he always had done, his father's reminder that Asa's voice belonged to the synagogue. After "En Kelohenu," Asa would make a beeline for the door, to be gone for the evening. But Harry knew it was at the Bijou stage door that Asa began the Sabbath.

3

Jolson himself seemed to enjoy telling the story of his boyhood rebellion against the family tradition of cantorship. At fourteen, he ran away to Baltimore, walked into a cafe—the Seamen's Inn—and asked for a job washing dishes. No dishwashers required. Asa said he could sing—he could be a singing dishwasher—he knew about singing waiters. Before the proprietor could say no, Asa sang a verse of "Kiss Me, Honey, Do." He got the job but he had no place to sleep. He had no money. The proprietor arranged two chairs for Asa's bed.

Asa lasted one week at the Seamen's Inn. Cantor Yoelson had finally located his son through chance information from a neighbor who had seen Asa cleaning tables and singing. The father stormed into the cafe, gripped the boy's ear, and dragged him out to the street. When the cantor asked Asa why he had run away from a respectable Jewish home, Asa replied readily enough that he did not want to sing in a synagogue—he wanted to sing in a theater.

In the train—all the way home from Baltimore—the father wanted to know why Asa was against carrying on the family heritage as the seventh cantor in an unbroken line. It was possible that in time Asa might even be blessed with one of the largest and richest congregations in Washington. Even the president of the United States might one day visit the synagogue to hear Asa as the cantor. Mr. Yoelson reminded Asa of the time the boy sang the "Kol Nidre" on the Day of Atonement. The congregation had never been so inspired. But no matter how earnestly his father argued Asa did not yield. He insisted he could never sing in a synagogue again, that he wanted to sing on a theater stage, and what was wrong with that? He told his father, as the train brought them nearer to Washington, that some day he would become famous and rich in the theater. Asa pleaded with his father to give him the word. But the father was as obstinate as the son. He called the songs of the theater "loafer songs." He made it plain to Asa that he would not permit any son of his to besmirch the good, religious reputation of the Yoelson name. He told Asa in no uncertain terms that the boy was going to be a cantor in spite of himself. He would move heaven and earth, if need be, to make this come true. Asa listened but said no more. He was tired, hungry, sleepy.

The train steamed into Washington. Home at last. His sisters, Rose and Etta, greeted him warmly. His brother Harry gripped his hand. Everyone felt quite sure Asa had come home to stay.

4

At fourteen he could not live with the one-sidedness of his father's viewpoint. His father followed the pattern of an orthodox conception to do as your forebears had done before you. The son of a cantor becomes also a cantor. The congregation would expect it.

And how could a fourteen-year-old boy convince his father that here in this land there was opportunity to lead an independent life? There was only one thing left he could do—run away, break the tie that bound.

As Al Jolson himself told the story, one night, instead of going to bed, he sneaked out of the house. He could picture his sisters grieving in the morning when they would find him gone. Well, some day they'd all understand.

He had no money but he had read about hoboes sneaking rides on freight trains and he decided to try it. He stole into the freight yards, picked out a likely looking box car with partly open door, climbed up and slid into the darkness within. He lay down and buried his face in his arms and thought of the family back in the house. He couldn't repress the sobs.

Presently the box car creaked. There was a thud, a rattle of chain as the coupling took hold. Asa's adventure into the outer world had begun.

It ended abruptly in the Baltimore freight yards where Asa was nabbed by a railroad detective and taken into custody. In due course his father was notified. Yoelson wasted no time in reaching Baltimore. The authorities advised a term for Asa at St. Mary's Industrial School for Boys. The lad could be set straight there.

It was a Catholic school for troubled youngsters. Since Cantor Yoelson's teachings and whippings seemed to have done no good, perhaps Catholic teachings and whatever they used instead of whippings would be the answer. (At a later date, Babe Ruth of baseball fame attended the same school.)

Asa did not care for the arrangement at all. He chafed at restrictions, and it was his nature to crave freedom. He could not stand any form of bondage. As he told it later, he begged his father to take him home; he promised he would never run away again. This time his father did not believe him. His son was in bad need of discipline, and at St. Mary's he would get it.

Yoelson held a conference with the superintendent, a kindly priest. The necessary papers were duly signed. Yoelson kissed Asa on the cheek, told him that when he saw him again he would expect to meet a settled young man. The superintendent took Asa by the hand and led him away.

4

1

From the first day at St. Mary's, Asa revolted. He sullenly refused to eat. He disobeyed the fathers. He refused to take part in the prayers and choir practice. He taunted the other boys. One boy, coming out of the chapel, saw Asa scribbling on the wall and threatened to "squeal" on him.

Without further ado Asa turned and swung at the boy with his fists just as the superintendent came on the scene. He gripped Asa by the arm, turned him around. After a sharp reprimand the priest told Asa that a few days in solitary would afford the boy time to mull things over. Confinement to Asa was insufferable. Anything but solitary. The superintendent did not yield to Asa's protests but led him to a room on the second floor, a cell-like room with a single barred window. He was sure Asa would emerge from the room a more considerate and compliant youngster who would give his parent no further trouble.

From the moment the door of the small room was locked and Asa found himself a virtual prisoner, he behaved like a wild young caged animal. He paced up and down, kicked the walls, tugged at the steel bars, shouted at the top of his voice. He screamed and yelled without letup.

The sound of his voice reached the ears of the teachers and attendants, and the other boys. It brought the superintendent quickly to the locked door. A key grated and the door swung open. The good priest told Asa to stop screaming. Cantor Yoelson was coming to take Asa home.

2

After his father brought Asa back from St. Mary's, the boy's stay at home was brief. Yoelson had once more grasped at the idea of training Asa for the cantorship, but it was a futile effort. At the end of two weeks, just before the High Holy Days, Rosh Hashana and Yom Kippur, Asa ran away again.

Once more he landed in Baltimore, with the resolve to break into show business. He plugged the theaters, hung around the stage entrances, did errands for the performers, carried their trousers to the tailor for pressing, went to the stores for cigarettes and soda pop, cleaned the dressing rooms.

Always, at any opportunity—for he never stopped pushing himself—he sang for them, hoping they could find a spot for him.

Once he sang "On the Banks of the Wabash" for Al Reeves, producer of a burlesque show. Al, an astute showman, recognized something in that boy soprano voice and hired him.

Al Reeves was a good coach.

He taught Asa the stage tricks, timing, the art of catching the attention of an audience and holding it.

Asa, with a show of eagerness, listened, then went on and sang in his own way.

At the same time he wondered—why couldn't his father understand? Songs were prayers; the audience was the congregation.

That night, after the half-nude chorines had finished their number, Asa sang "On the Banks of the Wabash" to a thrilled audience, for which he received two dollars.

There were a few more nights, and then Asa had a visitor backstage. It was his father who had hurried to Baltimore on receiving a letter from Al Reeves, who had written of his plan to train Asa for the stage.

Cantor Yoelson, at the sight of the amply proportioned but scantily dressed ladies of the burlesque show, threw up his hands and told Asa this was no place for the son of a cantor and, once again, took Asa back to Washington.

3

Harry had already left home for New York to try his luck in the theatrical world, and now Asa, following his older brother's example, had secretly saved up the train fare to New York. He knew that if he were to get anywhere in show business, New York was the place.

He had always hated to leave home without notice to his folks, but the attitude of his father toward the theater would have caused only needless argument and heartache. A clean silent break . . . so he ran away from home again.

On the train he kept thinking about his sister Rose, who was alone now, Etta having gone to Yonkers to stay with an aunt. Asa hoped Rose wouldn't grieve too much.

Some day, he hoped, the whole family would feel happy about what he was doing, and perhaps his father would eventually forgive him.

The July heat in the metropolis was killing.

Asa went from one soda pop stand to another, until his meager funds were exhausted. Penniless, with night approaching, he sought a place to sleep. There was Central Park. He found a suitable bench under a tree and staked it out as his temporary quarters.

It was dusk now, and the gas lamps flickered on the walks of the park. The galaxy of city lights lit up the night. He sat on the bench, his chin in the palms of his hands, dreaming of his place in this great city.

Presently he felt lonely, sick with fear. What was he doing here in New York?

He also felt hungry, tired. He was unwashed, and the prospect of sleeping on a park bench did not altogether appeal to him. A great wave of homesickness came over him, and once more he wanted to be back in Washington.

He made his decision. In the morning he would jump a freight and go back. He'd rather take the licking from his father than endure all this.

He unbuttoned his shoes and placed them under the bench.

He slept in starts and sudden awakenings.

Once he was certain there was a figure bending over him.

The sound of the waking city, the clatter of horses' hoofs and iron-tired wagon wheels on cobblestones brought him out of his sleep. When he regained his senses he found himself staring at his stockinged feet, and remembered that he had placed his shoes under the bench. When he stretched out his hand to retrieve them, he discovered they were gone.

He realized that going back home now was out of the question. He could not walk into the house of his father minus his shoes.

He rose, and the emptiness of his stomach buckled his knees.

He walked out of Central Park, and to the nearest eating place in his stockinged feet. This and the rumpled knee pants, his soiled blouse, and his shock of unkempt tangled hair caused people to stare at him and shake their heads in compassion.

Asa eloquently convinced a restaurant owner to trade a pair of shoes, a couple of scrambled eggs, and a glass of milk for a dishwashing and floor-sweeping job, with a song thrown in.

4

One thing about Asa, he had no qualms about talking up to people. At fifteen he felt himself a man; had not his father assured him that at his Bar Mitzvah he automatically had changed from boy to man?

He knew he had a voice. He wanted to sing anywhere, anytime. And he remembered that back in Washington at the synagogue, or on the street, people had been willing to listen. As singing regimental mascot for the Fifteenth Pennsylvania Volunteers, he had sung hundreds of times and the soldiers had always listened. In the Seamen's Inn in Baltimore he had serenaded the customers effectively enough to make some of them forget their dessert.

Why not in New York—and for money?

He walked to the theatrical district, and noticed a crowd of young and old men and women at a stage entrance. He joined them.

They informed him that the theater was opening with Israel Zangwill's *Children of the Ghetto* and that extras for the mob scene were required.

Asa did not hesitate but pushed his way through the crowd of would-be thespians; and he was hired at six dollars per week—his first theatrical job for real pay.

That night he walked up and down Broadway in celebration. He had made it . . . he was an actor.

Asa remained in the mob scene of the *Children of the Ghetto* for two weeks. He soon realized that the bit meant nothing, but he had twelve dollars for his trouble.

He bought for himself a new shirt and cap. He treated himself to enough food to make him forget for once that lingering hunger.

Then he made the rounds of the booking offices.

One agent sent him to the rehearsal stage of a show called *My Jersey Lily*. The director listened to Asa and nodded favorably, but he showed the boy how he wanted the song "belted" out. Asa agreed to do it the director's way, and he was engaged.

He made no mentionable impression and at the end of three weeks he was at liberty again.

It was during this period, between engagements, that Asa found some recreation in a community center on Delancey Street. Here he had a chance to relax a bit, to attend the Saturday night dances. But he was not much of a dancer. Usually he remained in the stag line, watching.

Al Jolson later recalled how eagerly he had grabbed at any opportunity of talking to bored pretty dance partners about his hopes and ambitions, his future in the world of the theater and vaudeville. He outlined to them his plans for his career. Naturally the young ladies avoided him like the plague.

5

Asa continued to make the rounds of the booking offices.

He had never anticipated such determined resistance; the answer he usually received was an emphatic No, in some cases a polite stall.

As Al recalled, one agent looked at his young boyish face and demanded his right age. When Asa told him he was fifteen the agent informed the boy about New York's Gerry Society that kept children under sixteen off the stage. The agent wanted no trouble with the society, so Asa trailed out of the office.

How in the world does one crack the wall?

He did not despair entirely. He tried other agents. He tried the theater rehearsal stages. He kept on and at times he sought refuge in Coney Island where he loved to watch the ocean breakers, how they hurled themselves on the beach again and again, retreating only to charge once more.

His spirit replenished, he would return to Manhattan and the booking agents. But always the answer was the same.

They seemed to be under the impression that he would not be capable of handling an audience. Too young. Lack of experience. Perhaps in a few years, when he'd be more mature. But Asa wanted to start now. He wanted to face the public, bring his message of song to them.

But there was no opportunity to do this, and there were moments when Asa was ready to throw in the sponge and call it quits, try to obtain a job as a waiter or a clerk in a store, or make something of himself in the world of business.

BOOK TWO

Vaudeville, Burlesque, Minstrel Years

1900–1911

With Harry Jolson
and Lew Dockstader

5

1

On the home front in Washington, Cantor Yoelson felt that it was time to take unto himself a wife to look after the household and the family. He remembered that back in Srednike his cousin, Perli Yoels, had had a rather acceptable daughter named Ida, some dozen years younger than himself, who now was widowed. Thereupon he wrote a courteous, careful letter to Perli, asking her for the hand of her daughter. In four weeks a letter came from Mrs. Yoels informing the cantor that her daughter Ida, now without husband and father to her son, George, would be more than honored to accept the proposal of the great Cantor Yoelson.

In the spring of 1901 Ida arrived at the Yoelson home in Washington, bundles and all, and Cantor Yoelson was duly married to her in a quiet ceremony in the social basement of the synagogue.

Asa, Harry, and Etta had come home from New York to attend the wedding. Rose had outdone herself in baking a masterpiece of a wedding cake. Introductions were made to the bride and to her son, George, somewhat younger than Asa.

The new Mrs. Yoelson held Asa's hand and smiled at him. Asa liked her at once. She was his own mother all over again, and she told Asa how she used to hold him on her knee when he was a baby back in Srednike. She declared how big *Hershela* (Harry) had grown, and then she embraced Rose and Etta who also had been under her ministrations back in Srednike. So the hugging and kissing went on in the Yoelson homestead while the cantor himself nodded proudly at his new *yidina*, approving her overflowing affection toward his family.

At the wedding feast the elders of the synagogue were regaling Cantor Yoelson with repeated "Lé cheiim's" as they emptied their glasses of shnapps and eased their appetites with herring and sliced onion. The neighborhood fiddler supplied *frailech* music for a few Russian *kasatchka* dances.

Asa and Harry supplied a program of comedy and song, and it was a night to remember.

On the following morning, Asa and Harry hurried back to New York and their careers. Etta would go back to Yonkers in a few days. Rose intended to remain. It would have been nice to have the boys at home but Rose had already learned from them—"the show must go on."

2

Back in New York Asa did find assignments, now and then, usually in burlesque houses and honky-tonks. During the years 1901 and 1902 he managed to eke out a meager existence, plugging sheet music in stores, but his extreme youth made these jobs short-lived, in favor of mature and experienced singers.

There was a boy's part in a new play being cast but the director took one look at Asa and shook his head. As Jolson remembered the incident. The director, without much diplomacy, informed him that he was not the type for the role. Asa, the director advised, was hardly the romantic type who would appeal to young ladies and their mothers. Asa understood the implication —legitimate drama was not his destiny. His destiny was to sing, and sing he must. Nevertheless he began to have doubts. So far he had accomplished very little—even as a singer.

Perhaps his father had been right, and his place was back in Washington, in the synagogue. As a cantor he had undeniable prospects. As a figure in show business he had thus far drawn a blank. Well, it wasn't too late to go back home. Until he would achieve his cantorship he could get a job in Washington. Then he thought about his brother Harry who was getting bookings in vaudeville, and seemed to be doing all right. Maybe, if Asa kept trying. . . .

At the turn of the century New York was a lusty, budding metropolis. Right here in this city there were plenty of chances to make good and become somebody important outside of the theatrical world. He saw young fellows like himself hurrying to their work in the mornings and he felt envious. He would join them. He would find a regular job. He'd study the help wanted ads in the newspapers. But in the next moment he knew he could not be happy in any kind of endeavor except show business. He had to be in or near a theater. His fulfillment could be found only in front of an audience. He was sure he had something to give to the public—and the mere giving would be his happiness.

Each day, after having finished the rounds, he would steal into a vaudeville house, slink into a seat in the gallery, and watch and study the performances. In his mind he would analyze the acts, throwing out a line here, a word there, revising until he felt sure of improvement. He would sit through the entire show and was always loath to leave the theater. Once outside, Asa would walk along the street into the increasing cold of the winter night. The wind would howl like a mad banshee as it swooped down between the stone and steel cliffs on lower Broadway. He would look at the theater marquees and picture his own name blazing away for all to see. Finally he'd go home, a single room in a tenement on the lower East Side. An iron bedstead, a dresser with a chipped mirror. The toilet was out in the hallway— "foyer"—and it was a community affair; sometimes, inconveniently, he had to wait his turn.

3

That spring Asa landed a job with the Walter L. Maim's Circus as an usher.

Without delay Asa told the owner-manager he could sing. Maim advised Asa he had been hired as an usher and that meant his job was to "ush." He was given a crimson uniform. He put it on, examined himself in the glass, thought he looked soldierly.

He guided the people into the big top. He made an effort to do his job efficiently so that he would be kept on.

He spoke to Maim again about singing. The owner informed Asa that people paid to see tightrope walkers, flying trapeze artists, clowns, elephants, bareback horse riders, dogfaced humans, Siamese twins—but no singing.

Asa was disheartened, but he did not give up.

There was a gathering of the performers to celebrate someone's birthday. Asa saw his chance. He sang a number for them and they were pleased. When the song was over, there were clamors for more.

Asa was called into Maim's office wagon. The owner announced that Asa Yoelson would go on in the Indian Medicine Side Show after the main performance.

That night, after the main show, Asa sang in the medicine tent —a side show, complete with Indians in full warpaint, extolling the magic cure-all wonders of the genuine Indian Herb Elixir. He sang "I'd Leave My Happy Home for You" and "On the Banks of the Wabash."

The crowd increased, little by little, until there were several hundred people pressing about the medicine show, listening to the boy sing, with that tremulous voice. And when Asa received encouragement, the sky was the limit. Something snapped within him like an electric switch and he was off, singing tune after tune out of his miraculous memory. Soon, the listeners started to call out to him the songs they wanted to hear: "After the Ball," "A Bicycle Built for Two," "The Band Played On," and a dozen more. From a single number Asa found himself suddenly deluged with requests and, of course, he was anxious to oblige. There seemed to be no letup, and the barker of the medicine show had to order him to stop. Otherwise there would have been no time left to sell the elixir.

4

When October of that year, 1902, came and the circus folded, Asa went back to New York. He was sixteen years of age, with no more fear of the Gerry Society, but his voice was still that boyish soprano. He was told by veterans of the stage that it would soon begin to change.

Asa found a room, this time in a tenement on the West Side, and at once began making the rounds.

He knew beforehand that it would be a matter of repeated rebuffs but he knew, also, that he had to keep on.

He even auditioned for an amateur operatic group, but the director, a man with long hair and thick-rimmed spectacles, told him that he did not have the voice nor the desired qualities.

As another winter set in, Asa, desperately in need of money to pay for his room rent and food, made his way to the Bowery. He asked for and obtained odd jobs in saloons and cheap cafes—sweeping floors, cleaning counters and tables, helping in crummy kitchens—anything that would keep him alive.

His whiskers were beginning to appear, and he could see in the mirror the semblance of a genuine mustache. He felt that perhaps if he didn't shave he would look older.

He saw life here in its elemental level. Almost every second person was in a state of near-stupor, induced by liquor. He soon became accustomed to the sight of red noses, bleary eyes, unshaven faces, soiled clothes, and he came to know only too intimately the stench of stale tobacco smoke, cheap whiskey fumes, and unbathed bodies.

At first he had been rather careful and wary of all this human misery, but soon he felt himself practically a part of it. He was, in effect, a near-candidate for skid row membership.

At sixteen he had grown taller and heavier, and the proprietor of one saloon assigned to him the job of bouncer, telling him to call out if anyone was too big to handle.

Shades of his boyhood fighting days. He still had the use of his clenched fists. But several young Bowery toughs beat him up and he was summarily fired.

Asa was discouraged. His father had been right. He would amount to nothing.

He came home to his room, feeling lonely, tired, cold, and sleepy. There were nights when he writhed through sleepless hours in close association with bedbugs. They stung him with a vengeance, and in the mornings he could see the red welts all over his body.

His earnings were meager, and he could not even afford to keep the room. He had to pack his things into a suitcase and trudge through the snow to a Bowery flophouse, fifteen cents for a night's lodging. He ate scraps.

He toyed from time to time with the idea of returning home.

Asa suddenly saw an opportunity in a Bowery theater—an amateur night for prize money.

He signed up and came out on the stage as one of the contestants.

The motley, leering audience began to yell, "Get the hook. Get the hook." Asa had just finished the first verse of "Hello, Ma Baby," when the stage manager motioned him off the proscenium. Asa pleaded that he hadn't finished his number. The manager told him that his voice was breaking all over the place. Asa was at the voice-changing age.

His next job was as a candy butcher in the Gayety Theater, a burlesque house on Fourteenth Street.

Asa again pleaded with the manager for a singing spot. But the manager warned him that the audience would eat him up alive. They had paid good money to watch the ladies wag their behinds and wanted no interruptions. Now if Asa were a female hootchy-kootchy dancer with a substantial torso, the manager would be ready to talk business. He was advised to attend to his butchering. He had to remember he was working on commission, and the more he sold the more he earned.

So Asa walked up and down in the aisles between performances while the house lights were on and made his spiel: Candy, soda-pop, prize bags. Find a valuable prize in each and every bag and the picture of a lady about to take a bath. Only ten cents—one dime.

He was fired because he spent too much time backstage.

Frustrated, his next job was as a dishwasher in a Jewish restaurant on Fulton Street on the lower East Side, his old haunt. He resolved this time to hold on to his job, to wash those dishes with ambition and earn enough to pay for a room of his own.

Asa told a fellow dishwasher that he was a singer. The man's comment was that if Asa sang like he washed dishes—that's why he was washing dishes.

Asa remained silent. He wondered how much truth there was in that.

3

1

Jolson often reminisced about the time he went off by himself
after a day's work washing dishes. He walked along the bank of
the East River and when he came to a vacant area—a rubbish
dump—he started to sing, just to convince himself that he had
not forgotten. He was practicing.

He jumped up on an old oil drum and looked out over the river
at the passing craft, not too great a distance away. There was a
group of small boys playing hide-and-go-seek in the rubbish
heaps.

His voice came out loud and strong, then suddenly wavered
and broke into a rasp, and he knew it was changing.

He might as well face it—right now he had no voice. Once, with
Al Reeves, the burlesque producer, he had done a whistling act.
Al had shown him how to whistle with thumb and forefinger in
mouth, and he had become quite expert.

He tried it now, and soon had an audience of small boys and
two or three ragged gentlemen of leisure.

When he finished they stared at him, the small boys glowering,
the hoboes grinning. One of the urchins threw a stone that struck
Asa on the shoulder.

One of the hoboes warned Asa to "skiddoo"—that stone was
an opening shot.

2

Asa once more considered the idea of returning to Washington.

In a letter to his sisters he noted that he was, by this time, quite convinced he probably wouldn't amount to much on the stage. Why should he persist in this madness? Here he was washing dishes in a greasy beanery. Surely, being a respectable cantor in a synagogue was better than this. All he had to do was to forget this insanity about show business and align himself with his father.

He thought about this possibility.

The prospect looked more and more appetizing.

He had been in New York two years, and what had he achieved? A few insignificant spots as a half-baked singer in vaudeville and burlesque, but mostly crummy jobs in foul-smelling saloons and greasy kitchens. Was this the life for a cantor's son?

But, on second thought, coming home now was out of the question. He had no decent clothes. He was penniless. What sort of an impression would he make on the neighbors, members of his father's congregation? He'd only disgrace the family. He knew, after all, that he must remain an involuntary exile.

And now he wondered whether he should take up another profession, but what? He had no schooling, no training, no experience.

He walked up Delancey Street, figuring his next move.

He could register at a trade school and become, for instance, an electrician. This was a new field, but he had no money for tuition. He could, perhaps, learn carpentry, or plumbing, or paperhanging by studying as an apprentice. He had seen paperhangers on the street, going to work, carrying their paste brushes and rolls of wallpaper on their backs. He could get a job with one as a helper, learn the trade, and go out on his own.

He would lead a normal life. He would find a nice girl, marry, settle down, have a family. His problem would be solved. All he had to do was to make up his mind.

But Al Jolson, telling of these things, admitted knowing all along that this was not for him.

3

Booking agents persisted in demanding hoofers, with canes and straw hats, who could dance fast and deliver fast comedy patter; also in demand were freaks, acrobats, trick-performing dogs, magicians, and partly clothed females.

Asa wasn't any of these.

Under the manipulation of the two giants, Keith and Willie Hammerstein, vaudeville was hitting the greatest stride of its career, and the thousands of theaters built in the larger cities and towns, and also in the hinterlands, were overflowing in attendance with the two-a-day variety shows. If a person was a Yiddish, Irish, or German dialect monologist, if he could tap dance, hard or soft shoe, if he could juggle or stand on his head, bark like a dog or quack like a duck, then he was in. Fame and fortune were invariably his.

Some of the vaudevillians achieved enviable financial positions. They acquired fine homes on Long Island; they began to drive the new-fangled horseless carriages; they took to wearing flashy clothes and fancy jewelry.

But for Asa Yoelson there was no place in this boom-world of show business. The reason? There was only one thing this sixteen-year-old boy could do—sing—and there were doubts about that in the minds of the impresarios.

He had no wardrobe to make a proper appearance when he walked into a booking agent's office; as it was, his unpressed suit, his stained tie, his unlaundered shirt, and his distorted cap put two strikes against him even before he went to bat.

He resolved to hold on to his kitchen job, put aside a certain sum each week until he had enough to purchase some new clothes.

Al Reeves had once told him that appearance—a "good front"—was all-important to an actor in getting bookings.

Asa would sit down on the front doorstep—the "stoop"—of his tenement and scold himself for thinking again of becoming an actor. First of all, it would be some time before his voice would readjust itself.

Meanwhile he would wash dishes or be promoted to a waiter, without the singing.

4

When the spring of 1903 came around, Asa grew restless. He knew he would have to quit his job, and he did.

He tried selling cosmetics from door to door—outside work.

There was a selling class on the tenth floor of an office building on lower Broadway. There was a morning "pep" session and a talk by the glib sales manager of the outfit. As Al himself liked to relate it, the talk went something like this: "Men, you are soldiers now—soldiers of salesmanship, the most vital occupation in the world. Without selling where would we be? Everybody has something to sell. We are selling cosmetics to the little lady of the house direct. We must always observe the principles of decorum, uphold the dignity of our products and our company. Before you go out into the field of battle, you will each receive an official badge of identification which you will wear on the lapel of your coats. You will also receive one carrying case containing samples of our merchandise which you will display to your customers. Each of you will be assigned to certain streets. Do not encroach on your fellow salesman's territory. And now we will sing the company anthem. Please rise."

Asa's voice, still in its uncertain stage, rang louder than the others and there were several "soldiers of salesmanship" who turned to look at him.

Asa sold nothing, not even one box of face powder. He threw the cheap cardboard case with the samples into an empty lot in the Bronx and went to see a vaudeville show at Proctor's 58th Street Theater.

He found a lone seat in the gallery for the matinee performance and he was in his glory once more. This to him was the epitome of living.

From the moment the curtain rose his eyes did not miss anything. He watched, he made his usual mental notations, he studied each act.

There was a chap on the stage who played the trumpet, cracked jokes, and sang, but Asa was sure that he himself could have done better with the songs. He felt an inward fury at the powers that were keeping him from the stage. He had so much in him to give out, to let the people hear. He knew he could make them feel what was in him, make them live through a song's meaning, make them thrill to its music.

But here he was, unseen and unheard, in the shadows of the gallery—watching other performers.

Asa remained in the theater, ate a box of Crackerjack he had bought during the intermission. That evening he was still in the theater and sat through the entire performance again as fascinated as in the beginning.

By May of that year Asa's voice had almost cleared up, had developed into a resonant tenor, with a tremor that was to cut a huge swath into the hearts of audiences yet to materialize.

An agent penned a note to the producer of the "Dainty Duchess Burlesquers": "Try this boy. Has fresh nice voice with promise."

Asa was booked for "Dainty Duchess Burlesquers" on trial. He put everything into it. He sang his best. This kept him in the show. He sang a number, "Be My Little Baby Bumble Bee," to the star of the show, a ravishing blonde displaying a lavish portion of her langorous curves to an excited, straining audience, ninety-five percent male. He sang the number as though his life depended upon it and one thing this did accomplish—it made a good part of the audience lean forward somewhat in their seats and stare at this boy on the stage, despite the disconcerting presence of a half-clothed female.

When he had finished the number, the applause was favorable and there were a few calls for an encore, but the director eased Asa off the stage.

The show continued for several weeks and Asa seemed to improve. He couldn't wait for each succeeding performance, and when it came he ran out on the stage with increasing confidence. He had his new voice now, a tenor, and he could sing to his heart's content.

When he asked the director whether he could sing an encore, he was told summarily to be thankful for the privilege of the one number.

So Asa delivered "Be My Little Baby Bumble Bee" twice a day, and always he received applause with a few calls for an encore which never came.

Asa's proximity to the scantily dressed ladies of the "Burlesquers" perhaps served to immunize him to an extent, against the environment of so much exposed feminine pulchritude. Though at the critical age of seventeen, he seemed to keep his equilibrium in the midst of all this allure. He was somewhat more mature than the average boy of his age. There were two or three chorines who gave him the eye, but so intent was Asa on his career that those charmers had to take second place in his agenda. If some young chorus girl whom Asa had seen prancing about the stage with breasts and buttocks in startling prominence invited him to escort her to her home, Asa accepted, not so much from the desire to be with her, but to preclude the possibility of offending her by a refusal.

Soon the others seemed to sense his absorption with the furtherance of his career, young as he was; and so they looked elsewhere.

While he was performing his number, some strange force seemed to possess him, and the emotions born within him were transmitted through his voice to his listeners to make them feel as he felt.

The "Burlesquers" folded and this time Asa did not have to wait too long.

Another brief booking came his way in a variety show at Hammerstein's Victoria, the goal of many a vaudeville player. But the Victoria audience was strictly partial to trained seals, tightrope walkers, Chinese jugglers, dogfaced freaks, and dialect comics, spiced in right proportion with heavy-thighed maidens in various degrees of undress. A boy singer only interrupted the mounting excitement. At the end of the week he was on the street again, "carrying the banner," the vaudevillian's expression for unemployment.

Once more the rounds of the agents. He received a number of promises. They were beginning to know him, what he could do. They assured him that as soon as the freak-show craze was over, things would be different.

5

Asa next took a turn as a singing waiter in a Hungarian restaurant on Seventh Avenue.

The diners at the restaurant were not too impressed with his serenading. These people were in the restaurant primarily to satisfy their stomach hunger, and singing was no substitute for Hungarian goulash. But it did serve as a sort of accompaniment to the movement of their jaws as they chewed and swallowed and looked upon Asa Yoelson with a certain degree of compassion, glad, perhaps, that they did not have to sing for *their* meals.

Once in a while a moneyed patron would hand Asa a fifty-cent piece. Chicken feed, sure, but a tide-over. The money he had earned from his last two vaudeville engagements had bought new clothes, had added to his confidence.

He took time out to write a letter to his parents, telling his new "Momma," as he called her, how much he missed being with her and getting to know her better, thanking his father for having been so patient with him, teaching him whatever he knew about singing.

It was the first letter he had written in five months.

He was booked at Tony Pastor's.

Here there was none of the sensationalism in entertainment. Pastor strove for refinement, catered to family patronage. Here people relaxed and listened to a song.

Asa was received warmly, but it was nothing to make him excited. Apparently the audience regarded him as just another young singer starting his stage career, and they wished him well.

Here Asa lasted one whole week, then found himself once more "carrying the banner."

He hated to go back to being a singing waiter or a dishwasher. The Albee-Keith people had put thumbs down on booking him for their circuit, citing his youth and inexperience. They told him to come back in a year or two.

Asa walked the streets.

Despite his resolutions, he had to take odd jobs again between spot bookings. His voice, in the months that passed, grew deeper, and developed a sensitive quality. His stage presence improved considerably and the gawkiness of the amateur gave way to the savoir faire of the young professional. It became easier for him to hold an audience during the time he was on stage.

7

1

In the early 1900s the vaudeville stage had definite classifica-
tions for dialect characters, which were the rage. It was the time
of a tremendous influx of immigrants from the "old country,"
every nationality being amply represented as they filed out of the
ships' steerages into the great steel and concrete melting pot that
was New York. Soon there were name-labels used freely in vaude
acts designating, with no chance of error, the various nation-
alities: an Irishman was a Mick; an Englishman, a Limey; an
Italian, a Wop or a Dago; a Jew, a Kike; a Chinese, a Chink; a
German, a Dutchie; a Bohemian, a Bohunk.

In his various vaudeville engagements Asa usually played a
straight man, with patter and song. When he teamed up with his
brother Harry in 1903 in a skit called "The Hebrew and the
Cadet," Asa, of course, was the straight man, or the cadet, while
Harry played the Hebrew. The act, starting in an uncertain
fashion, grew more finished until it was making the audiences
laugh. The jokes were fresh corn, adapted from other jokes or
stolen outright from other performers. A sample:

Asa calls Harry, the Hebrew, a monkey.

Harry is angry.

"A monkey! Did you call me a monkey?"

"Sure, I called you a monkey. Do you know what a monkey is?"

Harry thinks a moment, and then says, "No, I don't know vot a
monkey is. Vot is a monkey?"

"Well," Asa answers, winking at the audience, "a monkey is a fine person. Everybody knows that monkeys are wonderful people."

"Vell!" Harry remarks with a triumphant smile. "Sure, I am a monkey. Vot is more, I vant to tell you that my brothers and sisters are monkeys, my fodder and modder are monkeys, and all my ancestors vas monkeys."

And from the listeners there always came a laugh.

Under the auspices of the William Morris Agency they played such theaters as the old Keeney on Fulton Street in Brooklyn, Tony Pastor's on Fourteenth Street, Manhattan, and the Brighton in Coney Island, and here began a relationship with William Morris that was to last beyond the lifetime of these men.

Directly after the closing of "The Hebrew and the Cadet," Asa and Harry secured a booking with the Clift Grant "Little Egypt Burlesque Show," with which they performed a patter and singing act and during the intermissions bolstered their salaries—$17.50 each per week—by selling song books. To each fortunate customer purchasing a book, they threw in, "absolutely free of charge an amazing new novelty, the picture of a female dancer in scant Oriental costume that does the hootchy-kootchy right before your very eyes. All you have to do, gentlemen, is light a match like this and wave it behind the picture, like this, and there she goes, shaking away a mile a minute. Only ten cents, one thin dime, for the song book, containing the hit songs like "After the Ball," "Organ Grinders Serenade," and others by that master composer, Charles K. Harris. Get your song book and the free hootchy-kootchy dancer while they last, folks. Get them before the show starts. All right, Asa, this gentleman is taking one, that gentleman there, and another, and another. . . ."

Harry would do the barking and Asa would hand out the articles and take in the precious coins.

The show played the cities and the larger towns. Sometimes the theater manager would pressure the actors to "smear it" (to make the joke or the skit "dirty" or the show girl take off more) to attract customers. On these occasions there were times when the police stepped in. Once, while the show was playing a stand in a Pennsylvania town, the performers were arrested for obscenity, and Harry and Asa for peddling the "kootch" pictures, but the show's manager secured their release, with the condition the show leave town on the double. The boys continued their intermission hawking and their stage act with "The Little Egypt Burlesque Show" until it played its last gasping performance at the Unique Theater in Brooklyn.

Once again the brothers were stranded and back to "carrying the banner." Out of this experience Asa resolved to stick to singing and bona fide entertaining.

It was early in 1904 that Asa decided to make up a new act.

Harry, his brother, currently working in New York, had located Asa at Tony Pastor's on Fourteenth Street during one of the latter's engagements. It was a joyous reunion. If they had had differences in childhood days, these were now forgotten entirely. First, Harry assured Asa that Poppa, Momma, and the girls were fine.

Harry had some singing ability for, in generations of cantors, it was inevitable that the descendants should at least be endowed with the knack of singing a song.

In the course of his career thus far Asa had met, through Ren Shield, a vaude act writer, a young fellow by the name of Joe Palmer who was confined to a wheelchair, and who had introduced himself as a singer of fast and funny ditties, reinforced by fast comedy patter in a variety of dialects—Hebrew, Dutch, Italian, and others.

With his brother Harry and Joe Palmer, Asa formed a trio offering popular songs, fancy soft shoe and tap dancing, funny jokes and repartee. They billed themselves as "A Little Bit of Everything."

Palmer, being an incurable cripple, had to do his vaude act in the wheelchair, but he was a talented comic and never failed to get laughs. The audiences naturally assumed that the wheelchair was part of the act. They never suspected that Joe Palmer couldn't stand on his feet.

During the spring of 1904 the act was perfected by rehearsals, mostly in the partners' lodgings but sometimes under the open sky in Central Park, after which the ordeal of obtaining bookings began. After a series of rejections they obtained engagements in independent small variety theaters in the Bronx and Brooklyn, also across the river in Jersey City.

The act was nothing unusual. There were dozens of similar acts on the boards except for the wheelchair. It was not considered sensational enough or attractive enough to rate billing in the Keith circuit, or at Hammerstein's Victoria, or at the Proctor houses on 58th and 23rd streets.

But the boys plugged it and eked out a hand-to-mouth existence.

Asa felt that something was wrong, and he suspected that they just weren't good enough. They were received with lukewarm applause that sometimes petered out to positive frigidity. Their engagements were brief and their billing on the program was always the most inconspicuous spot.

Palmer suggested it would help the act if Asa and Harry would change their names to something easier to pronounce and remember. After a brief conference they decided on "Al" for Asa and "Jolson" for Yoelson. The act would henceforth be known as Jolson, Palmer, and Jolson, six letters in each name.

They managed to wrangle from William Morris the booking of a tour with the hope they would meet with better success on the road—the tour spanning the eastern half of the country and closing in New Orleans.

William Morris, at this time, through his agency, was valiantly trying to fight off the stranglehold on vaudeville by Keith, Proctor, and others who were combining to develop a trust, a show business octopus to be known as the United Booking Office. The booking of Jolson, Palmer, and Jolson was made by Morris on the strength of Al Jolson's singing talent rather than on the capabilities of the act as a trio. After the first few performances of the act Morris suggested that Al leave it and go on his own. Al refused point-blank. William Morris was not peeved. On the contrary, Al's decision won from Morris lifelong admiration, and he scheduled more bookings for the act than it rightfully deserved. The boys did try to iron out the rough edges. They tried somehow to dress the act up, to give it "moxie."

In a tryout of the revamped act at Proctor's 23rd before they went out on the tour, the reaction of the paying patrons was still too much on the negative side. But they still hoped that on the road the tide would turn in their favor. The tour opened in Philadelphia at the Bijou where the reception was somewhat more encouraging, but in Pittsburgh they were almost cancelled. The audience was restless. Eggs were thrown, and several cabbages landed at Al Jolson's feet.

They had a week's booking here and they stuck it out. Near the end of the week the audience grew more receptive, the act went off more smoothly, and on the closing performance Saturday night it didn't do too badly.

The act was a comedy stint and its synchronized rigid format imposed restrictions upon Al Jolson. This played havoc with his need for self-expression, put a clamp on his emotions. He had never liked the idea of mathematically timed cues. It gave him a feeling of being fenced in, sometimes almost to oppression, but for the sake of the act's success he adhered to the formulas they had laid down for themselves.

Though Al may not have defined it as such, his best work was done in a spontaneity of performance, where he could "let himself go." Otherwise, the thing became like the recitation from a text, without color, without impact.

They played the cities of Harrisburg, Reading, Erie, and Buffalo. In Buffalo a heckler threw a well-aimed overripe tomato that struck Al on the cheek and splattered his white suit.

They were forced to accept the truth that their act was a flop. What more proof than the increasing heckling, tomato and egg throwing? It had become a dangerous undertaking. They were suggesting to each other that perhaps they had better call it quits—maybe go out as singles. Some one-man acts were going over very big, including singers and comics. Singing would be Al's specialty. As for Harry and Palmer, it would be the comic stuff. But after discussion they felt it would be a shame to split up at this point. Maybe they could still make a go of it by changing the act, making it something special the public could not help but welcome. But meanwhile they came up with no new ideas. The best they could do at this time was to let it slide and appease their anxiety with card games.

They played a few games of poker with Al losing all his small change. But at least their problems were shoved—though temporarily—into the background. Right then and there Al fell in love with cards.

Al and Harry took turns watching Joe Palmer on their evenings off so that the other could go out for a good time. Harry recorded in his journal that in Chicago Al Jolson went out with a blond chorine who called herself Daphne.

They visited the Lake Front Inn. They dined, wined, and danced. Al's companion shrugged her buxom shoulders as Al made a brave but blundering attempt to lead her in a waltz. As a dancer Al was as graceful as a hippo. According to his own admission he must have stepped on the poor girl's toes a dozen times. Al could see her face growing red with the ordeal, sought the easiest way out, but was stymied. She did make an effort to show him the technique of the steps, but apparently it was a waste of time and energy. Al had always found it difficult to concentrate on what people were suggesting. "My mind," he once told an interviewer, "was always filled with the possibilities of shaping up a vaude act, to make it hot with the paying customers."

When they parted that night he forgot all about her at once.

A tough audience in Cincinnati, using the effective "colonial clap"—the clapping of hands in unison in staccato rhythm—counted out Jolson, Palmer, and Jolson, terminating their performance before its scheduled finish.

After an argument with the theater manager, the trio took his advice and left abruptly for their next stop, Minneapolis, where they found a more sympathetic and better behaved house. Al realized that perhaps he had been too hasty in building the act.

His brother Harry had been doing much better as a single. Palmer had been okay, too. As for Al himself, his own record was not very encouraging. But always he retained that spark of hope that the act would ripen and improve with additional experience.

The salary they received ranged from $80 to $125 for the three of them, and there was an understanding with each theater manager that if the response to their act was good, there would be a proportionate increase in salaries, but if their act went stinko, there would be a proportionate shrinkage. This was the setup, take it or leave it.

Al had resolved to follow his old mentor's—Al Reeves's—advice, to "put up a good front," and splurged his cash for a black derby hat, a flap pocket coat, a silk wide-striped shirt, fly-top pants, two-toned button shoes and spats.

He remembered the curvaceous blond Daphne's dancing lesson, and now he learned to dance, not only the waltz and two step, but also the latest innovations, the sensuous Maxixe, turkey trot, bunny hug, grizzly bear—new dances in a faster tempo—to a ragtime rhythm that appealed to Al for he believed this was the new lasting trend in American music and not a passing fad. It was the music he hoped to interpret in his singing—an inevitable breakaway from the staid past, an expression of growth, a reflection of the changing times.

Entertainment was in the process of changing too.

2

Toward the end of 1904 the first experimental moving pictures were publicly exhibited. By the middle of 1905 the nickelodeon began its invasion of the theatrical scene, snowballing rapidly in momentum, to become a looming threat to vaudeville.

This was especially true in the smaller cities and towns where the natives did not have too much money to spend on comparatively high priced live theater admissions. The nickelodeon took immediate hold and where buildings were not available, tents were swiftly put up, the screen and projector installed, and voila! a house of entertainment, showing "pictures that move and come to life before your very eyes"—all for the price of one nickel, and a little later, a dime for adults.

There was a fascination about the pictures that moved in lifelike manner. Here was entertainment that surpassed even the live stage shows, both legit and vaude, when it came to scenery and fluidity of movement. Outdoor action could be portrayed in its natural locale, whether it was a desert in Africa, a street in London, or the blue expanse of the Mediterranean, a feat which the stage could not very well duplicate.

This medium took hold of the imagination of the public, and one by one, at an increasing mortality rate, the traveling stock companies and the variety shows began to fold.

Jolson, Palmer, and Jolson had their first run-in with the nickelodeon when they watched the people in St. Louis crowd into a tent pitched on a vacant lot. In the opinion of vaude performers moving pictures were a child's toy—but there went their audiences.

3

Sample of 1905 stage humor in "A Little Bit of Everything" offered by Jolson, Palmer, and Jolson:

Palmer: You can drive a horse to water but a pencil must be led.

Another sample:

Harry, comic: What makes oil boil?

Al, straight man: I give up. What makes oil boil?

Harry, comic: The letter B.

And another:

Palmer, comic: I sent my wife to the Thousand Islands on a vacation.

Al, straight man: How long will she be away?

Palmer, comic: A year on each island.

And still another:

Palmer, comic (looking at a chorine's ample chest): Where did you get those eyes?

The corn grew tall and green those years. But it brought forth belly laughs which, in turn, transformed the green corn into long green at the box office.

Sandwiched in between such hilarious masterpieces of wit, Al Jolson would sing his numbers.

The listeners could not, at first, quite fathom Al's style. There was something about it that was different. It was not purely a rendition of the melody; they detected within it sounds and modulations that had nothing to do with the melody, and once or twice during the number, he spoke the words of the lyric and that made them wonder what it was all about.

Someone was trying to come out of the cornfield and that was always incomprehensible.

So that when the next gag came on with false black beard, false huge horse teeth, and false bulging eyeballs, the spectators were back in the corn and they sighed in relief and the belly laughs came loud and strong once more, and all was well.

4

In the fall of 1905, Jolson, Palmer, and Jolson came down to New Orleans from St. Louis on their tour. Their act now was being received with greater appreciation in the Southland.

But in New Orleans a misunderstanding arose. Joe had to be watched and helped with his food and clothing for he could not get out of his wheelchair and remain upright. He had to be held up or carried bodily. Al and Harry had to dress him, feed him, put him to bed almost like a baby; but Joe was an artist, and the gratefulness in his eyes was an expression that Al would never forget. It made Al always keep in mind the plight of the helpless and maimed.

But at that time he was too young to be broadminded about certain other things. When they came to a new town one of them would take care of Joe for the night while the other would go "out on the town." Harry had done his stint on the first night in New Orleans while Al had gone out. But on the following night Al insisted that he had to go out again since he had made a date with a girl, and asked Harry to stay with Joe. Harry refused point-blank, justly claiming his own night off. The two brothers argued to and fro. Meanwhile Joe's face was the picture of chagrin and anguish.

When Al looked at Palmer he saw him desperately wheeling his chair toward the open window facing the street three floors below. Al rushed forward and restrained the struggling Palmer. Harry, in a fit of anger, walked out of the room, and out of the act.

That ended the Jolson brothers vaude act.

Al stayed with Palmer for a while. They did a double together but bookings were hard to obtain. Soon they separated, tearfully, in St. Louis. Al was going to take the train to Chicago.

Al asked Joe to drop a line sometimes; promised to take care of him financially. Al would never forget that parting. Joe sat there in the wheelchair, asking for no help, insisting he would make it on his own. Hadn't he always wowed them even from his wheelchair? Al also would never forget Joe's evident act of nonchalance when he really could have broken down and cried.

Al took his suitcase, made his exit, knowing that Joe was watching him.

The two never met again, but financial help went from Al to Joe for the rest of Joe's life.

Al's road was an upward one. Joe lived long enough to hear the name of Al Jolson spoken by many.

Harry Jolson, as a single, was holding his own, playing the independent theaters that were still available to the William Morris Agency. He was also taking an interest in the organizing activities of the White Rats, the first vaudeville actors' union. When the Morris bookings ran out Harry went to the Keith office for engagements, but he was given the cold shoulder.

Al Jolson, heavy of heart from the breakup of Jolson, Palmer, and Jolson, expressed his feelings in his songs, let go of his emotions to the audiences, and now and then they would look at the performer before them with something like awe.

From Chicago Al's wanderlust took him to California, and San Francisco. On April 25, 1906, he arrived to view a sight he would never forget—a great city in smoking ruins.

5

From the people Al learned how on April 18 the ground had trembled, buckled, and given way, ripping open great ditches, and heaving up and down like a giant sea wave. Buildings had begun to topple into the streets. The end of the world seemed to have arrived. The city had been a bedlam of disaster whistles, mingled with the roar of falling steel and stone, and the moans of trapped humans. Horse-drawn fire engines had raced through the rubble-strewn streets. Pits had yawned open like huge hungry jaws.

Everywhere, from Bay Shore Line to Nob Hill, the flames had roared through the day and night, consuming the city, and the wails of anguish had gone on and on.

Al forgot show business for the while, watching the city dig out. He pitched in and helped. Gradually, order was restored to the demolished city, once beautiful San Francisco, the iridescent jewel set between the blue Pacific and white-capped San Francisco Bay.

Seeing all this misery and suffering made an indelible impression on Al. It made him feel, more than ever, the importance of human brotherhood.

He thought he'd stay in Frisco for a while. Maybe he could cheer up some of these people with his singing while the work of reconstruction began.

He remained through all of 1906, and decided to stay on another year or two.

He was booked at the Globe and the Wigwam theaters, where his singing began to take on a new depth and intensity and gradually made its way into the good graces of the audience. They grew more tolerant toward his style, and were finally beginning to understand its implications.

At the same time Al's delivery improved, and he was fast approaching the goal he had set for himself, a breakaway from the notion of "doing it the way it's been done before."

There was a tent set up for Hebrew prayer and services to replace the area synagogue that had been destroyed. A rabbi heard Al sing to a group of wounded in the hospital camp, learned that he was of the Jewish faith, and asked him whether he would care to attend the evening service. At once Al accepted. He also offered to assist the cantor.

Somehow he envisioned his father in front of him, standing at the pulpit, as they chanted the prayers in unison, and Al thought to himself that he had come home.

3

1

During his engagement at the Globe Theater, Al met a young, attractive, and aspiring actress named Henrietta Keller, who was in a short skit on the same bill. Somehow they became friendly and had long talks between acts. On the third night after their meeting, Al invited her out to a restaurant after the show.

Thereafter they had pleasant tête-à-têtes, and Al found himself welcoming these interludes which helped to dispel the loneliness he felt in San Francisco.

They were married before the end of the month and Al realized with a feeling of importance that now, at twenty-one, he had a wife, and perhaps soon a family. He resolved to buckle down and make something of his career.

In the beginning he couldn't wait until the show was over so that he could hurry to their little apartment, located on a pleasant residential street near the bay, with a view also of the blue mountains on the horizon. But show business in those hectic days was hardly conducive to a regulated marital co-existence. In the rare moments they were together—from past midnight to mid-morning—Al was either sleeping, having his breakfast, or dressing for another round of performances. Shows must go on. Theater managers did not sanction excuses for absences, for the audiences had paid to see a complete show as advertised. Al, trouper that he was, could easily accept that discipline, but Henrietta, though she did try to comply, found herself rebelling

against Al's preoccupation with his career. Al worried about his
wife's reaction.

Perhaps he shouldn't have married while in the throes of
launching his career. Henrietta was almost in a state of mutiny.
She made known to him her wish that he would get into some
other line of work. She had been willing enough to give up the
theater for his sake. But, as for Al, he sacrificed himself to the
stage. There was not a single moment of the day when he put the
theater out of his mind and paid more attention to her. Before it
could develop into an intolerable situation, she began to wonder
about her next move. She had anticipated finding in Al a husband
and lover; instead she had found a human machine, geared to
achieve only one objective—top billing on a theater poster.
Making love, as far as Al was concerned, was of less importance
than getting bookings as a singer. And yet, with all his sacrifice he
was, in Henrietta's estimation, making very little headway, especially in the matter of earning money.

2

But if Henrietta thought she was having a bad time, the months
that followed were even worse. Al announced that in time he
would have to leave San Francisco for New York. The real
opportunities lay on Broadway, but one had to be ready.

Al was singing his heart out in out-of-the-way variety theaters
and the waterfront bistros to rough-looking patrons, the greater
portion of whom were well under the bottle. Sometimes they
threw their wine glasses at him.

When he came home to her on these occasions and told her he
had been a target, Henrietta would huddle in his arms and sob
softly. In the days that followed she was fast losing her patience
when her husband came home with his suit plastered with egg
yolk, or his face bruised by a thrown wine glass. Definitely now
she was trying to convince him to quit this crazy business. He
was performing in the worst dens of Frisco, and he was getting
nowhere. He could have accomplished so much more in some
other line. But his answer, as he himself recalled, was if she would

ask him to stand on his head, he would do it; if she would ask him to swim across San Francisco Bay, he would dive right in—"but, please, Honey, don't ask me to give up show business."

Al and Henrietta remained in Frisco until 1908. Eventually he did most of his singing at the Globe Theater, where he established somewhat of a following.

But his performances were still no more noteworthy than those of the average vaude singer. He was considered capable enough, but only one of many who just about toed the mark to fill out a bill of entertainment. Al knew that he was not making the impression he had dreamed about. Just a singer—not bad but not spectacular. This could not satisfy Al. He wondered what he could do to lift himself above the crowd where the heights were more rewarding. Could it be that he had nothing special to offer and that the world would not miss him if he were to give up singing altogether and turn to something more dependable?

Once again he was ready to chuck the whole thing.

3

The people of San Francisco had dug themselves out of the rubble left by the earthquake, and rebuilding was in full progress. A majestic new city was to rise out of the ashes.

Meanwhile Al was busy trying to snag enough bookings to earn a living for his wife and himself. He played the burlesque houses and vaude joints along the Barbary Coast, and here he came face to face with the toughest elements of the population. He did not always please them and there were occasions when he had to walk off in the middle of his number.

In the apartment, he suddenly had the urge to write to his parents back in Washington, and he composed a longer letter than usual, assuring them that he would see them soon, and ending with, "and, Momma, wait till you see my wife—you'll love her."

A growing desire to return to New York took hold of him. He was anxious to try that seemingly impregnable fortress once again. He felt that he was now better prepared to storm those towering walls.

With Henrietta hanging on his arm, they strolled along the Embarcadero and looked out across the blue, white-capped waters of the great bay, and glimpsed the mountains in the north and Oakland to the east.

San Francisco, since the earthquake, was taking on a new, a more beautiful aspect. Sometime in the future he would be back—of this he was sure—how could he stay away from this enchanting land? With him the state of California would always rate first, the true locale of the fountain of youth.

On a fall day they boarded a train bound for the East Coast. Al was excited about going back, yet full of misgivings about the outcome of the pending contest.

4

In the beginning of the year 1904 not a single nickelodeon had been in existence. By 1908, two million people patronized the moving pictures each day, and two-thirds of this number were adults.

In New York the seating capacity of the new crop of "theaters" averaged up to 299 per house, since 300 or more necessitated the acquisition of a theater license. Stores, warehouses, restaurants were cleaned out, seats and equipment installed, and lo and behold!—a multitude of moving picture emporiums.

Al Jolson, back in New York as a "single" and twenty-two years of age, could boast now of seven years experience, one way or another, in show business. He was booked as a program singer in Manhattan, Bronx, and Brooklyn theaters, where patrons were being drained away by the infant film industry rapidly growing into a giant. Al sang his songs and earned a living, but it went no further than that.

There was always an oversupply of male singers for the ever-diminishing vaude shows, and there were times when he found himself at liberty, as in the old days, but now his earnings averaged enough to tide him and his wife over without the necessity of taking on survival jobs.

Vaude was being irrevocably undermined by this new form of show business, the "pix biz," which was able to offer to the working masses for a nickel or a dime a whole new experience in entertainment. Live shows were being forsaken without too much self-recrimination on the part of the deserters.

But vaude put up a battle for survival, even if it had to play second fiddle and end up as the prologue to the feature film presentation.

In time Jolson played the Palace in Cleveland, the Keith's in Boston, the Albee in Brooklyn, Proctor's 58th and Proctor's 23rd in Manhattan.

His experience on the road and his adventures in California seemed to have conditioned him for these appearances, and he gave a more finished performance. He also received special assignments to appear at receptions and benefit affairs at such gay New York night spots as Rector's, Shanley's, Bustonaby's, Keen's Chop House, and the fabulous Maxim's, and Henrietta began to find herself more and more a sort of show-biz widow. While her husband strove for the favor of the crowds and busied himself with his singing, Henrietta sat alone in their New York apartment, waiting—always waiting for Al.

His performances on his current bookings were adequate and satisfied the listeners. He overheard a few remarks by the patrons and these were in his favor. It was like being a cabinet-maker and producing a piece of furniture that pleased the customer, but nothing more. He was afraid his work was falling into a rut.

Perhaps to forget this impasse, he escorted Henrietta to Rector's on the first night he was at liberty.

Al was not the suave, smooth-talking, smooth-romancing type with the ladies. He was always himself, down to earth, out-spoken, aboveboard, holding nothing in reserve. He never got over a feeling of inadequacy in the presence of the feminine gender. He always experienced a sort of diamond-in-the-rough complex.

He was not, definitely, a waltz-dancing, hand-holding romeo, and he knew it. But in the company of Henrietta he found an enchanting sense of fulfillment. He could be himself—and yet, the way she looked at him, it made him feel quite romantic after all.

Al was between bookings. He sought relaxation and also a chance to inspect some current vaude acts.

At Hammerstein's Victoria at 42nd and Broadway Al—all by himself—watched the Salome dance on the stage. This was primarily an exhibition by a veiled buxom female nude, twisting and bending into a variety of positions that were intriguing if not graceful. He had just settled down to enjoy the other acts on the bill when his brother Harry ran blithely out on the stage and went into a fast, lively rendition of catchy songs and a routine called "The Ghetto Sport" in Hebrew dialect. He received a rousing round of applause that demanded an encore. Harry sang another tune with soft shoe accompaniment, and they made him come out for a third time before he was permitted to leave the stage.

Al leaned back in his seat, wiping his forehead with his handkerchief. A startling but pleasant surprise. Alive and bubbling, good old Harry! Absolutely wowing them! As soon as Harry's performance was over, Al hurried backstage. There ensued a first-class exchange of greetings and back-slappings. They hugged each other like two long-lost sisters instead of stage-seasoned brothers.

They met Willie Hammerstein himself, owner of the theater, in the lobby where—as was his custom—he was leaning on a marble-topped radiator, surrounded by a coterie of his subordinates and hangers-on, each one striving for his favor.

Willie Hammerstein was noted for his brassy showmanship. He was shrewd, kept his fingers close upon the pulse of the public, seemed to read its thoughts, and supplied what it wanted most to see and pay for. Week after week he displayed upon his stage freaks and abnormalities of every description, from bearded ladies to reformed bank robbers, in addition to a never-ending parade of trapeze artists, unicyclists, jugglers, contortionists, and performing monkeys.

5

Al studied the theatrical journals and magazines. He learned that besides the Keith-Proctor-Albee and Willie Hammerstein interests, another circuit, Klaw and Erlanger, Advanced Vaudeville, newly encouraged and boosted by William Morris, was offering hot competition and bidding up actors' salaries.

In 1908, though the movies had made terrific inroads into the green pastures once reserved exclusively for vaudeville, there was still enough grazing land left for the nurture and survival of vaude to keep it quite alive for the next decade.

During those days of struggle for recognition, Al Jolson had little time for the social life. At the age when most young men indulged in the pastime of girl-chasing and dating, Al, already a married man, was too busy with the formative steps of his career to let his attention wander from his prime objective. He knew that a girl named Henrietta, as radiant as any of the prettiest, was always waiting for him. Besides, he was not much of a party man. He could not flirt for the mere sake of flirting. His conversation invariably veered to the subject of the stage and his connection with it. And Al, though well-built, of solid proportions, was not what is commonly known as a handsome man. His nose was somewhat on the flat side and his cheek bones were high; his mouth was wide, the lips generous; his eyes were round and had the habit of rolling when he told some catchy story or cracked a joke.

He could be quite dull at times, especially when he was engrossed in a card game with "the boys" under a canopy of tobacco smoke. He did not drink; that was one vice he found he could ignore. His appearance, off the stage, was conservative; he had adopted turtleneck sweaters, and he could have passed for a typical young businessman. His too-brief education, having been limited to a few years in grade school, precluded any conversation on involved or technical subjects, but one seeing him on the street would have said that there goes a performer on the stage, or a singer of popular songs.

It was only Henrietta who had singled him out as somebody extra-special, though even as his wife she could hold onto only a small part of him, the public claiming the greater part.

Al Jolson, in his movements about New York, could not help but see the material advances being made in all phases of human life. The moving picture had blossomed into a reality and now was growing by leaps and bounds to become a tremendous force in the American way of life. In addition, he saw the perfection and acceptance of Edison's phonograph, a miraculous invention indeed, enabling people to sit in their own parlors and listen to entire programs of entertainment. Voices of their favorite performers were forever captured on a cylinder of wax so that they could listen to those voices wherever and whenever they pleased.

Also on the streets of the metropolis Al could see the inroads the automobile was making into transportation, and its effect on patterns of living. More and more the old hay-burners were being replaced by horseless carriages. Already there were so many makes—the Maxwell, Aericar, Wayne, Franklin, Elmore, Cadillac, Winton, Peerless, Packard.

Some day—perhaps soon—if things were well with him, he would certainly become the owner of an automobile and take Henrietta on long rides. Meanwhile he must concentrate on his immediate objective, which was to perfect his style of performance and become a top name on Broadway.

He sacrificed personal indulgence for the cause of his ambition. He must not disappoint his father, his mother, his wife. He must justify their faith in him. He had promised his father— back when he had been a small boy repeatedly running away from home—that he would amount to something. Yes—he would be the Yoelson family's seventh cantor, singing the songs of the people, but from the stage of a theater. He was sure his father in time would understand.

But thus far Jolson knew that he was nothing more than a plugger, a run-of-the-mill song man.

6

Al was appearing in a small theater in Brooklyn and his engagement was not going too well. He felt that something was lacking; in fact, something had been lacking in his work all along. He had a voice—he was sure of it. But that spark of greatness was not in it because, as he surmised, he had not yet found it in himself.

He sang as though it were a duty, and he always managed to deliver a fair performance. But he knew there must be something more than that. He did not inspire his listeners; he did not sweep them off their feet.

He was in his dressing room. He was to go on after the present number—a man-and-wife comedy act—bowed off.

He sat there, quiet, motionless, and looked into the mirror. There was no striking quality in his personality. He could have been an unheralded tailor or a shoemaker or a grocery clerk.

He was pretty sure he had gone as far as he could. He didn't even know the fundamentals of musical technique, having never taken a bona-fide music lesson. The fact was—he told himself bluntly there in the dressing room—if he had had any dreams about a glamorous future on the stage, these were now being dissipated. Even his brother Harry was making better headway. There were things his brother could do on the stage which Al could not—dancing and reeling off joke after joke in dialect. Al shook his head. Why in the world did he, Asa Yoelson, ever want to get into this business anyway?

How long could he keep up this mediocre routine? There had to be more to it. His performances had to be powerful enough to awaken and inspire a lethargic audience. But how? What was the secret? Then it happened, unexpectedly, suddenly. Al had a dresser—more of a friend, really—known by no other name than Ezra. Al had never learned the man's last name, but that didn't matter to Al. It was Ezra who offered a suggestion that seemed, at first, too far out, but gradually Al Jolson considered it as a possibility—to go on in blackface and sing the songs in the true Southland style. It was only a matter of applying some burnt cork to his face and hands, whitening his lips. He took the plunge, mainly out of curiosity, but still skeptical about the outcome. It was like grabbing at a straw. If he didn't have that something special within him, how in the world would this masquerade help? But he did put on the burnt cork and come out on the stage as a "collud gen'man," following Ezra's instructions. Ezra took one look at him and declared that Al could have passed as his own brother. Al thanked him for the compliment, but within himself he was a caldron of mixed feelings of fear, doubt, and wild hope as he awaited the signal for his walk-on.

He faced the audience, then went into his song, "Rosey, you are my posey—"

The audience watched and listened, quiet and tense. Al felt there was something in the air. He sang the number, strutting up and down the stage, spreading his white-gloved fingers in waving gestures, rolling wide open eyes that shone like fireballs, and to the spectators he was a new, lovable, shuffling "collud gen'man," easing his way through life, with a song on his smacking lips. The people looked on, entranced. The singing had a new inspiration, a plaintive note, a laugh and a sob in it that went straight to their hearts.

When Al sang out the final note and made his bow, there was a brief silence, then the applause started, grew in intensity, and did not stop. The applause went on and on. It seemed it would never stop. Presently it increased to a climactic outburst. He heard his name being called—"Al Jolson—Jolson—"

Finally the applause died down. The manager in the wings motioned to Al to give them an encore. Al went back on stage and sang another chorus. When he finished, the applause thundered forth again. He had to sing once more. The audience seemed to have gone wild in its demonstration. As he walked off the stage he could hardly believe it. It was a fantastic dream. The applause shook the theater even though he was now in the wings and out of sight.

The manager gripped his arm, told him he had done something to them, he didn't know what. Al had to give them another encore, or they would have torn the theater apart. Back on the stage again, facing the cheers. He sang another chorus, then he came backstage and saw Ezra, who sported a wide grin.

Blackface. That would be Al Jolson's mark from now on.

Al sat down in front of the dresser mirror, feeling faint, bewildered, excited, and fearful, all at the same time. He still couldn't understand it. What, really, had happened?

And so it was not long before the word spread in theatrical circles about a new blackfaced singer who was wowing them in Brooklyn.

At the end of his second week in the theater, in November of 1909, Al Jolson had a visitor backstage—Lew Dockstader, producer and star of Dockstader's Minstrels. He seemed to be impressed with Al's singing, offered him a contract to join his minstrels.

Al considered this a smile from Lady Luck. Lew Dockstader's Minstrels was one of the hottest shows on the road.

Al's dresser and friend, old Ezra, wore a grin that was wider than ever these days.

Jolson had no time to wonder about what was happening to him. Dockstader made him grind through rehearsals without let-up, teaching him with relentless drive the elements of good minstrel entertainment. To Al this was another step up the ladder to the big time.

Al often recalled his feelings during those bittersweet days. Life had suddenly taken on a new, fresh meaning. Being one of Dockstader's Minstrels was a gift from the angels.

1

Lew Dockstader was a member of the old formal school of
show business. He was rigid in his principles and wary of any
innovation that would deviate from the tried and true. His
minstrel show was a model format, with the group of blackfaced
members sitting in precise formation on either side of him,
tambourines on their knees, and Dockstader himself, the
interlocutor, occupying his chair of state with a pomposity that
was comic opera in effect. He took his occupation with absolute
seriousness and he expected the same from his minstrels. Any
member wavering from the rules laid down by Dockstader would
face the penalty of a layoff.

Al Jolson, on his second day with Dockstader, realized the
situation. It was as if he suddenly found himself in a military squad
with strict disciplinary regulations. He sat in his place next to the
end man through the entire performance, singing only with the
rest of them as one of the group.

At the end of the first week he had the dismaying sensation of
having passed into the shadow of an eclipse. His sudden success
in Brooklyn as a blackfaced singer had been choked off almost
before it had a chance to survive. At the end of the first month he
asked Dockstader for the privilege of doing a solo. To this request
the answer was that when Dockstader judged him ready for a
solo, he would tell him so. Al was further reminded by his
employer that none of the other members of the group over-

stepped the bounds of decorum set by Dockstader. They all worked as a unit, no one climbing over the other. Jolson had to learn that one fact while he was under the great interlocutor's wing. Dockstader tolerated no upstarts.

Al went back to his place and put his tambourine on his knee.

He remained a "cooperative member," as Dockstader had requested, and kept himself under control as they performed in New York and on the road. The minstrels played the larger cities and towns across the country. Always it was the same routine, the same songs and manner of singing them, the same jokes, the same everything.

Dockstader was a stubborn standpatter—he abhorred change, and he ignored the necessity for it. To him the minstrel show in its traditional form was perfection, and he felt obligated to keep it that way.

But Al, in his travels on the road—especially in the South, in New Orleans and its environs—had heard the Negro voices on the Mississippi levees, and had discovered in their singing a new rhythm, fascinating in its primitive appeal. It was a rising musical tide, held back by the conservatives, but which was seeping out across the barriers. Little by little this American folk singing was to feel its way up the Mississippi into Memphis, St. Louis, Chicago, and other centers along the river's course, and gradually to filter into New York to be re-echoed by the Negro singers and bands of Harlem.

They took a melody, loosened it up, and drove it into this strange new rhythm—a rhythm that, though novel to the general public, was as ancient as the Negro ancestry in western Africa whence it originated. It found its survival in the heart of New Orleans; later, in 1914, in Chicago, they were to call this music "jazz"—a derivative of "Jazbo," a term then used extensively in minstrel shows, usually as a nickname.

This Negro music was an interplay of free-floating notes and beats pulsating against the core of the tune itself. Slowly at first, but with increasing momentum, this irresistible syncopation took hold of the imagination of the younger element. Soon people were dancing to this faster, more exhilarating arrangement, to be identified as "ragtime," from a Negro clog dance in the deep South known as "ragging."

To Al Jolson this was the kind of music he had been looking for, the kind he wanted to sing on the stage. It was a provocative, accelerated tempo, and there were no set rules or prescribed methods.

Al became a devotee of this new form. He studied it. He listened to the combos playing it in the Southland when the minstrel show went on tour again in 1909. He listened to the Mississippi levee Negroes singing out their feelings of sorrow as they loaded the cotton bales aboard the paddle-wheel steamboats. The rising wail sometimes reminded him of a cantor's chant in a synagogue.

This was to be known as the "blues." The blues was the sadness and ragtime the gaiety of jazz.

Al went about humming the music to himself, singing it to a circle of friends at private get-togethers. It was not like anything heard before by the general public. It was the expression of freedom.

During an intermission Al spoke to Dockstader again about a solo spot. After a year's silence on the subject he could no longer restrain himself. Dockstader's reaction was that this Jolson fellow was giving him trouble. While the rest of the group were quite satisfied with conditions as they were, Jolson kept agitating for the spotlight. Dockstader did not encourage the superiority of one member over another. He strove to maintain equality among them, thus eliminating jealousies and group politics. To this policy he attributed the show's success, as evidenced by the ever-increasing audiences. Other minstrel shows playing to lesser houses were but sketchy imitations of the champions.

Dockstader dealt firmly with Jolson. He admitted to associates that the young upstart had a voice, a good voice, not yet fully developed in its power. But Dockstader did not intend to upset the applecart. He could not take the risk, no matter how tempting. And yet Al persisted. Lately he had approached the implacable interlocutor with that new brand of music. Al was sure it was going to be the big thing in America. Dockstader had listened to it, and had informed those about him that he had no use for it. This he made very plain to Jolson, and Al finally agreed to stop his pestering. Dockstader recalled later that Jolson satisfactorily performed his part in the show, that there was a certain refreshing spirit about him that audiences seemed to recognize and appreciate, and that Al was popular with his fellow minstrels. He further admitted that there was something Al Jolson had that the others lacked, but, again, the minstrel boss dared not focus the public's attention on Jolson's talent, lest the equilibrium of the show be endangered.

2

The ordeal of these performances was bearing down upon Jolson and causing increasing irritation. He saw no purpose in what he was doing. He was never given the opportunity of singing solo, the way he had started to sing that time in Brooklyn before Dockstader had found him.

Working in the minstrel show seemed a slow death to Al Jolson; he was beginning to feel the agony of frustration. Al knew he had security here but no progress. It was like working in a factory, doing a routine stint day after day, with no innovation. He broke the rule and spoke to Dockstader once more about a solo spot but the answer was the same—the great interlocutor would play no favorites. The only reason Al didn't walk out was his responsibility toward Henrietta. He couldn't let her down. They did have a sort of marriage, and the hundred a week Dockstader was paying him was the seal that kept the connubial bonds from snapping. A break in Al's career impasse finally did come.

While Dockstader's Minstrels were performing in New York, a quiet individual caught the act several nights in a row. Apparently he had come to look at the minstrels. But after the first night it was not the minstrels as a group who interested him. It was the spirited young fellow next to the end man, the one they called Al Jolson. The visitor was watching Al sing in the quartet and he studied the young man's performance from all angles. Sitting in a front seat, night after night, watching, studying, figuring—the stranger became convinced.

Beneath a front of self-effacement the quiet man made his way backstage and asked Dockstader for permission to talk with Al.

Dockstader was slow to agree, but the politeness of the visitor finally induced him to nod.

As Al Jolson himself recalled the incident, the quiet man placed his hand on Al's shoulder and uttered two words: "You're it."

Then he introduced himself as Arthur Klein, agent.

He told Al his talent was being stifled in the confines of the minstrel show; it was time to look to the heights.

Klein convinced Al to quit the minstrels. Despite Dockstader's plea, Al walked out of the group and looked to Klein for the next move. Klein had nothing definite to offer at the moment, but he'd keep in touch.

From time to time they had lengthy conferences; acquaintanceship ripened into friendship. They visited a Jewish restaurant on Seventh Avenue, gorged themselves on borscht, chicken liver knishes, and *lokshen kugel*, Al's favorite. Over these delicacies they discussed show business. Klein knew all the important theater people—producers, directors, operators of vaude circuits, theater owners.

Al began to see in his newly acquired agent the possibility of a turning point. To his sister Rose he wrote: "I can hardly wait for developments. I have an agent, Arthur Klein. Now maybe something will happen. How is Momma? Is Pop still wowing them at the synagogue?"

3

Arthur Klein was an astute manager. He had watched Al Jolson in Lew Dockstader's Minstrels, he had studied his possibilities, and he had come to a conclusion: this young man had a future in show business.

Given a singer with a great potential, would it be bookings in vaude circuits where his singing would be more or less muffled in the shuffle of hoofers, croaking seals, jugglers, heavy-thighed females, contortionists, and acrobatic dogs? Would it be minstrel shows where he'd be held down to singing in chorus with all the other minstrels, or perhaps in a quartet crooning stereotyped songs that were grandfather's favorites? A waste of time and talent.

Klein was determined to make something of Al Jolson. Sure, Al could sing, but so could a thousand others like him—some of them with operatic voices. But this Jolson was endowed with a unique quality difficult to pinpoint. It was something audiences could hardly fail to acknowledge. Klein, seasoned by years of experience, sensed it, felt it. Most of the times in his appraisals he had scored bull's-eyes. To hell with vaude circuits, burlesque, four-a-day cheap variety shows, even the minstrels. Not for his new find. Klein was going to have a talk with Lee Shubert of the Shuberts' show-biz empire.

He knew they were opening with an extravaganza, *La Belle Paree*, at the Winter Garden, the most impressive theater in New York. That would be the right move.

Klein brought Al Jolson into the office of the Shuberts. Of course they were too busy to see anyone—but Lee Shubert gave Klein a break.

Shubert looked at Klein's protégé. He saw before him a young man who did not look too much like an actor. He wondered why Klein was so enthusiastic.

Klein, gambling on a bold stroke, insisted that Lee put Al in the Shuberts' new spectacle. Lee's answer was No. But Arthur Klein abhorred the word No. He countered with the suggestion that Lee listen to Jolson sing. One song—no more. To get rid of them, Shubert agreed. One song. Al started to sing in a frightened, wavering voice. Klein glanced at him quickly. What was the matter with the young dope? This was his big chance and he was blowing it. Get hold of yourself, boy. Sing, damn you, sing. Lee Shubert was shaking his head. And then it happened. The Jolson power burst forth in a rising storm. *That* was singing. A verse and the chorus of "Alexander's Ragtime Band." Lee listened, awe taking the place of disgust. He detected a timbre in that voice, and something else—a performer vibrantly alive; a technique that would reach an audience. When Al finished the number Lee Shubert remained sitting at his desk, quieter than usual. Klein later called it a hypnotic trance.

Lee Shubert was too sophisticated to use superlatives, but the cold fact of the young fellow's audience pull could not be denied. However, he insisted he had no place for Jolson in *La Belle Paree*. The show was already cast and in rehearsal. Klein then

suggested the possibility of *making* a place in the show for his
client. Lee Shubert promised to think about it, and this was good
enough for Klein.

But it was not good enough for Al. He had to work to earn a
living for Henrietta and himself. He could not live on promises.
While waiting for the Shuberts to make up their minds, Al
proposed a return to the vaude houses. Klein tried to convince Al
that performing in the low-grade spots was harmful to his
budding career. He tried to show Jolson that the big time was the
only place for real achievement. All they needed was the one
break, bound to come soon.

But Al was impatient. He was worried. He had only to look at
his wife to realize that his marriage was in jeopardy. They could
not live on air alone, let alone love. He had tried to earn money,
like other men. He wouldn't mind going back to the variety
shows, even burlesque or, as a last resort, the minstrels. This
waiting and doing nothing—he was not used to it. He began to
resent Klein's interference with the normal aspects of his life.
Klein was going too far. Al would have it out with him. Al could
make his own decisions. He didn't need someone doing it for him.
This was his own life, his own career. If he wanted to sing in a dive,
then it was up to him. Nobody was going to tell him where and
when. He would tell Klein off once and for all. If need be Klein
could very well step out of Al's life.

Henrietta too was upset about Klein. She had given him the
cold shoulder from the first. Now it was up to Al.

When Klein came to the apartment, Al's resolve to castigate
his manager seemed to have evaporated. Instead, he found
himself listening to Klein, who was telling him he had interviewed
some of the leading producers of big-time shows on Broadway.
But nothing yet. Once again it was a matter of waiting. Al was
annoyed now. His temper was fast running out of control.

He told Klein of Henrietta's reaction. He was in peril of losing
her. When Klein asked for details, Al hesitated. He became
uneasy. He fidgeted. He looked away. Klein suspected something drastically wrong between Al and his wife, but he did not
press the matter. He could guess it had something to do with
their marital relationship. He had come across this with his

clients several times before. It was nothing new. Sometimes it was the career that put a damper on lovemaking. He suspected that was Al's trouble.

Al himself informed him. There was a rising barrier between Al and his wife. She was more than he could handle, if Klein knew what that meant. She wanted something he couldn't give her, children. Klein asked Al whether he had seen a doctor. Al shook his head. He had no family doctor. He did not want a doctor. It was something that had been wrong with him for a long time. It was something that would have to work itself out, or remain as it was. Klein listened attentively, but did not press. It was Al himself who supplied the answer: a case of impotence. Klein assured him it would clear up in time. Yes, it had been with Al for a number of years. Maybe it was his deep involvement with his career. A psychological condition. One had to concentrate on a marriage—that was Klein's opinion. He had seen it happen before. Some of the greatest matinee idols on the stage were impotent in the real-life relationship with their wives. In time, there was a chance of it passing. Al need not worry. It was a matter of diplomacy, of treating Henrietta with kid gloves. The main thing now was to focus his attention on his career. That was what really mattered. According to Klein, that was the destiny prearranged for Jolson.

Al could accept this declaration—but this idleness. He wanted to work. Anything, please, Klein, you dog. But Klein shook his head. He was a mild man, and cool. He never raised his voice. He made his decisions quietly, and he stuck to them. He insisted his client stick to these decisions as well.

It was the price of fame, of success, of winning the public. The big time. Al Jolson, you've cast your lot with the big time. Klein patted Al on the shoulder. The two men looked at each other as they ate their *kreplach* in their favorite Jewish restaurant on Seventh Avenue. The big time, Al. Hold on. But hold on to your marriage, too. Then and there Al knew the score. He could not dispense with Klein. That quiet man had become the guiding force of his existence.

They finished their *kreplach* and *flomen comput* dessert; walked out of the restaurant into the autumnal air of Manhattan.

They took a long walk up Broadway. Al kept looking at the
theater marquees. As in that earlier period that now seemed so
long ago, he envisioned his own name in the electric lights.

4

Klein was deliberate, persistent. On the very next day he found
Lee Shubert at the Winter Garden Theater watching the
rehearsals, and spoke to the producer about Al. Shubert tried to
satisfy Klein with a promise for the next production after *La Belle
Paree* but Klein would not accept the subterfuge. Shubert then
promised a conference with Hammond, the director, and Edgar
Smith, the writer.

Meanwhile Al was feeling discouraged about the whole thing.
He knew he could be booked in vaude but Klein had put his foot
down. Al wondered whether they were not knocking their heads
against a stone wall, trying to achieve the impossible.

But Jolson and Klein saw Shubert in his office the following
day, and the director was present. The director admitted he
could squeeze Jolson into the second act between Mitzi Hajos'
dance number and the solo by Kitty Gordon—but it would have
to be a short bit. Klein shook his head. He insisted his client be
given the time and spot where he would have room to maneuver.
Al Jolson was no amateur. Given the right support, that boy
would bring the house down. That was Klein's guarantee.
Hammond accused Klein of trying to run the whole show. Jolson
would go on as and when the director indicated or he wouldn't go
on at all. Take it or leave it. Klein calmly agreed to the arrangement—for now.

Al shook hands with Hammond, the director, Frank Tours, the
composer, and Edgar Smith, the writer, and several members of
the cast, including the gay Mlle. Dazie and Barney Bernard,
comedian. He was of course introduced to Mitzi Hajos, the
radiant star of the show, who gave him an encouraging smile. Al
was beginning to feel at home.

After a conference with the director, a song number was selected with Al's sanction: "I Want a Girl Just Like the Girl That Married Dear Old Dad."

He felt confident that he could do justice to the song.

Jolson and Klein, after all this, went out into the New York winter evening air. They stopped at a lunch counter to grab a sandwich and both were too excited to care or enjoy what they were eating.

As they sat at the counter, Klein leaned forward and put his hand on Al's shoulder, telling him they had finally made it. Somehow he had finagled a part—a small one, true, but a part—from the hard-hearted director. Now it was up to Al.

They walked along their favorite promenade—Broadway. They discussed Al's prospective debut in a real Broadway show. Al enjoyed every minute of this anticipation. He forgot his immediate problems. He forgot his impasse with Henrietta. In fact, he did not think of her at all. He could see only the stage before him. He was already enjoying the vision of a large, approving audience. He was already hearing the applause. He would not disappoint them. He would not let Hammond down, nor his friend Arthur Klein, who had made all this possible.

They came slowly back to Al's apartment. Henrietta was already in bed. Klein came in for a final cup of coffee. They talked some more. Al was living in the excitement of a great dream coming true at last. When Klein left, Al finally thought of Henrietta. He didn't wake her now. Let her sleep, the poor kid. She was having a hard time of it. But wait until she heard the news: her husband in a genuine Broadway show. He tried to undress quietly as he prepared for bed. He stole into bed, careful not to awaken her. Her sleep was deep. He would make her happy. There were other ways, he was sure, of making Henrietta happy besides having children. The thought entered his mind at this time: why not adopt a child? As soon as he was up there in show business and earning real money, he would broach the subject to her. He lay awake for two hours, thinking of himself on the stage, the hundreds of faces upturned toward him, the hundreds of eyes watching him.

The following morning he woke to find Henrietta standing at the window. She was already dressed. Her face had that hurt, repressed look he had become familiar with. These days she rarely smiled. He remembered how gay she had been the first months of their marriage.

He told her of his good fortune, and assured her he was on the way to the top.

Her answer: she had heard that story a hundred times.

Al insisted to Klein that he must do his act in blackface. Blackface had become his trademark. Remember how he had wowed them in Brooklyn when first he appeared in black? And then his performances with Dockstader's Minstrels. Klein was skeptical at first, but after a while he saw the plausibility of Al's argument. When he suggested to Hammond that Al would go on in blackface, Hammond almost blew his top. He ranted, he raved. Positively no blackface. Nobody was going to hide his face behind burnt cork. This was not a cheap minstrel show. Thousands of dollars were sunk into this production. It was high class, for high-class paying customers. Hammond announced that Al Jolson would go on in his natural state as a white singer—or nothing doing. Klein brought this declaration to Al. Al was downcast, disappointed. He knew that blackface was his own infallable gimmick. The greatest effect of his performance would be lost in the natural. They could see no way out. Hammond was a very determined man. He believed in his decisions being carried out to the letter—or else it was curtains for the dissenter.

Klein hit upon a solution. Al could rehearse in natural, but when the real performance took place on opening night, he would come out in blackface and Hammond would have to accept it. There would be nothing else the director could do. If the audience went for it, then it would be blackface permanently. If not, either Al would be out of a job or he would sing in the natural.

Al agreed to the plan. He was playing for big stakes. If he lost, it might mean the end of his career. Henrietta, on hearing of the plan, thought it was sheer folly. Why did Al have to wear a mask? If he was such a good performer the audience would recognize his ability. She was also impatient with Al's constant staying away from the apartment. She rarely saw him. He was always immersed in his rehearsals, or he was with Klein, or he attended other shows. Every night he came home long after she had gone to sleep. Going or coming, Klein was always at his side. Henrietta grew despondent. She felt out of it—a spectator—hardly a wife. Where was their home, their family? She knew, by this time, that it was not in Al's power to give her a child. She would have to live with that realization, the frustration, the futility. Resentment grew and grew in her.

Hammond listened to Al sing during the rehearsals. He had a puzzled expression upon his face. He demanded to know from Klein what kind of "style" Al was using. It was not the singing he had anticipated. Al sort of twisted the tune and seemed to add uncalled-for notes. It was not the way the other singers rendered their numbers. One could understand and enjoy their music, but coming from Al Jolson the song assumed a strange arrangement that almost obscured the melody. That disturbed Hammond's sense of hearing. Klein assured the director that this was something new, something up from the South. It was "jazz" and the audiences would go wild over it. Klein swore to that. Hammond, still skeptical, finally agreed to permit Al to sing the songs as he pleased. Another victory for Jolson and Klein. Al breathed in relief. Now he was ready. Now he could go to town. He would teach the public an entirely new system of music, a new incantation, a new rhythm. In time they would grow to love it. Klein beamed broadly. Actually, he gloated, they were pioneers in the entertainment jungle.

5

After the regular rehearsals, when all the performers, and Hammond as well, had left the theater, Klein and Al remained. They held their own secret rehearsal, with Al putting on the burnt cork and performing in blackface. Al sang his songs with appropriate gestures and expressions, and Klein was fired with enthusiasm. He saw this as a sensational bit of innovation. He also recognized in Al a performer who never seemed to tire.

Jolson could belt forth song after song with no apparent letup.
The voice held. When Klein asked whether he was hungry, Al
shook his head. He would not permit anything to interrupt him
when he was going full blast. He strutted to and fro upon the
stage, a minstrel straying from the flock, a minstrel scaling the
heights of inspiration. Klein watched, fascinated. What had he
found in this man, so nondescript in appearance, this lonely
figure?

Finally Klein convinced Al that this was enough for one night. It
was, in fact, near dawn. Klein reminded him of a waiting wife in
the apartment. Al replied that anyway she was fast asleep. Klein
wondered whether Al realized what he was doing to her
emotionally. Al was listening to the applause of audiences yet to
materialize. He was seeing their upturned faces, all watching him.
He was seeing his name blazing in electric lights. It was all to
come true at last—was it not, Mr. Klein? Klein assured him, yes,
yes. It was coming true, but hadn't he better go home? It was
possible that Henrietta was really worried. Jolson conceded that
Klein was right, so they made their way to the apartment. Klein
said good-night, watching Al go in.

Al tiptoed into the bedroom, tried not to waken his wife. But no
need for caution. She lay there, her eyes wide open. She asked
him how long this was going to keep up. She was lonely,
miserable, neglected. She told him she counted for nothing in his
life. Wouldn't it be better for both concerned if she were to bow
out? Al suddenly became frantic. He had not bargained for this.
He approached the bed. He got down on his knees. He pleaded.
Henrietta, whatever you do, honey chile, don't leave me now.
Something important is about to happen to me, to both of us. I'll
give you everything you want. But don't talk about breaking up
our marriage. She did not answer. Al did not say anything more.
For him, no sleep. He had to satisfy his two great obsessions—
the theater on the one hand and Henrietta on the other. He came
into bed quietly and lay very still, careful not to disturb her. He lay
there for the rest of the darkness, staring up at the ceiling,
desperate, fearful, bewildered. If only Klein were in the room, to
comfort him, to advise him. Quiet—quiet—he dared not talk any

more, lest he break the spell. He was listening to her muffled sobs. He was afraid even to put his hand on her shoulder to solace her. When the sobbing stopped he knew she was asleep. Thank heavens for that. Sleep on, fair girl. But whatever you do, don't step out of my life. His eyes were brimming. The soft bit of femininity beside him was his very heartbeat. For her sake, and her sake alone, he had to succeed. There was no alternative.

6

On the night preceding the opening of *La Belle Paree*, Klein and Jolson took a taxicab to Central Park.

They strolled along the paths and breathed deep of the cold night air, and discussed tomorrow's event. The sounds of the city hummed about them, muffled by the barricade of the evergreen trees. Here one could think without distraction. Further on, the nostalgic sight of the bare-boughed maples that lined the walks reminded Al so much of those that arched his home street back in Washington.

Jolson was also remembering another night he had spent on a park bench, when his shoes had been stolen.

He told Klein about it and the latter laughed.

Klein informed Al that tomorrow night would be the turning point of his life. Either Al went up the ladder of success or turned backward toward that bench in Central Park.

After a brief period of silence they both laughed and made their way home, Klein still figuring the angles, Al with a head full of dreams. . . .

When Al was in his apartment he wrote a long letter to his parents, telling them of his lucky break and promising them an early visit home. He ended the letter with a row of crosses indicating kisses for his mother.

Henrietta, seemingly more at ease and somewhat reconciled, approached him from behind as he sat at the table. She leaned

against him, put her arms over his shoulders, inquired about all those crosses at the bottom of the letter. Kisses for his mother, he explained, then pulled her down over his lap and told her that kisses for her he delivered in person.

Which he did, most emphatically.

BOOK THREE

Broadway Years
1911–1927
Shubert's Winter Garden Shows

10

1

March 20, 1911—opening night of *La Belle Paree*.

Hustle and bustle behind the curtain. Scenery shifters busy, electricians arranging and testing lights, makeup men busy with the principals of the show, chorus girls in various stages of nudity preparing for their numbers, assistant directors calling last-minute instructions. Hammond conferring with Lee and S. S. Shubert in a heated discussion. Everything was fast and frantic in anticipation of the curtain's ascent.

The Winter Garden Theater was rapidly filling up. The attendance would be better than expected. As Shubert had prophesied the audience would be a sophisticated one, the social register being amply represented.

In the pit the orchestra was tuning up and there was electric tension charging the interior of the great house.

Al had a small cubicle of a dressing room, being considered one of the lesser members of the cast. But he had his paraphernalia ready: his greasepaint, his burnt cork, and his costume.

Klein squeezed in with Al to keep a sharp lookout at the door, for he didn't want anybody to suspect that Jolson was going to perform in blackface. So far so good—no one suspected. The surprise was going to be thorough, Al and Klein were sure.

Curtain time drawing nearer.

Klein advised Al not to put on the cork now. He wouldn't go on stage until the second act. Klein suggested they go up and join Henrietta in the boxes and catch the first act as spectators to get a line on the show. They found places with Henrietta. She, too, was tense with the ordeal of waiting.

Al could not control the shaking of his hands. He was nervous and admitted this to Klein, who advised him to "take it easy." Just another show, and Jolson was not a beginner.

But it was a new kind of show. Al had never been in a musical revue before. It was different from the vaude circuits or the minstrels.

The moment came for the curtain to go up as the orchestra struck into a lively number.

The house was packed. Al felt that he was standing on the brink. This was the fateful hour.

2

Klein was quite calm, studying the house, the stage, as the curtain ascended.

The Winter Garden's leggy, full-breasted chorines danced out upon the stage, and the show had begun.

The scenery was lavish, the action smooth, the songs well-sung, but in the strictly orthodox manner, following tradition and sticking close to the bare melody and rhythm as composed. It was all very correct, somewhat stiff. The audience applauded generously after each number. There was a thread of story in the revue—boy wins girl, loses girl, wins girl, all in Gay Paree—with appropriate romantic situations, garnished with ballads, between Kitty Gordon and the tenor playing opposite her. These two gave a satisfactory performance, as did the supporting cast, but on the whole thus far there was nothing unusual, nothing of special note, nothing actually new. The patrons felt, however, that they were receiving their money's worth. The costumes were striking and costly, the sets luxuriously designed and furnished.

Al, watching all this fantastic display of glamor and glitter, felt suddenly out of place, as though he were a poor relation come to visit fabulously rich relatives.

Henrietta took Al's hand. She felt the trembling.

As Klein had done, she reminded Al that he was not a newcomer to show business. Al asked them how he could possibly fit into all this—this shiny razzle-dazzle. Klein reassured him. Let them have their fill of this razzle-dazzle, the wiggly girls, good old Kitty and her Parisian romeo. When Al finally got out there, it would be a welcome sight. Something different at last. But Klein's enthusiasm did not dispel Al's misgivings.

He took a deep breath and clasped his hands. He could feel his heart pound.

The critics, too, were down there at the front, keeping hard impartial watch upon this latest splurge of the Shuberts. They would—in their reviews in the morning newspapers—either breathe life into this opus or crucify it.

The first act ended, and the intermission was the signal for Al and Klein to leave Henrietta and make their way backstage to the dressing room. The stir in the theater among the patrons in no way compared with the tumult backstage. Al ran into a hornets' nest: the cast members scurrying about, the directorial staff and the Shuberts holding a hasty meeting to compare notes.

Klein deftly steered Al out of their way. He did not want anything to crop up to deflect his client from his course. They had worked hard for this one chance. It was the deciding step and Klein was determined to have Al take it right.

Back in his dressing cubicle Al began to apply his makeup.

Klein pleaded with him to take it easy, not to get upset, to consider this as just another vaude engagement or a minstrel show. He must take his time. Intermission wouldn't be over for another ten minutes. After that, the first act would be Mitzi's dance number, scheduled for a full five minutes. And then the spotlight would beckon Al out upon the stage.

He had faced audiences before—hundreds of times. But this— this was different. A ten-year dream come true. Al felt faint. The cream of New York theatergoers were present—furs—dia- monds—evening clothes. Klein tried to assure Al that despite all this they were just people.

Nevertheless it was a far cry from the old vaude circuits.

Al's hands trembled as he applied the burnt cork. Klein stepped forward and helped to blacken the space behind Al's ears, and the back of his neck. Al smeared his lips with white greasepaint. He put on a white starched-front shirt and a white celluloid collar; then he put on black trousers. He fastened a black string tie about his collar, pulled on a satin-lapeled black tuxedo jacket and a pair of white gloves. He was ready.

By this time intermission was over and Mitzi Hajos' dance number was in progress. The audience was unusually quiet. Al's mouth felt dry, especially with the white greasepaint on his lips.

Klein himself was beginning to feel the pressure. He was unconsciously pulling his fingers and snapping them. Was this dance number going to end or would Mitzi dance forever? The music rose to a high pitch, then fell into a trough of subdued notes, followed by a rattle of the drums, and then silence. The dance scene was over. Al and Klein heard the burst of applause— a good hand, as Mitzi took her bows.

It was a critical audience, enjoying on that night a fiesta of extravagant production numbers. What would be their reaction on seeing a lone blackfaced figure coming out to entertain them? Al began to sweat beneath his makeup. He looked at Klein who was still snapping his fingers. Both tried to smile but all they could manage between them was a weak grin.

3

Al was waiting at the dressing room door for his cue.

Klein was trying to be calm, his eyes staring, saying nothing. Words were of no use now.

Mr. Jolson—Mr. Jolson—you're on.

It was the cue boy calling. The moment had come. The turning point.

Al straightened, took a deep breath. He patted his perspiring face with his handkerchief. Klein continued to stare.

Al had gone out of the dressing room. He was walking across the space to the footlights. There was a spot of white light waiting for him at one side of the stage. He stepped into it and it brought him out to the center of the stage. There seemed to be a shock of disbelief in the audience. From the wings Al could hear the astonished and dismayed voice of the director: What the hell do you think you're doing, Jolson? What's the idea of blackface?

Hammond was gesturing to Al to come off the stage but Al was with his public. He bowed to the audience, and gave them one of his wide grins with an introductory rolling of his eyes. I have a little song for you, folks. The audience, somewhat bewildered, could only stare at him, and Al could sense their coolness.

He looked out over that vast assemblage fading into the darkness of the theater. All he could see were eyes—hundreds of eyes staring back at him. Up in the galleries it was the same thing. Everyone was focusing bristling attention upon him, waiting for him to begin. Al, in his fascination, almost forgot the words of the lyric, but he went into a shuffling walk and once in action, the words came back to him. He waved his white-gloved hands in rhythm as he began his number, the orchestra coming out of its surprise with the accompanying music. Jolson's voice—after a few initial tremors—came forth clear and vibrant: "I want a girl just like the girl that married dear old Dad. . . ."

The audience listened. The opening song seemed to reach them and they leaned forward, still wondering. Al felt himself growing stronger, more confident in what he was doing. He would disregard his orders. He would give them more—much more. An emotion surged up within him, and eagerness to move his listeners, to inspire them . . . he would give them a medley of Stephen Foster songs. He started off with "Camptown Races."

Camptown ladies sing this song,
  Doo-dah! Doo-dah!
Camptown racetrack's five miles long—
  Oh! Doo-dah day!

The theater was presently resounding with his voice. He was not Al Jolson meekly asking for a chance. He was Al Jolson, star in the making, shaping his own destiny.

His voice was now in full power. It rose and fell in fine gradations of emotion. It interpreted that new rhythm he had striven to express, that new vitality of music. His listeners could

see him now only as a performer communicating with them—
blackface or white—it didn't matter—it was the singing—

I dream of Jeanie with the light brown hair,
Borne like a vapor on the summer air.

There was rapture in those upturned faces, for the people had
never heard this kind of singing before. It was new, it was fresh, it
was of the earth. There were tears in it one moment, laughter in
the next.

Oh, Susanna, Oh don't you cry for me,
I've come from Alabama
With my banjo on my knee.

In the wings the Shuberts, Hammond, Frank Tours, Edgar
Smith, Mlle. Dazie, Kitty, Mitzi, and even the chorus girls
watched, hypnotized. To them, inured to the surprises of show
business, this performance was a revelation. They had heard no
one in their experience like this Jolson fellow—and they could
see that the audience was truly moved.

Oh, weep no more, my lady,
Oh, weep no more tonight,
We will sing one song for my old Kentucky home—

Al shuffled his way across the stage, shuffled his way back. The
spotlight accompanied him, like a halo all his own.

His voice was rich, sweeping. He felt a rising power within him.
He knew now that he was going over, and it was an ecstasy he
could not derive from anything else, an ecstasy every time he
would face an audience in the future.

Here on the stage he was Al Jolson, inspired performer. Off
stage, he was plain Mr. Citizen whose pastime was a good game
of pinochle, who awakened no special response in those he met.
But in front of an audience he was a man transformed, as by a
miracle, into a dynamic personality.

Finally, he concluded his performance in a final burst of vocal pyrotechnics with the minstrel march-on song by Dan Emmett, "Dixie"—

Den I wish I was in Dixie,
   Hooray! Hooray!
In Dixie land I'd take my stand
   To live and die in Dixie—

The performance had ended.

For Al it was like coming out of a dream into the world of reality. He bowed, waved his hands to the audience, heard the beginning of the applause. It came in waves, louder and louder, and then the applause was full-blown, filling the theater. He walked from the footlights to the wings.

It was Hammond who turned Al around and sent him back to the proscenium to give them an encore.

In the wings, also, Arthur Klein had almost bitten away a good part of his fingernails. But his boy had come through. In celebration Klein grabbed a chorus girl and kissed her. Then he looked at the Shuberts and Hammond. What did I tell you, eh? That's my boy out there—Al Jolson. So now the name means something. By the way, Shubert, I want to discuss a new contract.

Al had finished his encore. The applause was, as before, deafening, but he came off, promising the audience he'd sing again tomorrow.

11

1

Congratulations were in order. The Shuberts, Hammond, Tours, Smith were all smiles as they greeted him. Mitzi Hajos came forward and put her arms about him. Al Jolson, what happened to you? You seemed like a different person. You've put this show right on top. Tell me, darling, where do you come from?

A question. Al stared at her for a fleeting moment. He might have said to her: *From the ghetto of Srednike in Lithuania,* or *From the synagogue of my father, the Sixth Cantor of the Yoelson family and, believe it or not, I am the Seventh.* But he had no chance to tell her anything.

He hastened to see Arthur Klein and hear what he had to say— the man who had taken Al in hand and brought him to this.

Al managed to reach his dressing room and was surprised to see Henrietta waiting for him. She reached up and kissed Al impulsively, told him he didn't seem to be at all like he was in vaudeville. Had that audience eating out of his hand. And in blackface, too. I told you, honey. I told you we'd make it.

Klein entered the dressing room and pulled Al out. He was instantly surrounded by a pressing crowd of admirers. Mlle. Dazie was there to give him an enthusiastic kiss. Klein found himself pushed aside. Henrietta felt keenly neglected. She was out of it. She stood at Klein's side. Klein took her hand, and assured her everything would turn out fine. After all, this was Al's hour of triumph. He had worked and hoped a long time for this.

Finally the crowd melted away. Klein and Henrietta found

themselves alone at last with Al. Henrietta came close to him. Al put his arms about her. Honey, from here on in we're in clover.

Klein suggested they go home now. Al needed rest to be ready for tomorrow. From now on he must watch his health. Al was loath to leave the theater. He was overwhelmed with the excitement of it. Lee and S. S. Shubert came forward and shook Al's hand. Lee Shubert told him he didn't mind Al going on in blackface. Apparently the public had accepted it unanimously. Al thanked him. He promised a better performance.

Klein took Al's arm. He repeated his suggestion that they leave the theater. Henrietta looked at her husband speculatively. For the moment she seemed unable to decide about Al's attitude. Apparently, she would have to accustom herself to this new circumstance. If fame came to Al, Henrietta, as his wife, would have to readjust her life.

Klein reminded the Shuberts that a new contract was in order. The Shuberts told him they had expected this.

Al was telling Henrietta he would write a letter home to the folks in Washington. He had to tell them of his triumph. As usual, his half-brother, George, would read the letter to his mother— poor Momma, she couldn't read a word of English—then she would relay what was in the letter to Cantor Yoelson and maybe garnish it up a bit to make the cantor feel pleased. Cantor Yoelson still harbored a grudge against his stage-struck son for deserting the family tradition, but the news of Al's hit would surely serve to make the father relent somewhat.

The Jolsons and Klein finally took a cab home from the theater. They first drove to Klein's apartment and let him off. After that Al and Henrietta were alone at last. Al had his arm about her as the cab sped homeward. He was talking a mile a minute, describing the wonderful things he intended to do. No more honky-tonks for him, no more cheap variety shows. For him there would be bigger and better musical extravaganzas. And as he talked, Henrietta found the Al Jolson she had known slipping farther and farther away from her. He could no longer belong to her. He belonged to the untold thousands who were even now waiting to hear him. She knew she would have to recede into the background. That was inevitable.

She was also certain, by this time, that Al could not give her any children. She could have overlooked that were he to show her the love and affection she had once received from him, but as it was, a barrier began to rise up between them. She could not reach him. Maybe he didn't want to be reached. All his energies were reserved for the world of show business. She began to see him as a man who craved public attention, public approval, and he would strive to attain it. She could see no way to make him regard her as something more desirable than her glittering rival—the theater.

They got out of the cab. Al forgot to pay the driver. Henrietta took the money out of her purse and paid the man. Al walked on ahead of her toward the apartment entrance, still talking about his performance.

2

After the opening of *La Belle Paree* there was a new star in the theatrical firmament—a star that was destined to shine brighter with each succeeding performance, and it was not long before the name Al Jolson began to be spoken and printed. His individual style became the subject of imitators.

He was imitated at amateur night shows, in burlesque houses and variety theaters. And with this increasing publicity his astute manager, Arthur Klein, did have his conference with the Shuberts and Al was raised from $250 to $400 per week.

In the space of a few weeks Al Jolson had left his days of penury and want behind him, never to know them again.

His blackface stage presence transformed him into a spellbinder who held an audience under control for the duration of the performance. He found it increasingly less difficult to gain their confidence. They grew to like him, to consider him not only as an entertainer but also as a personal friend.

Outside of the theater, Al Jolson took a great interest in card playing. He spent most of his spare time in some friendly game from which he almost invariably came out the loser. Somehow he could not develop skill in handling the cards; even in shuffling them he never lost the beginner's awkwardness. Often Klein would sit in with him, but Klein had no special devotion to the game—he could take it or leave it.

At twenty-six years of age, Al found himself on the brink of fame and fortune and he felt that this would make Henrietta quite content. She must understand that from now on he would be closely preoccupied with his work, and his recreation would be pinochle rather than noisy parties. Once in a while he would place a modest bet on a horse to satisfy his growing urge to gamble. But this would have no weakening effect on his personal character or on his work on the stage. When he gambled and lost he accepted it quite calmly as part of life's scheme. His sincerity, his sympathetic regard for his fellowmen, had not been damaged by his improved financial status. As for Henrietta, he would give her anything her heart desired.

He had also a natural inborn shrewdness which governed his regard for money and which came to his aid during the economic depressions that were yet to appear. He saved religiously at the bank and he noted the balance at $3,800, which was the most money he had ever accumulated.

But performing to an audience was his greatest pleasure. He felt at his best and happiest while standing at the footlights in blackface, singing his songs.

The show was going over nicely and it was set for a long run. It was the opinion of the other players, and even of the Shuberts themselves and their staff, that it was Al Jolson who had instilled a flow of vitality into the revue that kept it hot at the box office with no sign of diminishing returns.

At the same time the reviews in newspapers and magazines had further publicized the name of Al Jolson. He received invitations to receptions, parties, special occasions, but he steered clear of as many of these as possible. He had too much to do.

3

There was one particular night, after the show, that Al noticed Henrietta's weariness as she waited for him backstage. He told her to go on home, that he'd be delayed. Just a friendly little game with the boys. You know how it is, Honey. She asked him whether he could skip it tonight. Sugar, you don't want me to let my friends down? She relented, beseeched him not to come home too much later. I'll be home sooner than that, Sugar.

It was 4 A. M. when he came into the apartment.

He asked her whether she could forgive a repentant sinner.

They looked at each other and the woebegone expression on his face made her forget her chagrin and break into a dimpled smile. Al, you're incorrigible. Honey, you're right. My father thought so too. He even got me into a Catholic home for boys. How he got me in there, I don't know. But then my Poppa has a special understanding with God.

He described the experience to her, and other adventures of his running-away-from-home days, and Henrietta forgot about bawling him out and they both laughed and Al was completely happy again.

4

But with the continuing springtime and the advent of the Passover holidays, Al felt that the time had come for him to pay his parents a long-postponed visit.

He conferred with the Shubert management and arrangements were made for him to skip an evening's performance so that he could make his visit in time for the *seder* meal on the first night of Passover. He had written to his mother, and his half-brother George had answered his letter saying they were expecting him and that "Momma was so overjoyed, she cried all night."

Al read the letter to Klein who remarked, if I were you I'd have made that trip long ago.

On a warm afternoon in April, Al and Henrietta took the ferry to Jersey City where they caught the Washington train. Sitting in the coach as the train moved out of Jersey City, Al leaned back in his seat, and with Henrietta cuddling close against him, he closed his eyes and reviewed the past few years, the struggles, the disappointments, and finally the first triumph.

He had left home as a penniless runaway, without a friend in the world. He was coming back on the verge of worldwide fame and with a million friends. But dearer than that million were his "Momma"—the one special friend—and his father who, Al hoped, had become more lenient in his attitude toward the theater.

The train glided onward, across the spring blossoming countryside of New Jersey and Pennsylvania, through the historic city of Philadelphia, where some day soon he hoped he would sing; then a brief stop in Baltimore, a city of memories for him. Everywhere signs of new growth—trees, shrubbery, flowers. So much to see. Honey, some day soon you and me are gonna do some traveling.

Then finally Washington, the familiar depot, the streets, the federal buildings, the Capitol, the White House, the Potomac with its green banks. A taxi took them to his own street. There was the house—it looked so small—his boyhood home. He told his wife, Sugar, this always gets me. Wait till you meet my step-mother—my "new Momma" I call her.

He had faced large and small audiences across the land; hundreds of times he had faced the critical moment preceding his cue to go on stage, but here was a moment that almost caused his heart to stop beating—the moment of homecoming.

He pulled the bell-cord and the door opened. His "new Momma," smaller, grayer, stood before him. He was a little boy again, and it was the same thing. Al tried so hard to keep the moisture from his eyes, but his mother was not fooled. Asa, so why do you cry? This is your home. I'm sorry, Momma. I just haven't grown up, I guess. This is Henrietta, my wife. You two have lots to talk over.

He looked up, saw his father in the familiar skullcap and the black silk jacket with the handkerchief hanging out over the side pocket, standing in the front doorway. Asa, *Sholom Aleichem,* my son. His father came forward and put his arms about his son. To Al this was fulfillment. Well, Poppa, are you still ashamed of me? Do you still think I'm a *bologula*? Cantor Yoelson shook his head. No, my son. Now I think well of you. You are a big manager. But Poppa, I am not a manager. Then what? Poppa, I am a star. A manager earns much less than a star. The father shook his head in disappointment. But in time he realized that the public wouldn't honor someone for nothing. His son, even as an actor, was somehow a great man, and he permitted himself a little indulgence in feeling proud of him.

Al's mother busied herself with Henrietta, showing her the new furniture Al had provided, downstairs and upstairs.

Al's half-brother George approached and held out his hand. Welcome home, Al. Al inquired about Harry. George told him Harry was out on another vaudeville tour. He had been in Washington three weeks ago.

That night came the Passover feast—the *seder*—that Al had enjoyed so many times in the years before. The white linen tablecloth, the wine glasses, the *matzoth*, the brass candlesticks, the shiny brass samovar for tea.

At the request of his father Al recited the *Four Kashes* (four questions), beginning with the so-familiar *Ma-nish-ta-no ha-li-lo ah-zeh* (Why is this night different?). And Al was surprised that he had not forgotten his Hebrew. To Henrietta it was a greater thrill than his performance on the stage. But to Al it was as if the intervening dozen or so years had not happened at all. He was a boy again.

Henrietta was enchanted. To her this was a scene from *The Arabian Nights.*

5

Al read the Passover service along with his father. After that he partook of the *matzoth*, the egg and salt water, the bitter herbs, the sipping of the wine with the traditional wine prayer, "Pe-ri ha-go-fen." A glass of wine was reserved for the prophet Elijah whose spirit would come in through the half-open door sometime later in the night. Mrs. Yoelson began to serve the meal proper: the gefilte fish and *chain*, the *knaidlech* in hot chicken soup, the boiled chicken, the *flomen comput*, and to cap it all, Mrs. Yoelson's delectable apple strudel, with steaming hot tea fresh from the samovar. Cantor Yoelson, in accordance with custom, leaned back against a pillow on his chair and read the Hebrew delineation of the Passover story: of Moses and his struggles with the Egyptians, of the sufferings of the people of Israel under the cruel pharaohs, of the Israelites' flight from the pursuing hordes and the parting of the waters of the Red Sea to let the refugees through into the Land of Promise.

After all this Al related to them his own struggles with his own pharaohs of adversity, and of his final success at the Winter Garden in *La Belle Paree.*

Cantor Yoelson gripped Al's hand as he had done a dozen years ago when Al had sung the "Kol Nidre" on the Day of Atonement. And Al knew that now he had received the word from his father.

Henrietta could not help but feel a glow of pride for her husband. If there was a barrier between them it was now, for the time, invisible. It was a happy Yoelson reunion. At the end of the evening's ceremony Cantor Yoelson and his sons chanted the concluding fable, "Chad-gad-yo" (an only kid).

On the morrow Al accompanied his family to the synagogue where his father, proud as a king, chanted the Passover prayers. Henrietta caused a flurry of excitement as she took her place in the gallery at Mrs. Yoelson's side. She overheard the hushed whisper, a *shiksa* in the synagogue.

The congregation, however, looked on Al as a visiting potentate. All those present, including the feminine group in the gallery, felt a personal pride in Jolson, for they considered him one of their own. Al Jolson—now a famous figure in the outside world—at one time little Asa Yoelson who used to stand on the dais each week through the Sabbath services and chant certain passages of the Torah with his father; little Asa who had recited so eloquently his Bar Mitzvah portion of the *maftir.*

Al himself was fascinated now by the entire service. In his boyhood all this had bored him. But now he did not leave until the last prayer had been intoned. He had found special interest in the auctioning of the Torah readings to the various descendants of the twelve tribes of Israel, beginning with the *Revee-ee,* the fourth portion of the scroll.

Six shillings, *Revee-ee.* Six shillings, *Revee-ee,* the sexton called out, traditionally acting as auctioneer. Eight, from a bidder.

Eight shillings, *Revee-ee*. Do I hear ten? A voice called ten. Ten shillings, *Revee-ee*. Who gives twelve? A man bid twelve. No one topped the bid and the sexton chanted twelve shillings the first time, twelve shillings the second time, and twelve shillings the third time. Sold. And then the auction continued for the fifth or *Chomishee* reading.

Al outbid the others for the *Chomishee* with one bid at four hundred shillings, and Cantor Yoelson stood by his son's side as he read from that portion of the scroll.

That afternoon there was a reception for Al in the Yoelson home. Neighbors and members of the synagogue crowded into the small house and spilled out into the street. There were toasts of "Le'cheiim" with Cantor Yoelson's homemade grape wine, and personal well-wishing to their own Asa Yoelson and his good wife. Their praises reached an apex when Al wrote a check for two hundred dollars payable to the synagogue fund. And to climax the occasion Al succumbed to their demands and sang "Eili, Eili," "Yiddisha Momma," and "Ah Brievela du Momma" ("A Letter to My Mother"). Then he surprised them with "By the Light of the Silvery Moon," which they thought very nice, and were impressed by his stage mannerisms.

It was a performance the listeners were to talk about for the rest of their days.

One elder suggested that Al come back and be the next cantor. Cantor Yoelson was growing old.

Al replied that maybe he would. You never can tell. The Seventh Yoelson Cantor.

12

1

On his return to New York and the Winter Garden, Al Jolson threw himself into his career with vigor. He developed his mode of presentation with finesse during the long run of *La Belle Paree*. His popularity sprouted.

The show closed after 104 performances, and rehearsals were immediately started for the next production, *Vera Violetta*. Al became the favorite "good fellow" of the cast. The producers were concentrating on the elaborate costume numbers, the glamor queens, and the romantic ballad singers, regarding Jolson's blackfaced act as something in the nature of a fad, only a novelty that had attracted the temporary attention of the curious public. The director, therefore, following the example of his employers, focused his attention on the production numbers, the dancing, the conventional singing.

When the rehearsals were over and the show ready for an audience Jolson realized at once that he had been demoted. The progress he had made so brilliantly in *La Belle Paree* seemed to have been plugged up and slowed down considerably. He had a spot in the new show to sing two numbers with the proviso that, if the audience showed evidence of wanting more, his role sub-sequently would be expanded.

Klein was not pleased with this arrangement at all, but he himself did not fully comprehend the potential of Al Jolson's ability. He realized that Al was a blackfaced performer who could belt out a song; but what about other talents? As a dancer he rated a near zero, as a monologist he had far to go. He could do no juggling, no magic tricks, no acrobatic stunts; he was hardly the handsome Romeo type. It was all in his singing, but as the director of the show intimated, an audience could grow tired of an act lacking in variety. It was folly to have an unchanging Jolson pop up like a jack-in-the-box in the various scenes with irritating frequency. There were much more agreeable and pleasant things for an audience to enjoy. In a revue such as *Vera Violetta*, which was planned to be another extravaganza of color and glamor— to surpass even *La Belle Paree*—a blackfaced singer could be considered as an intruder.

2

The extravaganza *Vera Violetta* opened on the memorable evening of November 20, 1911. Book and lyrics were by Harold Atteridge and Leonard Liebling. It was taken from a German play by Leo Stein. Additional songs were created by Edward Eysler, composer.

The star of the show was the effervescent French importation, Gaby Deslys, with the sexy voice and curvaceous gams. Her leading man and dance partner was an American, Harry Pilcer. The show was built about these two when it started. In the revue also were Jose Collins and a youthful newcomer, Mae West. Other well-known names were Van Renssaler Wheeler, Barney Bernard, Billie Taylor, Mellville Ellis, Kathleen Clifford, and the coon-shouting Stella Mayhew.

In this show Gaby and Pilcer danced the "Gaby Slide," the music of which was expressly written for Miss Deslys. Songs for this gala musical were also composed by the brilliant Louis A. Hirsch: "Come and Dance with Me" and "When You Hear Love's Hello."

One of the lighter numbers that the new minstrel man, Al Jolson, was selected to sing was the 1890 classic "Ta-ra-ra-boom-der-e," while the chorus ladies in wisps of silver cloth about hip and breast came out kicking, twisting, and stretching like mad to Al's ragtime beat.

In the second act he was brought on to sing George M. Cohan's appealing composition, "That Haunting Song," and with this number he was a tremulous Al Jolson bringing up the sadness and the tears.

A week later the Shuberts stretched a point and permitted Al to sing a lively, intriguing number created by Jean Schwartz, "Rum-Tum-Tiddle," which brought down the house, the audience clamoring for encore after encore until Jolson found himself singing a few other numbers as well that had no connection with the revue. This was the portent of what was to come.

Al, in his blackface routine, was a sensation. It was his individual style—the personal appeal to the audience, the rolling of the eyeballs, showing much white, the wide mischievous grin, the talking of part of the song, and the "ragging" up of the prime melody to give it an irresistible sprightliness, the forerunner of swing, boogie-woogie and rock and roll.

With each number he sang in the succeeding performances he became more and more of a celebrity, and the general public began to hum the tunes a la Jolson.

The Shuberts now saw which way the show-biz wind was blowing.

Al Jolson began to ride the crest of the wave of his snowballing success. From a single spot in *Vera Violetta* he ended up with most of the show built around him.

His singing had created a shock wave the repercussions of which were to be felt for a long time, to be echoed and re-echoed down memory lane of the musical world. The star of the show, Gaby Deslys, took second place to Al Jolson, the new sensation of the stage. He was drama and he was comedy. Songs like "I Love My Wife But Oh, You Kid," "Casey Jones," "Becky, Do the Bombashay," he sang in the lighter vein, miraculously switching to the dramatic or the wistful with songs like "Girl of My Dreams," "My Little Grey Home in the West," and "Don't Wake Me Up—I'm Dreaming."

His salary was increased to $500 and then to $750 per week. The Shuberts were riding high with him in competition with Flo Ziegfeld and the others. Jolson became to the Shuberts their most valued performer and they made sure that he was satisfied in every way with his present status.

3

The Jolsons lived comfortably now in a small but nicely furnished apartment off Fifth Avenue, not too far from the scene of his Winter Garden operations.

Al would sleep until 9 or 10 A. M. and Henrietta would prepare his breakfast for him. He would eat it and praise her cooking and wisecrack about the world in general and himself in particular. Then he would dress and go out, giving her a husbandly kiss, and she would not see him again for the rest of the day until he returned after midnight, unless she herself attended rehearsal or the regular performance in the evening. Of course, she knew he was occupied with his theater work but she knew also that he spent considerable free time playing cards with "the boys" or running off to a racetrack, to be back in time for the performance.

It was Henrietta who suggested that now they could do things together as they used to do in the beginning. Al didn't have to rehearse *every* day. She told Al of her loneliness. Sometimes she even felt despondent. Al readily promised, Honey Chile, tell you what, from now on I'm going to be with you every hour I'm not working. You'll get so tired of me hanging around, you'll be kicking me out. He kissed her. She was pretty. She was concerned about his welfare. She wanted him near her. Al considered this: she was a good wife. What more could a man want? Well, he was going to make her happy. From now on no more gallivanting around. Klein and the others would have to carry on the game without him.

For four days he stuck to his promise. He spent more time in the apartment between performances or, if he went out, it was with his wife, strolling in the park or on the avenue.

He bought her a Pekingese and they took it walking.

But on the fifth day he told her he just *had* to go to the theater in the afternoon to go over some new songs with Gaby Deslys. He'd be back pronto and he'd take Henrietta to dinner at Delmonico's before show time.

Al did return home, but it was well past 2 A. M. Henrietta was sitting up in bed. She reminded him of his promise. He said he

was mortified. She shook her head. And tomorrow, more
conferences, more excuses? He called himself a low-down dog,
but he had a bit of news for her. He knew he shouldn't have done
it, but he thought they could use a little extra dough, so he had
booked a vaudeville engagement at the Victoria, matinee
appearance only. Promised Hammerstein a long time ago.
Wouldn't interfere with *Vera Violetta*. Just three songs at the
Victoria in the afternoon, then back to the Winter Garden.

Henrietta's face was pale. She asked, Only one afternoon? Al
spread the fingers of his right hand. Five. Ain't that great? One
grand in cold cash. Get you a new fur coat. She told him she
didn't want a fur coat or anything. She just wanted them to have
some kind of life together besides sleeping in the same bed.

He explained to her that he could not stop now. He was on the
way. Honey Lamb, we'd both be crazy to let go now. He implored
her to be patient. When he would finally be up there—among the
stars of the theater—he would give her anything her heart
desired; he would take her places, see the world. Live like king
and queen. What do you say, Honey Chile?

He tried to make her see it as he did. The thrill of being a hit
performer—the thrill of the admiring crowds—the fame and the
money. The thrill of his name in electric lights, blazing away into
the night. That was it, Honey Baby. That was it.

She listened. She had learned, of late, to be a listener. When he
started talking, with his eyes round and shining, his hands
gesticulating, she found herself quite helpless. She *had* to listen.
But there was no enthusiasm on her part. She herself could not
explain it—but she did feel a growing resentment at being thus
shunted aside for a rival she knew she could not beat—the
theatrical vampire. She listened. She nodded. Sure, Al, sure.

4

With his ever-increasing success and popularity Al Jolson,
though he had never meant to preen, did begin to feel a sense of
power, of being able to do and get what he wanted. His wealth
had grown considerably and his accounts showed handsome

balances in six different banks. He had begun, on advice from Klein, to invest his money in gilt-edged securities—railroads, telephone and telegraph, steel, utilities. He had a natural shrewdness in the handling of his money and he made sure it was not put into any risky enterprises. He was wary of numerous high-pressure confidence men trying to put a dent in the armor of his resistance.

At the same time he felt he could afford to have some fun. Being on top, he felt more at ease; the tension of the struggle uphill had now subsided; he could lean back somewhat and relax. To relax meant playing cards—pinochle—and betting on horses. He lost sizable chunks of cash which he wrote off as amusement expense; but there was always more coming in from his show contract, from phonograph records—something new to him— from music publishers who used his picture and name for the promotion of their wares.

He had purchased a sporty Packard two-seater automobile, color bright yellow. He went in for flashy clothes in the manner of the top-notch vaudevillians, to Henrietta's rather scorn-tinged amusement. He had his pinstripe and checkerboard suits tailor-made and his Chesterfield overcoats trimmed with fur collars. He fancied himself, at this stage of the game, a man about town and, acting the role, frequented the night spots after theater hours with a somewhat appeased but embarrassed Henrietta on his arm.

On these jaunts he would joke, dine, and do some dancing, but so far as he was concerned, drinking was practically nil. In his late twenties he became a well-known figure in the night spots of New York. But, actually, to Jolson, it was all a great splurge of play-acting.

In the midst of all this, one thing he did not forget—the weekly letter and check to his mother. Occasionally he visited his parents in Washington, but perhaps not so often as he would have liked. His father, older, and recovering from an illness, was no longer the chief cantor in the synagogue but acted in the capacity of a relief cantor.

His mother had grown to love Henrietta as her own daughter after discovering that a *shiksa* was not different, really, from any Jewish girl, and the two were always together from the moment Henrietta made her entrance at the old home.

In New York Al dressed well, ate well, lived like a king with several retainers always at his beck and call. Klein, however, had a difficult job trying to keep the chiselers, the money borrowers, the con men away from his golden boy. All sorts of propositions came Jolson's way but an astute manager saved him from many a headache as well as a lost buck. Jolson continued to make his investments in solid stock, acquiring nothing on margin but everything outright, with a modest but safe yield.

At the same time his personal life outside the theater was divided between his wife and his two favorite avocations—card games and following the ponies. He began to bet larger amounts and play for bigger stakes. His losses, in consequence, were heavier, but again he wrote all this off as the price for his pleasure.

He was not a drinker and he had little use for bars and liquor-drenched bistros. He confined himself to an occasional glass of wine, a mild cocktail, or perhaps a prudent drink of champagne, while a tolerant but resigned Henrietta clung to his arm.

He became interested in automobiles, traded in his yellow Packard for a Wayne, then changed this for a Franklin. He found driving them an exhilarating diversion, with his wife an occasional backseat driver.

He also discovered a sudden interest in moving pictures, admiring the dramatic impact of this new theatrical form. At the suggestion of Klein that Al might consider acting in the "movies," he shook his head and grinned. He knew he was not a Maurice Costello or a Douglas Fairbanks. Give Al his blackface and the Winter Garden and he was in his own world, and happy. Klein adopted a "wait and see" attitude.

5

Sunday morning in the apartment. Jolson reading the reviews. Henrietta buttering a piece of toast. She glanced up at him. She remarked they were married seven years and had no children.

She wished they had at least one. Al seemed depressed. Henrietta suggested they were now, for certainty, paid-up members of the club that goes to an orphanage. Al knew what she meant. Adopt a child. Al asked her to wait a little longer. By some miracle maybe they could have their own child. She pouted. She reminded him that if they'd wait too much longer they'd be too old to even *adopt* a child. He evaded the issue. Let's think about it for a while. Agreed.

She nodded, and he took her in his arms and kissed her. It was then that he had that moment of awareness—that he loved her dearly. He was worried. He sensed, somehow, that he could not ameliorate that dissatisfaction within her. Always there seemed to be some cause for complaint on her part. Al himself began to feel an undercurrent rising between them, forcing them apart.

13

1

In these tumultuous days he could not make out what had happened; it seemed that the whole world had suddenly become aware of Al Jolson. He received a string of offers to sing in vaude and musical comedy, to cut records for the phonograph which was fast being adopted as an integral part of the American home.

But primarily Al Jolson's kingdom was the Winter Garden. People in New York and elsewhere began to associate the two together—Al Jolson and the Winter Garden. One without the other would be incomplete.

After *Vera Violetta* came *The Whirl of Society* in 1912, and Al continued to ride the crest of the wave. It was a rising tide that carried him to new heights, and the money kept rolling in.

It was a rare phenomenon. No matter how many times the people heard him sing, they came back again and again. For *The Whirl of Society* Jolson's faithful followers packed the house. He gave them "You Made Me Love You" and "Take Me to That Swanee Shore," and their applause was consistently enthusiastic. Jolson became, in time, a sort of ragtime demigod—or the Winter Garden cantor.

The reviews in the newspapers were usually favorable and they couldn't safely be otherwise. For those who criticized him would face the wrath of his army of fans. For him they would have committed mayhem if need be. Reviewers and critics, beware! The cynical and wordly wise, of course, disdained his flamboyancy, the narrowness of his musical technique, and what

impressed them as his expansive, extroverted ego. But this in no
way deterred or slowed down the human dynamo that was Al
Jolson.

Instead of easing off and growing more subdued with the
advent of success and money, Jolson, on the contrary, seemed
to pick up new energy and ambition to inspire his listeners. On
sudden impulse he would hurry off the stage and move up and
down the aisles, singing directly to his patrons at close range, face
to face. This was another adventure for them to remember and
tell their grandchildren.

His singing, his personality, continued to have a marked effect
upon his listeners. It might even be described as a sort of
evangelistic influence, for he gave to their lives a fresh buoyancy.
He showed them in song that living was an exhilarating experience. Those songs, in turn, were destined to become classics.
Down through the decades they would be remembered: songs
like "Waitin' for the Robert E. Lee" and "Moonlight Bay"—
remembered in the way they were sung by Jolson.

A new voice in the theatrical world that left the domain of the
theater itself and came into the homes of the people. From the
youngest to the oldest, they all learned to know him. Mothers
rocking their babies to sleep would croon the Dixie melodies as
Jolson crooned them; people going about their daily work would
hum "Rosey, You Are My Posey" or "Take Me to That Swanee
Shore." Teachers in school assemblies would lead their classes in
singing in the Jolsonesque manner.

2

At this time Jolson, as if he didn't have enough to do with the
nightly performances of The Whirl of Society, instituted a special
social program on Sunday evenings at the Winter Garden,
exclusively for his fellow show people and their friends. The
existing laws prohibited regular theatrical performances on
Sunday; only so-called private concerts were permitted, without
costume, without makeup. It was because of this that Al Jolson

gave these special performances "informally" for his friends. At these impromptu sessions he did not wear the burnt cork and there were no shaded, colored lighting, or spotlights. However, the law did permit the use of the regular house lights which were on in full brightness, and Al would say, Now I can see you people as you are. Yes-sir-ee, folks, you ain't heard nothin' yet. You name your songs and I'll sing 'em, no holds barred. I'm at your service, folks. I brought you all down here and I'm on the stage, so you better make good use of your chance while you can. You call 'em, folks, and I'll sing 'em. Do I hear any bids?

The requests came, one after the other, and Jolson sang them. No sooner had he finished one song than another waited its turn. But he missed no one. He put that prodigious memory of his to full employment, and his listeners were amazed that he could retain in his mind so many different tunes and lyrics and sing them without any show of hesitation.

Sometimes he would step down from the stage and walk up and down the aisles and quip with the listeners and sing his songs from the floor of the theater, directly to the group of people closest at hand.

After that performance, though Henrietta pleaded with him that it was enough, that it was time to leave the theater, Al would linger, assuring her he'd stay for just one more number, Honey Lamb. You know your hubby by this time. He lives on singin' and it's hard to stop him once he gets started. Ain't it so, folks? Al inquired of his audience.

This ignoring of her pleas—with no malicious intent on his part, but with the assumption that she would be a good sport and play along with him—only added to the tension between them. It was these continual slights that grated against Henrietta's forbearance. On these occasions she felt belittled and embarrassed, though she covered these feelings with an outward smile of indifference. Most of these concerts—when Klein and Henrietta would finally succeed in convincing Al to walk off the stage—would end well after midnight.

Klein himself, when interviewed by reporters, could not explain how Al Jolson, after seven nights of performances, could still be going strong. How could his voice hold out like that? It must come from iron lungs. Sometimes Klein thought of him as half-a-dozen men rolled into one. How long could he go on like this?

As his wife, Henrietta could only stand aside and wait.

3

A blackfaced figure upon a great stage, strutting up and down before the footlights, clapping his white-gloved hands together, rolling his eyes in sheer hilarity. A blackfaced figure, extending his arms in supplication and pleading with his audience, or getting down on one knee and talking the words of a song in heartbreak.

Laughter—tears—exaltation, with sincerity to enchant a nation.

A man who handed out five-dollar bills to panhandlers on the street and gave generously to every charity that came along. A man who did not pass by anybody who needed his help.

In those first feverish days of success Al Jolson was concerned wholeheartedly for his audiences and their reaction, and perhaps that was why he tended to overlook those little attentions to his wife. His head was always in the clouds, in the purple heights where dreams come true. Women, in general, regarded him with adulation as he stood before them on the stage. Perhaps they loved him in a companionable sort of way and not with the romantic passion they had for the handsome debonair matinee idols.

4

1913 was a great year. The Big War had not yet spewed itself upon the earth, and under the new president, Woodrow Wilson, this country seemed to be rolling along in an easygoing, languid manner, but the pace was forward, slow but sure.

In that year of 1913 Jolson had to face the odds of formidable competition.

There was W. C. Fields and his famous Indian club juggling act, as well as his hilarious golf skit. The great Sarah Bernhardt played the Palace on the same bill with Fields. At this time, also, a newcomer was beginning his own theatrical conquest, Eddie Cantor in *The Kid Kabaret*. The (Three) Marx Brothers were already going strong. Fannie Brice, recently of burlesque, was singing songs like "Lovey Joe" and "Grizzly Bear." Mae West, fresh from *Vera Violetta*, was going into her sex-accentuating career with her muscle-flexing exercises, causing near-riots in college towns. Eddie Leonard was "wah-wah-ing" on the crest of his singing career. There was a specialty act on the boards with "Ben Benny, the Fiddlin' Kid," who later played his violin as Jack Benny. An English comic called Charlie Chaplin was clowning in an act, "Karno's Wow-Wows" (before the baggy pants and cane of the screen). Eva Tanguay blitz krieged the vaude stages with her titillating "I Don't Care" mélange. Bill (Bojangles) Robinson was peppering gaping audiences with his machine-gun tap-dancing feet. Willie and Eugene Howard were knocking 'em dead with their Hebrew dialect act; Leo Carillo ditto with his Chinese dialect. Then there was the melodious Scotsman, Harry Lauder, garnering a cool $4,000 per week for "Roamin' Through the Gloamin'." Bellowing out her ear-scorching "Red Hot Momma" routines was the indomitable Sophie Tucker. And there were a host of others, including Julian Eltinge, female impersonator; Ed Wynn, the winsome; Pat Rooney, soft-shoe; Jimmy Savo, slapstick; Blossom Seeley, coon-shouter; Texas Guinan, the happy singing and dancing cutie; Leon Errol, rubber-legs.

Against this array the blackfaced singer at the Winter Garden swept through his house-packed performances with unabating gusto, as though all these others—as far as he was concerned—did not exist.

5

In the spring of 1913 Klein broached to the Shuberts the subject of a new contract for his client.

Lee Shubert, who did most of the managerial work of the concern, had, of course, expected this for quite some time now in the face of the spectacular rise of this Jolson fellow. Lee was entirely cognizant of the fact that it was Jolson who was selling the Shubert revues to the public with overwhelming box-office success.

In the new contract Klein wanted $3,000 a week for Al, in addition to equal starring status with Gaby Deslys for the Shuberts' next revue, *Honeymoon Express*.

Lee protested, claimed it was impossible. In the first place, it was the Shuberts who had given Jolson his big chance. But Klein argued that it was Al who packed them in, hence he deserved proper consideration, financially and otherwise, and Klein was determined to achieve this for his client. He reminded the Shuberts that their competitors were howling for Jolson, but, of course, they had first option.

The Shuberts felt themselves being pulled through the wringer, but their sense of showmanship came to the fore. In a moment like this their prime performer could slip out of their grasp, leaving them high and dry. Equal billing, agreed the Shuberts, but their financial terms were these: a $10,000 bonus to sign a seven-year contract at $800 per week, thirty-five weeks guaranteed each year.

Klein held out for $1,000 a week, or no contract. He rose and turned to go. The Shuberts called Klein a robber but acquiesced. They wanted Al for seven years.

So a new contract was drawn up, giving Jolson equal star billing with Deslys, and at the agreed salary, this contract to run for seven years.

As in previous productions, Jolson in *Honeymoon Express* proved to be a smash hit and this definitely established him as the singing star of the year.

Klein basked in the reflected glory of his client and told him after a "socko" performance that Al was now way up there. Sometimes a star eases up and leans back a little on his past glory. But Al assured Klein he was not leaning back on anything. Singing was his life, and he was not slackening. Klein apologized for even mentioning it.

Al was surrounded by the usual backstage mob—newspaper men, theatrical critics, well-wishers. Besides, his card-playing henchmen were waiting to celebrate in their own way.

Henrietta made him promise again to break away at a decent hour.

As usual Al stole into the apartment just before the break of dawn.

In the morning, when he got out of bed, Henrietta turned her face away as he attempted to kiss her. When she did look at him, her eyes were cold.

She wanted him to stop associating with those card-playing friends of his.

Al clenched his hands and unclenched them. He started to turn away, to choke the whole thing down, to let the matter rest. In the past he had done just that—many times—to avoid the continuation of an argument and its development into something more serious. In the past he had been able, on such occasions, to control his temper—but when she insisted that he give up his "card-playing friends" Al did lose his temper. He slipped up on his code of behavior and before he quite knew what had happened, he had raised his voice to her for the first time. In later years he often declared he regretted that first loss of self-control. He accused her of bellyaching just because he spent some time with his friends. Whatever he did failed to please her. He told her that all of it—the Winter Garden, the vaudeville engagements—was all for her. But apparently she didn't seem to appreciate anything.

That was all she had to hear. Her cheeks were burning.

She turned, walked stiffly to the closet. She placed her traveling bag on the bed, then she began removing dresses from their hangers.

As Jolson told it later, the sight of his wife preparing to leave him was the first unnerving shock he had experienced in his life. He stood there in the room, stunned, watching her, feeling himself helpless to prevent the catastrophe. But he felt, also, the urgent need for action to try to stop her. He could feel his world already trembling before the fall. He made his plea. He begged her to give him another chance. He would make it up to her. He tried to make her see that all his success, money, affluence, didn't mean a thing to him unless she was there to share it. All his achievement had been possible because of her inspiration. She and she alone was his motivating force. She wouldn't regret it— giving him another chance. He promised her on his knees.

She did listen to him. But she had heard his promises before. All right, he admitted, he had not kept those promises before— but from now on, just watch your Jolie, Honey Chile.

Her hand, holding a dress, dropped to her side and the dress fell to the floor. She stood there, quite motionless, staring at Al and wondering. Then she started to replace the clothes in the closet. Al stepped forward, put his arms about her, kissed her eyes, lips, cheeks, throat. She told him he was simply impossible. She was smiling suddenly—to Al it was the sun bursting through the rain clouds.

For a long time he held her in his arms as though he were afraid to release her, lest she slip away from him.

14

1

In *Dancing Around,* the Shubert extravaganza that opened on October 10, 1914, at the Winter Garden, Al Jolson was, in effect, the star of the show. The music in great part was composed by Harry Carroll, with sketches and lyrics by the brilliant Harold Atteridge. The cast was an impressive one which included Bernard Granville, James Doyle, Harland Dixon, Clifton Webb, Cecil Cunningham, and Melville Ellis.

Composer and director Sigmund Romberg created the two theme songs for the revue: "My Lady of the Telephone" and "He Is Sweet, He Is Good." There was Gaby Deslys as the dancing star and the famed Winter Garden chorus beauties.

In this show, as he had begun to do in the previous one, Al Jolson followed no set script and no prescheduled song list. He would come out before the audience after the closing curtain— around 11 P.M.—and sing one song after another, including request numbers from the people. He belted out in his individual rhythmic and emotional style such tunes as "Waitin' for the Robert E. Lee," "You Made Me Love You," "That Old Girl of Mine," "You're a Great Big Blue-Eyed Baby," and "Oh, You Beautiful Doll."

There were times when the audience would sit there, transfixed, watching him project his personality volubly to each listener until well past the midnight hour.

As "Gus," the stock character in blackface he portrayed in these Winter Garden revues, he had made for himself a unique and permanent reputation in the entertainment world.

With each smash success the Shuberts, mainly through the prodding of Arthur Klein, his manager, raised Jolson's salary until it hovered around the $2,000 per week mark.

2

Al began to live up in the clouds, from which he found it ever harder to descend to pay some attention to Henrietta. She saw him claimed more and more by the general public, including the irrepressible reporters, columnists, playwrights, producers, and even his fellow actors and actresses. They all vied for his attention, mostly, of course, to further their own ends.

And Henrietta found it increasingly difficult, with each success, to maintain for herself some relationship with her husband. His first romantic attentions, the fond embraces, the kisses, those affectionate caresses grew less and less frequent.

Henrietta began to see that it was not entirely his gambling. It was the theater that could be a jealous mistress, demanding too much of the body and soul of her paramours, and Al Jolson was no exception. Henrietta found herself alone for lengthening periods, a "show-biz" widow indeed.

Sometimes she would stand by, quite helpless, while a crowd surged about her husband, blocking her off.

Honey, I'll see you later. Honey, wait around a bit—I'll be through in a minute. Sugar, I'll only be a while with these reporters. I've got a special rehearsal, Honey Chile. New song. Won't take long. This was the refrain she heard from him these hectic days. She was always waiting. But it was not a matter of waiting for minutes—sometimes it was hours. It was like living with a will-o'-the-wisp, in constant motion. Al Jolson had taken on more of the semblance of a legend than a flesh-and-blood human being. In fleeting moments she came face to face with him, for instance, in bed in their apartment; but even then he was out of her reach, fast asleep from the day's seething activity.

One morning she told him, Why didn't he take it easy? Did he have to see *all* those people? Did he have to be everywhere and do everything all in one day? Sometimes he didn't even know she was around.

His answer, He was flying high, wide, and handsome. Everything was finally coming his way. He wanted to keep flying. He would stop one of these days, but right now the winds of success were blowing his way. Henrietta could only shake her head in resignation. She still felt skeptical, even when he promised her a second honeymoon.

Dancing Around rang down the final curtain on its 145th performance to a rousing demonstration from the audience, and Jolson entertained them with his own concert after the show. He received a thunderous ovation and promised that he would soon come back in another Shubert extravaganza. And now, folks, you ain't heard nothin' yet. Gay songs, sad songs—one after another he sang to them, and his listeners wondered: where did this man get all that energy, that tireless spirit?

3

In the days preceding the start of rehearsals for the next opus Al, instead of taking that second honeymoon he had promised Henrietta, signed up for a vaudeville tour with the Keith circuit for $2,500 per week.

He was to start in New York, and then visit the cities of Boston, Philadelphia, Pittsburgh, and Chicago. It was to be a gala triumphant sweep through the east. He broke the news to Henrietta, assuring her what a glorious time they would have in all those different cities.

Henrietta was standing at the window of their apartment, looking down into Fifth Avenue, and her face expressed anything but happiness. Her eyes were filled with pain. Her mouth quivered. She informed him she would remain here, that he should go on without her. She'd be all right. But Al came close to her. He put his arms about her waist and kissed her. He told her he wanted this to be the second honeymoon, as he had promised. He was sure it *could* be. All those places they'd visit—the people, the excitement of the different theater engagements. She would be part of it. She would be at his side. Don't you see, Honey Lamb?

She was quiet. Then she told him it was really all his—the tour, the adulation of the audiences—all his. She surely had no part in it. In fact, nothing would change: they would hardly be together at all. It would be the same as in Manhattan. Once again Al had to plead, begging her not to talk like that. She was his strength. Her faith in him gave him the ambition to keep on, to climb upward. He asked her to look into his roly-poly eyes. Look close, Honey Lamb, and what do you see? Love. Now will you stop pouting and come along? Or must I drag you, woman?

She insisted he did not want to understand her. He told her that when she talked like that he could not hope to understand her. But without her, there would be nothing. With her he was alive. He kissed her again. Now suddenly, he was the lover, in his own way. He told her how beautiful she was. Now, woman, will you go quietly or must I carry you? She dimpled. The rays of light were coming back into her eyes. Al knew he had won. He informed her that she had scared the living daylights out of him this time. And so they started to pack for the tour. This, then, was to be their second honeymoon, after nine years of marriage.

Or was it to be, in reality, just another vaudeville tour for a blackfaced singer riding on a tidal wave of applause that swept everything before it?

Henrietta was sorry—not for herself, but for this overly dedicated man with the slight Southern drawl in his voice, who would never break out of that glittering, bespangled realm—the never-never land of show biz.

4

In those busy days Jolson was not one to slow down or to stop working. On the contrary, he seemed to apply himself with greater zest and energy as the impact of his successes increased.

Already, as soon as his vaude tour was over—it was hardly the honeymoon he had promised—work was begun on the next Shubert Winter Garden revue, *Robinson Crusoe, Jr.* Rehearsals were soon in progress and Al was the star as well as taking an active part in the construction of the show, in the selection of songs, and even helping with the composition of the book.

He worked through long hours and that put an additional strain on his married life. His wife was patient with him, though often she felt that she was hanging on to a meteor zooming through space.

The show was finally whipped into shape and opened on February 17, 1916. It was a Sigmund Romberg production with additional music by Joshua Hanley and lyrics by Harold Atteridge and Edgar Smith. Supporting Al Jolson in the cast were Barry Lupino, Kitty Doner, and the usual array of hoofers, chorines, and glamor queens in tantalizing costumes accentuating when not revealing the feminine anatomy.

In this revue Jolson, in blackface, sang "Robinson Crusoe," "When You're Starring in the Movies," and "Minstrel Days." There was also a comedy song that he made into a smash hit, "Where Did Robinson Crusoe Go with Friday on Saturday Night," and this was followed by another "sockeroo," "Yacka-Hula-Hickey-Dula," which brought the house down.

It seemed the public could not get enough of this Jolson bombshell. Night after night he was on that stage, indefatigable, indestructible, a man of boundless energy, not only belting out the songs that were part of the show itself but, as was his practice after the closing curtain had descended for the evening, strutting out on the stage, still in his blackface makeup, raising his hands, and calling out his customary plea, Folks, now don't go away. It's only 11:30 and you ain't heard nothin' yet. He gave them his wide grin, he rolled his eyes at them, saying: I've got a million of them. And once again he regaled them with song after song and, strange as it may seem, he never failed to call forth their tenderest emotions or their most pleasurable laughter, as the nature of his delivery indicated.

Finally he would sing out his last note for the evening—or rather the first hours of the new day—and then with his: See you all next showtime, signal that the performance was over. The audience would thunder its final applause and gradually emerge from its hypnosis, as wraps and coats were put on to leave the theater.

Robinson Crusoe, Jr. proved to be another smash hit and ran for a total of 130 consecutive performances.

5

It was at this point that President Woodrow Wilson declared a "state of war with Germany" on April 6, 1917.

At once, Al Jolson, along with many of his fellow performers, tried to enlist, but he was deferred from active military duty, not passing the rigid physical examination. Disappointed, he resolved to serve voluntarily in Liberty Bond selling campaigns. He wasted no time. From the stages of theaters and auditoriums he sang his songs to sell bonds for Uncle Sam, as so many of the other top theater and screen personalities were doing.

Between performances on his regular bond selling tour, he found time to sing at veterans' hospitals, and this, coupled with his special engagements, made people wonder at the fortitude of this man and how he could stand the gruelling pace week after week. Even when the new Shubert revue was in the rehearsal stage Al continued his bond-selling campaign unabated.

He was informed by his draft board that when his age bracket came up, he might have the chance of going overseas as a doughboy.

It was a bitter war. Reports of the changing fortunes on the battlefront came through in the glaring headlines of the New York newspapers—the battles of the Meuse-Argonne, Chateau Thierry, the Somme, Belleau Woods. Al chafed at his immobility for not being in it, but he found some solace in doing his share at home. Appropriately, he sang "Keep the Home Fires Burning."

During that trying year of 1917, President Wilson, a devotee of the theater, considered Al Jolson one of his favorite entertainers, and honored him with an invitation to lunch at the White House. Journalists, magazine writers, columnists made much of this incident.

Being in Washington, Al dropped in to see his parents. His father was more excited than usual as he greeted Al. When Al informed his father that he had had lunch with the president of the United States, Cantor Yoelson stared at his son in amazement. Only in America were such things possible. In America a jazz singer became a man of importance and respect. Maybe he had been wrong about Asa becoming a cantor after all.

Al put his arms about his father. They reminisced about the old days: the whippings the cantor had bestowed upon his recalcitrant son, those first days when little Asa kept running away from home to break his way into show business.

It was a happy reunion—Henrietta and Mrs. Yoelson together again, Al discussing the theater with his father, his sister Rose, and his half-brother George. And Al advised all of them if they ever needed financial help, they knew where to get it. The evening ended with Al singing a few of his Broadway hits. Henrietta glowed with pride and, for once, enjoyed the miracle of Al Jolson separated from his public, even though for the one night only.

But, on the morrow, after their return to New York, the madness of show business swept them into its vortex without further ceremony.

While Al rushed about the country, Henrietta felt she was living in a squirrel cage. The rapidly accelerating pace kept up by her work-possessed husband left her entirely confused, frustrated, and wondering whether in reality she *had* a husband. At times he would be away for weeks at a stretch, on a bond-selling tour or special concert engagements, spanning a continent. When the rehearsals came along for the next show toward the end of 1917 and beginning of 1918, she saw more of him, but his thoughts seemed to be a million miles away from her. It was as if she were looking at him over a widening chasm, though for several hours each night they slept in the same bed. But for all his attention and response she might as well have slept alone.

6

When *Robinson Crusoe, Jr.* closed, Mrs. Jolson had been sure that now Al had had enough for a while, that he would relax and perhaps forget about show biz. But once more she was disappointed.

He told her that now he was starting rehearsals for a brand new show, *Sinbad*, something that would "knock 'em for a loop." Henrietta wanted to know why he couldn't wait a bit before starting work again. He told her—and it sounded so familiar to her—he couldn't stop now—he had to keep going. He had to sing to his people. When the time comes, Honey Lamb, ol' Massa Jolson is jest goin' to set hisself down in that li'l ol' rockin' chair an' call it quits.

She told him he was impossible. He agreed with her but he assured her he was doing all this for her, and for her alone. The first chance he had he was going to take her on a long trip, maybe a sea voyage to the South Pacific. They would have themselves a time. Just wait and see, Honey. But this was an old story with Al. She had heard that promise so many times before. And so Al immersed himself once more in the work of rehearsal. He supervised everything, overriding many times the instructions of the director. Henrietta finally realized that her complaining was wasted effort. She resumed her role of neglected wife. Her husband was back in the arms of his greater love, the theater. Henrietta grew more and more resentful. She felt frustrated, cheated out of the normal aspects of a woman's life. So far there were no indications she would bear Al Jolson's children. She had once suggested they adopt a child. He had definitely sidetracked the idea. After that she had suggested he visit a doctor. But that had touched a sore spot in Jolson. He had lost his temper. She had painfully insulted him. He tried to make her believe there was nothing wrong with him, physically. Time was what he needed. Time until the flood tide of his all-demanding career would begin to ebb. He tried to make her see he could not divide his emotions. It was all or nothing; and at this particular period it was all for the stage. The rehearsals for *Sinbad* went on apace.

For the opening night of *Sinbad* at the Winter Garden on February 14, 1918, there was a sold-out house, every available seat taken.

Included in the cast were Laurence D'Orsay, Kitty Doner, Constance Ferber, and Forrest Huff.

From the start Jolson burst forth in full force with "Rock-a-Bye Your Baby with a Dixie Melody," music by Jean Schwartz, with lyrics by Joe Young and Sam M. Lewis, which was received with a cannonade of applause that shook the old Winter Garden to its rafters. After that he followed up with "Hello, Central, Give Me No Man's Land," by the same composers, and then a number with the suggestive title, "Why Do They Take the Night Boat to Albany?"

With these songs delivered in the best Jolsonesque manner, with Al cavorting all over the stage, the audience forgot about the rest of the show. More than ever they were electrified by Jolson's performance and salvo after salvo of applause rang through the theater. It seemed that those people would never get enough of the blackface singer. The hard work of these extended performances was beginning to tell somewhat on Jolson, and Klein, standing in the wings, began to worry. But cries of "Sing 'Rock-a-Bye' again!" came from the audience. Klein advised Al to give them the chorus only, then come off. Al sang the chorus and then, while the listeners went wild with their demonstration of gratitude, took his bows and came off the stage.

Sinbad became the talk of New York and its reputation spread to the hinterlands, bringing the small-towners to Broadway in droves. With the show's fame increasing, the fame of Al Jolson also increased. Through the eventful year of 1918 the Winter Garden was always filled to capacity with seats at a constant premium. The performances were sold out weeks in advance.

7

During this final year of the Great War the songsmiths were busily engaged in turning out war songs, both dramatic and humorous. There were purely patriotic numbers like marching songs about the doughboy and the girl he left behind.

Al did justice to many of these, introducing them in his special performances after the nightly curtain had descended on *Sinbad* proper, just as he had done with other songs in previous shows. With his usual gusto, his individualistic gestures and expressions, he sang the tunes as they flowed out of Tin Pan Alley: on the heart-rending side, there was Richard A. Whiting's "Till We Meet Again," Billy Baskette's "Good-bye, Broadway, Hello, France," Albert Von Tilzer's "I May Be Gone for a Long, Long Time" and "Au Revoir but Not Good-bye, Soldier Boy," and Fred Fisher's "Lorraine, My Beautiful Alsace Lorraine."

And with equal vigor Jolson sang the wartime songs of a gayer nature, melting the melancholy into smiles: Fisher's "Oui, Oui, Marie," Irving Berlin's "They Were All Out of Step but Jim" and "Oh! How I Hate to Get Up in the Morning," Walter Donaldson's "How Ya Gonna Keep 'Em Down on the Farm." There were also such frothy ditties as "If He Can Love Like He Can Fight (Oh, What a Soldier Boy He'd Be)," "K-K-K-Katy," "Oh, Frenchy," and "I Don't Want to Get Well." And to cap it all there was the war song of all time, "Over There," created by the incomparable George M. Cohan.

Sinbad reached and passed the Armistice of November 11, 1918, which saw the boys starting their homeward trek to take up life where they had left it.

Of course, things were changing fast. The automobile age had arrived. People were being educated to purchase autos with down payments. Wages were higher, as was the cost of living.

In the theatrical world vaudeville was fighting a valiant though one-sided battle to survive, in the face of the tremendous advance of the motion picture. Here was a new entertainment enterprise that was a combination of an art form with modern expansive industry in all its financial, productive, and distributive functions.

The film industry had come into its own and was now measuring its capital outlay and gross income in millions of dollars. Theaters especially designed for screen entertainment sprang up in every city and hamlet. In the larger cities motion picture houses were palaces of elegance and comfort, reducing the legit theater to the status of a poor second cousin. Screen stars like Douglas Fairbanks, Mary Pickford, Charlie Chaplin, Rudolph Valentino, and Gloria Swanson captured entirely new audiences that had never set foot in a legit theater.

But the Winter Garden was doing a land-office business. As though they had never heard of the movies, Al Jolson and Company in *Sinbad* were still going strong. Night after night Jolson held his audience captive to the end of 1918 and into the following year.

8

At a party given by Kitty Doner there was a young man with dark hair and dream-filled brown eyes, who had the greatest admiration for Al Jolson. In turn Jolson felt, as did everyone else in the musical world, that here indeed was America's own troubador, a young genius who wove the very characteristics of this country into his music—George Gershwin.

He had just written a song—"Swanee"—for his first Broadway show, *La, La, Lucille,* for which he had also created the rest of the music. Now, at Kitty's party, he played this piece on the piano for Al's benefit. Al immediately thought he would like to use it in *Sinbad.*

It was all right with Gershwin. He was sure Jolson was just the one to put it over. Al told Gershwin this song was made to order, and asked him to be at the Winter Garden the following night. Gershwin promised to be there.

On the following night, right after the show proper, Al ran out on the stage and greeted the audience. There was, as usual, a packed house. Folks, I have a new song for you tonight. It was written by a dear pal of mine—a young fellow you're going to hear from quite a bit, George Gershwin. The song, "Swanee." There was a burst of applause in honor of the composer and then Al, still in blackface, went into his song.

And when he hit the chorus, the rapt faces upturned to him held expressions of sheer ecstasy.

Swanee, Swanee, how I love you, how I love you,
   My dear old Swanee—
The folks up north will see me no more
   When I go to that Swanee shore—

Jolson finished the song in a crescendo that swept mightily through the theater, followed by a salvo of applause for Al himself. He took his bows, and with this performance the name of George Gershwin was made dearer to the American public and the song "Swanee" became, like so many others, a Jolson classic.

15

1

But Al, in this eventful year of 1919, achieving the purple heights of his career, idolized and admired by millions of fans, walked into his apartment one night after the show—somewhat earlier than usual—and found Henrietta, fully dressed, sitting on the sofa, instead of being in bed as he had expected.

In a later year, in a reminiscing mood, he recalled the incident, even the words that passed between them. Sugar, waiting up for me? Al, I've come to a final decision. I've been thinking about it for a long time. Honey, you talk like a judge. Al, I really think it's better for us to separate. I didn't just want to walk out. We're old enough to come to an understanding. Now, wait a minute, Honey Lamb. Wait a minute. Al, it's late and let's not have an argument. No argument, Honey. Nothing like that. All I ask is you listen to me for a couple of minutes—a couple of minutes. Al, you're going to try to convince me to stay. You've done it before but this time it's different. Maybe I'm not good for you. Besides, there's really nothing to hold us—no children—I once asked you to adopt a child—but it's too late now. . . .

Al stood motionless, staring at her, still unable to believe this was really happening. He knew now he had a fight on his hands— a fight to hold onto her. He could not accept the idea of going on without her. After thirteen years of marriage he had grown to think of her as a very part of himself. He must try to convince her to stay. He would be willing to make the supreme sacrifice—give up the theater. All this he told her, there in the apartment, as the first streak of dawn pierced the night.

Again he pleaded, this time with desperation. Yes—he would throw everything aside. They'd go away together, travel, Europe, Asia, Africa. She would never regret giving him this final chance. She listened quietly. She finished her packing, closed the suitcase, and stood there listening to him. She remembered hearing those same words before. But she listened. She had to give him that much. He was sincere in his plea. He was ready to sacrifice his career.

All she had to do was to unpack and remain in the apartment. On the morrow she would see things differently. He was sure of that. For a moment it seemed she was going to heed his plea. She sat down on the bed and Al dropped to his knees and put his arm about her. He kissed her mouth, cheeks, forehead. He kissed her hands. He kissed each of her ten fingers. Henrietta saw the tears in his eyes. It was strange to see Al Jolson like this.

She finally spoke. She told him she did not expect nor want him to give up the theater. That was his life. She wanted him to be a fulfilled man, and in the theater, with his audiences, he would find his happiness. She assured him that, in time, he would look back at all this and wonder why he had tried to divide his attention between two alliances—the theater and his wife. In the end they both knew well enough it would be the theater.

He told her he was going out. He would let her be alone for the remaining hours of darkness to regain her perspective. He would go to a hotel. In the morning he would come back. They would both be in a more tolerant mood. From then on he would live only to make her happy. Just wait and see, Honey Chile. That's the way it's going to be from now on. It's going to be you. The hell with the stage. Do you believe me, Honey?

She did not say anything. She just sat there on the bed, the packed suitcase on the floor at the bedside.

He left the apartment, his world beginning to crumble about him. He walked for miles. He told himself over and over, It's my fault. I should have been with her more. Why didn't I see that? Can't blame her. She really had no life with me. I promised her it would be different but it never was. Tired, exhausted, he finally entered a hotel.

In his room he fell on the bed without attempting to undress. Before troubled sleep overtook him, he had a glimmer of hope that in the morning he would return to the apartment and find her there waiting for him.

In the morning he did go back to the apartment. No one was there.

2

But the show went on. *Sinbad* remained a smash hit all through those weeks of 1919. In time he received a letter from Henrietta telling him quite calmly that she was living in Oakland, California, establishing a residence. He knew what that meant. In the fall of that year he received a formal notice of a court decision granting Henrietta a divorce from him on the grounds of mental cruelty.

He went off alone after the performance. He walked to his hotel, shaking his head in disbelief along the way. He had not believed she'd go through with it. Mental cruelty. Maybe that's what it was. But he had been too busy to see it.

After this, in his singing at the Winter Garden, the critics were aware of an increased note of anguish in his voice.

Each night when he came out on that stage he was Al Jolson, the showman, the trouper, the clown in blackface—with a theaterful of friends—but after the show, he was a man lonely, hurt, bewildered.

During these lonely days, with Henrietta out of his life, Al walked about in a mental fog. He snapped out of it only when he had to go on stage, obeying the theater's prime creed, that the show must go on, heartbreak or not.

Klein did his best to cheer Al up somehow, told him sure it was a shock but that he'd get used to it. Life would go on. But Al knew now he had taken her too much for granted. He chided himself. The Great Jolson—he could hold a thousand people at one time and make them stick with him, but he couldn't hold onto one little girl.

3

In February 1920 a song—"My Mammy"—written by Joe Young, Sam N. Lewis, and Walter Donaldson, was selected by Jolson for his opening number for that night's performance of *Sinbad*. He figured he could do full justice to the song. The director considered it a rather hackneyed piece, with a moronic simplicity. He wanted something more substantial, a song with some depth to it. After all, Jolson was not going to sing a lullaby to a roomful of five-year-olds.

But strangely enough, Al seemed to like the greeting-card sentimentality of the song. Perhaps he was thinking of his own mother and all those years of separation. The production staff became aware of Al's strong preference, and so "My Mammy" was the choice.

There was an air of expectancy in the theater as, of course, there had always been with the Shubert revues. But somehow on this night it was different—the air of expectancy seemed more intense. It seemed to hover over the theater like a weight. They sat there—a sophisticated, critical audience, an audience that had paid top price for seats.

As the curtain rose the Winter Garden chorines—"the prettiest girls ever assembled on a stage" as announced in the advertisements—went through their paces with military precision. After that came a lavish production number, not intrinsically different from what they had seen in other revues.

But the audience anticipated something in the way of a bonus. Most of them knew they were waiting for a blackfaced singer.

The Shuberts and their production staff were worried—the audience reaction was below par. In fact there was a rustle out there, though slight, nevertheless a sign of boredom. For the opening numbers the applause had been lukewarm. Every now and then there was a chuckle in the house when a performer hit them with a punch line. The producers and their staff exchanged strained glances.

There was some laughter, and perhaps a few stifled yawns— evidence that people could grow weary of the same rich dish. They seemed to be waiting for something, though they listened politely to a song by the beautiful Kitty Doner. In acknowledgment, polite applause. Polite—but not the "oomph" response the Shuberts would have liked to hear.

Messrs. Shubert looked at Klein and shook their heads. They knew they were depending too much on Jolson. After all, how much can one man be expected to do?

Klein assured them they could depend on Al. He wouldn't let the show down. No matter how things were going, he was a trouper. The Shuberts admired Klein's faith but they still insisted one man didn't make a show.

Klein told the Shuberts to calm dowr Al would go on, sing, and then march off to applause. Simɣle as that. So relax. Have a cigar.

There was a love scene between Kitty Doner and Lawrence D'Orsay, another song by Kitty, and the audience grew restless once more.

And then the lights went out except for a blue-white spot that moved to the right wing. The spot hesitated there, and then a blackfaced figure, wearing a dark suit, a black string tie, and white gloves, ran out upon the stage and the circle of light followed him to the center of the proscenium.

Absolute silence in the theater, then a slight stirring, as hundreds of eyes stared at the figure before them. A blackfaced song and dance man—those who had never seen him perform were skeptical. But their attention was riveted upon that minstrel figure in the blue-white beam of the spotlight. His eyes seemed to light up and sparkle in reflection. He smiled, more like a wide grin, and then he rolled his eyes and clapped his white-gloved hands together and the audience stopped stirring. And then the blackfaced man went into his song. The audience forgot its impatience. There was no time for that, but only time to watch, to listen to what this blackfaced man had to say about his "Mammy"—

Mammy, Mammy,
The sun shines east, the sun shines west—

That catch in his voice—a sob. A note of sorrow in a voice that cried out to them one moment and reassured them the next.

But I've just learned where the sun shines best.
Mammy, Mammy,
My heart strings are tangled around Alabamy—

The blackfaced man singing with greater impact, his resonant voice filling the theater. Ladies' handkerchiefs came out and eyes were dabbed. Women of the social register, from Fifth and Park avenues. Masculine lips were trembling—men from Wall Street and Madison Avenue. In the galleries people from the teeming sidewalks of New York, caught in the same current.

Al Jolson—Asa Yoelson, the Seventh Cantor, with "My Mammy" as a prayer. . . .

The blackfaced man got down on one knee. He stretched out his hands in front of him, and there was grief on his face and tears in his eyes. This time he did not sing—he talked the words:

I'se a-comin'—
I'm sorry, Mammy—I'm sorry I made you wait—
Mammy, Mammy, I hope—I'm not too late—
My little Mammy—Nobody else's Mammy—

He got up from his kneeling position, held out his white-gloved hands in supplication to the audience. Now he sang out to them in militant, stamping rhythm:

I'd walk a million miles
For one of your smiles—
My Mammy—

On the word "Mammy" his voice caught on another sob.

The song was over. There was silence, but only for a few seconds. And then the first handclap—another handclap—and the applause had begun, increasing in volume until everyone was applauding. It was a responsive outburst, an ovation that went on and on without abatement. Calls of "Al Jolson—Al Jolson—" rang through the theater. "Encore—encore—" came the demand. They had heard the blackfaced man—now they would always want to hear him.

Unexpectedly this night had turned out to be a triumph for the Shuberts, and all the members of the company, down to the last scenery shifter, basked in the reflected glory. It would be theatrical history, that a minstrel man sang a song called "My Mammy" and immortalized it.

And so the curtain came down on that night's performance of *Sinbad*.

Al Jolson had fulfilled his promise to his father that even from the stage of a theater, he would indeed be the Seventh Cantor—in blackface. . . .

4

Klein was an astute judge of human nature.

There was always the danger of overwork on the part of his client and friend who was packing them in with *Sinbad*. Klein had to get Al away from his work at appreciable intervals. A little recreation might lend new zest to Al's performance. Klein therefore suggested that Al take out one of the young girls in the show. There was Kitty Doner's understudy, a dark-eyed, black-haired young lady of great promise who was billed as Francine Dubois. Al hedged. He was wary about becoming involved; he found it hard to forget the debacle with Henrietta.

But Klein did not give up. He was determined to see Al go out with Miss Dubois, especially when he found out that she was a nice Jewish girl whose real name was Esther Silverman. Al objected. He was leery of feminine association at present. At any rate, he had never really been a success with the ladies. Somehow, sooner or later, they had become bored. He was not, essentially, a lover. He could not concentrate, when the time came, on the charms of a female companion. His mind was always filled with the problems of his career. But he did confess to Klein that sometimes he felt lonely. If only Henrietta would come back.

Klein was smart enough to see and understand Al's reaction. Klein could foresee, also, that as the days wore on the inevitable would happen. Some young chick would show a sign of interest and Al would proceed to make a fool of himself.

On this particular night, when the performance was over, Klein asked Al to wait a minute. All Klein wanted was for Al to give the little Jewish lady a break.

The theater was almost empty and Al was growing impatient. He could have enjoyed a good game of pinochle instead of wasting his time with some stage-struck maiden. He wondered whether girls were really a necessary phase of a young man's life. He was doing pretty well as he was—free and unattached.

Klein returned with an attractive dark-eyed young woman in tow. Al realized it was too late to run. At any rate, he could not help but see that she was a beauty. Klein introduced her as a nice Jewish girl. Made to order for you, Al. A talented actress. Cooks a fine strictly kosher meal—Francine Dubois—real name, Esther Silverman. Al was somewhat embarrassed. He asked the girl not to mind Klein. That man was an intrepid exaggerator but a pretty good manager. Miss Silverman gave Al a reassuring smile. Al, strangely enough, began to feel at ease. His fear had melted away. He felt his confidence returning. He gave her his arm and they left the theater. Klein lingered behind, grinning broadly. Things were shaping up the way he wanted them to. A nice Jewish girl. After all, it had to be remembered, Al was the son of a cantor.

Al found it not too difficult to talk to Esther. She was his own kind. She was "family" from the first moment. It was as if he had known her some time way back. They were outside, now, standing on the pavement of busy Broadway. Al was determined to dispel any uneasiness between them. He wondered what she would really think of him as a companion.

It was almost midnight. The spring night was close. There were warm air currents fanning through the skyscraper canyons. Al whistled down a taxicab.

"Maxim's," he told the driver.

5

At Maxim's the headwaiter recognized Al and showed them to a corner table. A waiter appeared, deftly took their order, the roast duck dinner a la Maxim's.

Al informed Miss Silverman that the food here was not kosher. She told him her own cooking was definitely kosher, inherited from her mother. But when she dined out she was not too particular. But she did observe the code of not eating meat and dairy dishes together. She asked him whether he thought her too old-fashioned. He assured her of his approval. He was, after all, the son of a cantor; in fact, he was supposed to have become a cantor himself. Family tradition. He assured her he had not relinquished his faith. He was proud of his ancestry. But now he urged her to forget faith and family tradition and enjoy dinner at Maxim's. She put her hand on his arm, smiled at him. For once, in a long, long while, he had stopped thinking of the theater.

He was not too good at the small talk that usually went on between young couples. He could try to talk to her, perhaps, about her future career as an actress. But his problem was soon solved. She was quite clever, as he found out. Almost without realizing it, he was drawn into talking about himself. On that one subject Al could do quite well. Given a willing listener, he wasted no time in waxing dramatic over the details.

He told her briefly, but with gusto, the story of his boyhood and of his father's insistence that he develop into a cantor. He told her of his repeated runaways from home, of his stint in Lew Dockstader's Minstrel show, of how Klein had found him and brought him to the Winter Garden.

6

They did not finish their dinner. Untouched food was left on the table. Instead, they had become wrapped up in each other's life stories. Al now listened to Esther's story. She had completed high school, had starred in the school plays, had always dreamed of the stage. Finally she had come to New York. Nothing mattered but a start in the theater. She could dance, sing, act. She secured her first role, a walk-on, with one or two lines. Then came somewhat larger roles. Finally, she reached the plateau of being an understudy. She thought a great deal of their current show, *Sinbad*, but sometimes she thought of other things as well.

Marriage, for instance. Children. Family life. Being an honest-to-goodness housewife.

Al had been increasingly interested until her mention of marriage and children. He suddenly felt uneasy. He wanted to terminate the conversation. He wanted to take her home to her hotel. The evening had been an enjoyable one. But he had a feeling about Jewish maidens. More than once he had told Klein the first thought in the mind of a Jewish girl was to marry and become a Jewish mother. Nothing bad about that. In fact, what could be more wonderful? But this was one scene into which Al could not hope to tread. He had no business kidding himself or fooling the girl. He was the wrong man for children and family. Had he been capable, he could have prolonged their acquaint-anceship. Maybe it could have deepened into something more. He remembered Henrietta. He would not dare to make a similar mess of this young girl's life, to spoil her dream. He could see the question mark in her eyes. He did not have the answer she expected.

She asked him what he would do after the show closed. Once more he was back on his favorite theme. He told her he would go on singing—in other shows. His manager, good old "Kleiney," would see to that. He told her he was truly happy only when he faced an audience. He lived for their applause. His reward was not only the money involved but the approbation of his fans. That was his meaning in life, his own brand of personal fulfillment—to make them laugh, to make them cry. If he could keep on doing that. . . .

The orchestra music was intriguing. She leaned forward. By her expression he knew she wanted to dance. They joined the other couples on the floor in a waltz. Al's dancing was an improvement over his earlier attempts, and Esther glided on gossamer wings.

7

It was after 2 A. M. before they walked out of Maxim's into the fresh night air. The city was quieter now, but the lights still gleamed and the night life of the metropolis was in full swing and in some places would continue until the first gray streaks of dawn.

They strolled up Broadway, and Al had never talked so much for a long time. He had a good listener.

They finally got into a horse-drawn hansom cab, and when he stood at her apartment door, he was still talking about his career as though nothing else in the world mattered. The look in Esther's eyes seemed to hint of disappointment. She had hoped, perhaps, that he would stop talking long enough to pay attention to her in a more personal mood. He didn't even attempt to kiss her good-night. He started away. Al Jolson, there was reprimand in her voice. He stopped, turned around. What's the matter, Honey Chile? Al Jolson, you never even tried to kiss me—not once—not very complimentary, you know. He answered, I'm a fool.

He came back to her. He leaned forward, brushed his lips lightly to her cheeks and gave her a decorous peck. She put her arms about him, drew his head down, and placed her lips firmly against his. Al Jolson received a kiss he would not soon forget. She told him now he could go. He told her she was wonderful, that he would ask her to go out with him again some time soon. He had a wide grin as he left her, standing there, wondering. He hurried away to his all-consuming romance with someone else— a multiheaded siren called an audience.

16

1

Al made one of his periodic visits to his parents in Washington.

As usual, neighbors and fellow congregationalists dropped in to share in welcoming the famous member of the Yoelson family.

Cantor Yoelson, mellowed somewhat by the additional years, beamed proudly. That was his son, Asa.

After the guests had departed, Al put his arm about his mother. He sat with her, telling her of his experiences.

You will not forget every week to write? Now, Momma, you know I've been doing that. But I don't want you should stop. Momma, you know I wouldn't stop. He gave her a hug and a kiss. Asa, tell me, since the divorce you have maybe met a nice girl? You know, Momma, I've met hundreds of nice girls. They're around me all the time. I don't mean hundreds, Asa, I mean one girl. Momma, if I tell you I've met one girl, good-looking, educated, talented, would that make you happy? You mean it, Asa? You are not joking? You know, Momma, I wouldn't joke about a thing like that. Tell me, Asa, she is not, I hope, a *shiksa*? I guarantee she is a honest-to-goodness Jewish girl. Believe it or not she cooks strictly kosher meals and to the bargain she's a peacherino. What means that, Asa? Well, it means she is almost as pretty as you, Momma. But I am an old woman. You'll never be old to me, Momma. You're still my sweetheart. Asa, be serious for a minute. This girl—what is her name? She calls herself Francine Dubois in the show but her real name is Esther

Silverman. Now I know a *shiksa* she is not. And you are going to marry her? I just met the gal. Marriage? I don't know—the audiences—they like me, Momma. I'm making a hit with them. So I'll just wait a while before I ask any girl to marry me. Asa, to wait too long is no good. This Esther—soon another young man will steal her away from you. It could be. Don't worry, Momma. Just give me a little time. One of these days I'll come home with a brand new wife. Now give me a kiss and it's up to bed with you. Good night, Momma. Good night, son. Don't forget to ask that nice Jewish girl to marry you.

Later, when the family had retired and he was in his own bed, Al remembered how it had been long ago. He was fourteen again, planning to run away. . . .

The next day he left with the morning train.

Life was strange sometimes—he had to keep running away from the ones he loved.

When he came back to New York he telephoned Esther as soon as he arrived at his quarters. He was informed she had checked out of her apartment the day before. The next day he discovered she had left the show—to be married.

2

There was a backstage party at the Winter Garden for the cast in celebration of *Sinbad*'s closing after a total of 164 performances.

There was one girl who seemed to catch Jolson's eye and he found pleasure in conversing with her. She was extremely young, but somehow for Al feminine youth had an irresistible attraction. In this young girl's beauty he seemed to find a new incentive, a replenishment. In her clear fresh eyes he saw the eagerness of life.

And the girl, under the name of Ethel Delmar, was in a contemporary hit show on Broadway, *Scandals of 1920*. She had been invited over by her friend Kitty Doner.

Al danced with Ethel for the rest of the evening. He learned her real name was Alma Osborne, born and brought up in Easton,

Pennsylvania. Al seemed to have thrown caution to the winds. This was exactly what Klein had feared. Al was gravitating toward a mere child. He was almost twice her age. Was this to be Al's weakness? A mania for young girls? Klein was deeply perturbed. This was not merely a passing fun-thing. The girl, apparently, had been hypnotized by Al Jolson, the legendary singer. On his part, Al found her exhilarating. He was sure she would understand his needs. They strolled away from the center of the party, found an isolated corner of the stage where they could talk without being interrupted. Alma Osborne did not hesitate to express her feelings to Al. She told him she had always idolized him, had, in fact, kept every phonograph record he had ever made. Her youth intrigued him. He could not explain this in so many words. Klein had cautioned him to watch his step. Al shrugged. He could take care of himself. So what if she was young? At eighteen a girl was a woman. No better time to get married.

Al led her back to the party. They danced some more. She pressed close against him. He wondered about her perfume. He liked perfume on ladies. Alma gave him worshipful glances. He felt like twenty once again.

Klein urged Al to leave the girl alone. She is too young for you. Wise up, pal. But Al didn't listen. It was just because she was so young that attracted Al. And she preferred to be with him instead of consorting with any one of a dozen younger men in the show. Al was suffering what Klein called a "swelled head." Al, you're letting yourself in for a fall. This girl is just a kid. She doesn't know her own mind. Let her go, Al, let her go. Al turned a deaf ear to Klein's plea. He dated Alma. He took her to other shows. They dined and danced at the liveliest cafes. He liked the way she clung to him. Klein warned, she's taking the zing out of you, so what will be left for the show? I'm talking to you like a father. Watch your career. Al assured Klein he would give better performances with Alma as his inspiration. Maybe I love her. Do you understand, Kleiny? Maybe I'll marry her as soon as I'm free from Henrietta. Then Al was suddenly silent. The very mention of Henrietta's name emphasized an ecstasy lost.

Maybe marriage with Alma would stick. But Klein knew Al, knew what would inevitably happen, especially with Alma so young, so alive. The fulfillment this chick would expect would not be forthcoming, not from Al. Klein searched for a way to convince Al to set her free, and thus free himself.

But there was no way.

Unless Henrietta returned.

3

One afternoon Al had a few friends—mostly from the Winter Garden—in his apartment. With Alma Osborne nestling in his arms, they danced to the strains of a player-piano. The tune was one of the Jolson smash hits: Gershwin's "Swanee."

It was strange, even to Al, that this attractive young girl should make him forget all that had happened only a short time ago. He was fascinated by her almost childlike devotion to the Jolson legend. He couldn't tell whether it was merely a schoolgirl crush or something more. But he did know that holding her in his arms during the dance gave him a pleasant buoyancy. Someone had inserted another roll of music in the piano, this time a waltz, "Beautiful Ohio," a dreamy, lilting melody that made one think of moonlit waters and shadowy pine groves.

Al told her he wouldn't be the same man again. Why? Honey, baby, it's holding you like this. You're just a kid and you're frightening the daylights out of me. She laughed. Incredible. The great Al Jolson talking like that. She wished he'd be as comfortable with her as he was with an audience. The way he put himself down. Was he really afraid of her? But Al could not dispel his feeling of guilt. He was not the man she probably thought he was. Would she ever be close enough to learn the truth? Klein could tell her, but Klein would never do such a thing. Not Kleiny.

The music stopped. The people in the room were all talking at once, laughing, calling out to each other. Almost without realizing it Al was saying aloud, Jolie, you dog, you've done it again. You ought to be ashamed of yourself—taking advantage of a teen-aged babe. Alma was quick to counter with, Mr. Jolson, a babe of eighteen can be the mother of five children. Then they both laughed and for Al the broken pieces of his world were forming into place again.

He invited her to dine with him at Rector's after the performance. She did not hesitate to accept. Maybe that's what he liked
about her. She responded, quickly and directly. She didn't keep
him dangling.

This was the beginning of a pleasant courtship. Al, though he
might not have stopped to consider it so, was experiencing one of
the happiest interludes of his life. To him this girl was an angel. He
felt complimented by her companionship and he sincerely
wanted her love.

Meanwhile Klein was always there to remind Al there was work
to be done. Rehearsals were started for a new Shubert revue. So
important in the show-biz realm had Jolson become that a
theater was opened bearing his name, Jolson's 59th Street
Theater. Rehearsals were transferred to the new theater for the
next extravaganza, *Bombo*, which was to be bigger and better
than all the previous revues.

Jolson worked hard, but now with Alma at his side, he felt an
added impetus. Alma continued with her stage work, though
most of her time was taken up by Jolson. They visited the race
tracks together. They saw the Broadway shows. They went
dancing.

Al drove his new Packard along country roads in New York
state, in Connecticut, in New Jersey. They took a longer trip and
visited his people in Washington, and when Al brought Alma into
the house, the first thing Mrs. Yoelson asked him when she had
him alone, Asa, she is the Jewish girl? No, Momma. This is a
different one. Not Jewish. Asa, you mean she is a *shiksa*? Then
let it be with luck.

Mrs. Yoelson accepted Alma. If her Asa liked the girl, that was
enough. Cantor Yoelson greeted Alma with a degree of caution,
but with no resentment. She was part of Asa's world. This was,
after all, America. Intermarriage was nothing new here. The
nature of democracy. The essence of freedom. Let them be
happy. He would pray for them. The Lord would forgive them.
He knew his son had become an important figure in the land and
he, the father, should feel proud. But he would have felt much
prouder had Asa become a cantor.

That summer of 1921 Al lived through some of the happiest
moments of his life. Sometimes he shook his head at himself in

the mirror while shaving in the mornings. You lucky dog. You've got everything now—including that little cutie-pie—and she's stuck on you too. Imagine a smart young chick like that going for an old bugger like you. Jolie, I say again, you're a lucky dog.

There was one month's vacation that summer and Al took Alma everywhere. They even rode the subway to Coney Island where they had a field day adventuring on the various thrill rides. Later they threw baseballs at targets for prize dolls. For supper they ate hot dogs. After that they visited the Brighton Theater to listen to Sophie Tucker belt out her "red hot momma" songs.

4

In September of that year Jolson knuckled down to serious work on *Bombo*, putting on the finishing touches in dress rehearsals. It was to be an even more elaborate spectacle than *Sinbad*, and songwriters, choreographers, directors, electricians, and the cast were all busy with their tasks.

Klein had announced to Al that he was rather tired and would like to be released. Actually there was no formal contract between them and Al begged him to stay on a while longer, until *Bombo* was safely launched. But Klein insisted he couldn't continue. He felt he required rest. A man gets older, Al. Maybe you'll find that out when you reach my age. Jolson took a deep breath. Me get older? I'm going to be just the same as I am now. I'll keep on singing. Nothing's going to stop Jolie. Man alive, Kleiny, you're not *that* old. Stay on with me. What's the word? The word was that Klein would not change his mind. It was just after the rehearsal of *Bombo*. Al and Alma insisted that Klein dine with them. A sort of farewell party. Klein accepted the invitation. At the table at Rector's, Klein suggested several names of possible successors. Men who had good reputations. You see, Al, no one is indispensable. When the time comes a man can be replaced.

Al took Alma's hands in his. With this gal to back me up I'm one bugger that's goin' to keep on and on. Just wait and see. Klein remained quiet, ate his dinner. He had been determined to launch Al on his career. This he had done. Now his task was finished. From here on in Al must propel himself under his own power. And as Al himself put it: Nothin' was goin' to stop Jolie.

5

Among the manager-prospects suggested by Klein was one Lou Epstein. Al's eyes brightened. He remembered the name. A burlesque theater in Scranton. Lou Epstein was the manager. Al played a one-night stand there—back in 1912. Epstein—a swell guy. Al told Klein, Good old Lou. He thought I was the greatest.

Klein considered the choice ideal.

So Lou Epstein became Jolson's business manager—and personal confidante—to remain with Al until the end.

17

1

On October 6, 1921, *Bombo* had its gala opening at the Jolson 59th Street Theater, and the furs, diamonds, and evening clothes invaded the theater in resplendent array.

Supporting Jolson in the cast were Forrest Huff and Janet Adair. There was Sigmund Romberg music, including the songs "In Old Granada," "Oh, Oh, Columbus," and "Jazza-Da-Dadoo." Like the previous Shubert revues, this one had the usual lavish costumes and settings, and there was a packed house for each performance.

Jolson in blackface as Bombo, servant of Christopher Columbus, was all over the stage, singing his songs, a good percentage of them repeats from former shows. But the audience seemed never to tire of listening to them.

However, in this show there was a new number that immediately proved a great success—"California, Here I Come," created by Buddy de Sylva and Joseph Meyer, with help on the lyrics by Al Jolson himself. Al put this number over with a bang, and before long it was hummed and sung throughout the nation—the birth of another Jolson classic.

In the free time available to Al, he squired his girlfriend, Alma Osborne, to cafes and cabarets, and on Sundays, if they had no party or show to attend, they motored out of New York. Al loved to drive, and with Alma at his side the world was his.

Bombo sailed full steam ahead, and the box office clicked along with it. It looked like another long run and Jolson settled down to it. He wrote regularly to his mother, sending her checks, and he always asked about his father. Cantor Yoelson was semi-retired; he often asked about Al and when was he coming home again. Over the years Mr. Yoelson had finally been reconciled to Al's chosen profession, realizing that perhaps he had been wrong in trying to force his son into a cantor's career. As it was, everything had turned out for the best. Al had become world-famous as a singer of songs for all the people and this gave to Cantor Yoelson a feeling of secret pride.

2

Back in New York at the Jolson 59th Street Theater, *Bombo* was going over "socko." But one night the audience was treated to another of the Jolson surprises. He was to sing a number that would once more stir their emotions and send them away to remember.

There was a song written by the team of de Sylva and Louis Silvers, entitled "April Showers."

The show had settled down to an even pace. Night after night the customers came and were satisfied with the music, the dances, the sketches, and now it was time for something climactic. So once again the blue-white spotlight encircled the blackfaced singer and escorted him out to the center of the stage. As in his previous great hits, he went through the motions of clapping his white-gloved hands, rolling his eyes, and stretching his white greasepainted lips into a wide elfish grin.

Though April showers may come your way,
   They bring the flowers that bloom in May . . .

The people listened, their eyes focused upon him, their faces rapt. It was Jolson at his best. Every once in a while he came out with one of these super-performances.

There was not one person in that packed house who did not thrill to that voice:

So if it's raining, have no regrets
   Because it isn't raining rain, you know,
It's raining violets . . .

His voice was clear, of a deep timbre. It flowed like a great tide
of sound through the space of the theater. As he sang to them,
they could see the sun bursting through the clouds, the daffodils
dancing.

And if you see clouds upon the hills
   You soon will see crowds of daffodils . . .

The audience was stunned by this magic. On the crest of the
melody came the concluding words of the song—

So keep on looking for a bluebird
   And listen for his song,
Whenever April showers come along . . .

And then he made his bow in that brief moment of silence
preceding the burst of applause which soon thundered and
multiplied until the walls of the theater shook.

Al took his bows. He had to give them another chorus, and
after that he was finally able to shuffle his way off the stage. When
he saw Alma backstage he told her, Honey Lamb, your ol' Jolie
really gave them something tonight. Al, I saw and heard it all. She
leaned against him impulsively and kissed him.

Al's cup was brimming. Another smash hit—a worshipping
host of fans—a pretty girl who loved him. It was not his nature
to weigh the permanency of all this or to consider even the
possibility of a future change.

To Al Jolson every waking moment of the present was what
mattered: the past was gone, the future was for dreams, but the
present was for living. He was flying high. He inhaled deeply of the
giddy atmosphere. He was a conquering hero. There were
thousands of people who thrilled at his presence before them.
Al had tasted of the wine of success and it was sweet and
intoxicating. There was no way he could stand still now. He was
too excited to settle down to calmness, to reflection upon the

vicissitudes of life. The river of good tidings was flowing his way, sweeping him along in the current. The feeling was ecstatic. He wanted Alma to enjoy it too, close to him. He suggested they go out and celebrate. They must always celebrate. Honey, let's go where there are people—music—dancing. Maxim's. Al, don't you ever get tired? Jolie get tired? Baby doll, this is Al Jolson you're talking to.

3

And yet, sometimes, when alone—offstage and unattended— he was an ordinary figure of a man, a little clumsy, perhaps, in his movements and, even if he didn't admit it, a little weary, too, and more so as he grew older. A man who sat in the Moskowitz and Lupowitz Restaurant, the refuge of the Broadway membership, eating his bagel and lox on a Sunday morning, or on a weekday, his blintzes and sour cream. . . .

4

There was a party in the apartment of Janet Adair, one of the principals in the cast of *Bombo*. Members of the theatrical world were present, crowded into the space of the rather confining quarters.

There were several discussions going on among the writers, directors, producers, and performers. The discussions, of course, were in the main technical and somewhat involved, and Al, with Alma at his side, began to feel like an outsider looking in.

He could not take part, since when it came to the technical aspects of a subject, even of his beloved theater and its allied arts, he was at a loss. Alma understood at once his discomfiture and she drew him aside and talked to him about the things he did understand, but Al was not to be fooled. He knew the score.

As he told it later, sometimes he felt sorry he didn't go on through school and acquire an education. When you come right down to it, what do I know? Oh, I can sing, I suppose, in my own way, and keep an audience from being bored, but what do I really know about music—the technique of it—you know, the science of it—the way some people do—for instance, an opera singer like Caruso or a composer like Georgie Gershwin.

Alma tried to assure him that he was an artist in his own field. Someone composed the music, wrote the song, but Al was the one who gave it life. And the way he did it—well, there was only one Jolson. The proof? *La Belle Paree, Vera Violetta, Honeymoon Express, Sinbad*, and now *Bombo*. All smash hits. Why? Because of a blackfaced singer.

Al stared at her, realizing now that she was not such a child after all. She really thought he was *it*. Thanks, honey. For a minute there I thought I was the forgotten man. But, no kiddin', there really is so much to know, so much going on around us all the time. New inventions—movies, phonograph, telephone, automobile. Boy, oh, boy. You know what, sweetheart? One of these days I'm goin' to take myself some time off and read up on these things. I'll go to night school. I mean it. She smiled. Sure, Al, sure.

Jolson could not long be ignored by any group. Soon the conversations going on about the apartment grew boring and attention was transferred to Al. Come on, Al, we're waiting for you. Alma squeezed Al's hand. She glanced up at him, nodding. Now, what did I tell you, Al? Sooner or later it's Jolson. The requests began to come. Give us a song, Al. How about "Mammy"? Al, sing the one that goes "Rock-a-Bye Your Baby." Please, Al, "Swanee." And so the rest of the evening belonged to Al Jolson. He sang the songs and they applauded, and they requested more and more. The party became another Jolson rally.

5

In August of that year, 1922, Al Jolson and Alma Osborne were married in a quiet, civil ceremony, and there was a gala party in celebration backstage at the Jolson 59th Street Theater. The ecstatic couple moved directly into an apartment, and the honeymoon had to be postponed because of Al's absorption with *Bombo*. He reassured her on the morning following their wedding, Don't you fret now. We're goin' to have the biggest honeymoon ever. Remember, this is Jolie talking and it's a solemn promise, so help me.

It's all right, Al. I know you can't break away from *Bombo*. When the show closes we can go then. I'm a very patient wife. Al beamed. Sugar, all I know is I'm crazy about you and I want to see that smile on your face at all times, day or night.

6

Al suggested to the Shuberts that *Bombo* would go well on the road, that there were thousands of people outside of New York who were only too anxious to see a Shubert revue. At first there was strong opposition to Al's plan. The cost would be devastating and might result in a heavy loss. However, Al persisted. He had been thinking about this for a long time, and he had a feeling that it would be a successful venture. If they broke even, it would still be worth it.

Consent was finally obtained and a train chartered for the purpose. A dozen coaches were necessary to transport the personnel, the scenery, and the props, but *Bombo* did finally take to the road in the late summer of 1922, and the tour from the very beginning played to S.R.O. in whatever city they hit. The house was always sold out far in advance, and Al himself was surprised to see the tremendous impact he had created upon the people of America. He heard himself called "the greatest entertainer of all time."

Al had his newly acquired bride, Alma, along with him on the first leg of the tour, which became for them also a honeymoon. These were the most fulfilling days for Al. He was king of all he surveyed. He had seen other stars of Broadway fade into oblivion after a few seasons of acclaim and success. He had seen them come and go since 1911 when he had first come to the Shuberts, but here he was, more popular than ever, with the world at his feet.

He was sitting in the parlor coach with Alma as the train sped through the countryside. They could look out and see the trees, hills, flat lands, mountains—all whirling by, minute after minute. Al had his arm about her, holding her close. He talked of their future together. Alma was telling him she wanted children, at least five. He was silent now. How could he tell her that with him there would be no children? He could not spoil her dream. So he agreed with her. Five would be fine. Or maybe enough for a baseball team. They both laughed. Al tried hard not to think about the future, not to examine it too closely. All that mattered was now—their honeymoon. Alma suggested she would be willing to convert to the Hebrew faith for the children's sake. Al assured her it was not necessary. He was broadminded. Besides, in America intermarriage was not a forbidden thing. Then he kissed her and told her everything would be fine. Alma repeated her wish to convert. Honey Lamb, if you insist, you can become anything you like, so long as you're healthy. She explained otherwise our children would be neither Jewish nor Gentile. Mongrels, really. You will see to it, Al? I do want to convert.

Al tried to be pleasant through the rest of the tour. In the nights he would get out of bed and pace the floor of the train coach or the hotel room. He began to be harassed by a growing doubt. Maybe he should not have married Alma. A woman—any woman—thinks of marriage as the way to children. It was a natural expectation. Alma became aware of Al's anxiety. Is anything wrong, Al? What is an old bastard like me doing with a young kid like you? Mr. Al Jolson, you're not *that* old.

It was Lou Epstein's voice that brought them back to reality. Sorry, folks, to interrupt your honeymoon but, Al, there's some problem to be ironed out regarding the schedule. The Shubert strategic command is waiting. Okay, Lou. Come along, honey, and watch Jolie in action.

7

The explosive thrust that set off the roaring twenties like a red-hot rocket was the advent of prohibition in the first month of 1919, as an amendment to the Constitution. This led to a new way of life, a revised evaluation of the American scene. It was the inception of a new double standard of morality, the observance of the laws of the land with the exception of one.

By 1922 the manufacture, sale, and distribution of the prohibited liquors was entrenched well underground, controlled by violent, insensitive men whose sales argument was the "pineapple" and the "tommy-gun."

Violence took the place of due process of law and the resultant bloodbaths painted a crimson blotch of shame across the face of the nation. Political graft, police bribery, and corruption flourished while the watered-down "imported Scotch" gurgled noisily down the parched throats of "law-abiding" citizens.

Show biz felt the effects of this exciting situation—beneficially. The legit cabarets and night spots shut down their bars, and the resultant loss of revenue forced most of them to close their doors entirely or to discontinue entertainment and survive, if they could, merely as restaurants.

This forced the public, desirous of live entertainment, to turn to the theaters. Vaudeville, variety shows, and musical comedy received increased patronage, and the actors, musicians, writers, stagehands—as well as the producers—began to reap this new windfall harvest. From out of the bistros—the "speaks"—operating under the cloak of secrecy with little peep-hole windows where the password was "Joe sent me," came the jerky and uninhibited dances that soon invaded the legit dancehalls and even the private living rooms of the American public—the "Charleston," the "Black Bottom," with the "Big Apple" just around the corner, and a wild assortment of "rag" steps generally identified as "Collegiate." The music was blasted out by hot jazz combos, featuring muffled horns and saxes and eccentric drums.

Jazz, that new form of music that Jolson had so diligently advocated all these years, was not only here at last but was extending itself into strange and erotic forms—almost grotesque in some of its manifestations.

A devil-may-care attitude was developing, as a result of the Great War's aftermath finally come to roost among the people, as well as the impact of the unpopular prohibition laws.

In 1922, with Harding as president, a tremendous Mardi Gras began that was to continue until the Great Depression, a decade away. The night life in the cities seemed to be the very purpose of living. Dancing became an obsession, even extending into daytime "dansants." Gigolos and lounge lizards flourished. The people went on a binge of self-expression: flagpole and tree sitting, English Channel swims, marathon dances, six-day bike races, goldfish swallowing, racoon and bearskin coats worn by college boys, tight dresses above the knees, unbuckled flapping galoshes, spit curls and bangs, knickers for the boys, pajamas for the girls, beach parties, hip flasks, the word "chemise" appearing daringly in print, Elinor Glyn's *Three Weeks*, F. Scott Fitzgerald's *This Side of Paradise*, Sinclair Lewis' *Main Street*; Rudolph Valentino in *The Sheik*, Al Jolson in *Bombo*, Eddie Cantor in *Kid Boots*; phonographs and player pianos churning out "Love Nest," "Japanese Sandman," "Whispering," "A Young Man's Fancy," "What'll I Do," "My Isle of Golden Dreams," "Ja-Da," "Oh, Katarina," "The Sheik of Araby," "Swanee." 1922—a golden year, the symbol of an era.

For Al Jolson the apex of his Broadway career. . . .

Meanwhile money began its wild rampage. The stock market began a climb that was to reach a dizzy, precarious pinnacle. Everybody was clambering onto the bandwagon, buying stock on margin like mad, making fat, juicy profits—on paper.

Al Jolson and Company received a share of the demand for entertainment. The box office could not accommodate all the people who wanted to see *Bombo*, first at the Jolson 59th Street Theater, then on the road in the various cities it played. Always the house was sold out and perhaps just as many customers were turned away as the number of those admitted.

There was another element—the lower income segment of the population—that had little to do with the legit theater. These people were patronizing in ever-swelling numbers what they considered their own private ecstasy—the movies. Here was entertainment they could afford. For a fifty-cent piece, the flickering cone of gold-white beams from the projector transported them to frozen landscapes of the far north, lush green tropical jungles, strange cities and towns of other countries—as well as showing them alluring bathing beauties, suave lovers, sword-swinging heroes.

That new mass of potential listeners Jolson had not yet reached, except in phonograph records. But the time was not far off when Al Jolson, the jazz singer himself, was to come face to face with this great new audience through the medium of the screen—when it would begin to talk, five years hence.

18

1

In Chicago, *Bombo* was packing them in at the Apollo Theater. At the Wood Theater, Cantor's *Kid Boots* was doing the same. In the dressing room backstage, Epstein shook his head. He looked at Jolson with concerned eyes. Al, you're in no shape to go on. Your nose is running, your eyes are watery, you've got a fever, all the symptoms of what could develop into a serious illness. Call the show off for tonight. You're not a machine. Stop acting like the human dynamo they say you are. Lou, you know the situation—Eddie Cantor is at the Wood Theater in *Kid Boots*, remember? How would it look if I close the show now? You know what *Variety* would say? That Eddie Cantor ran Al Jolson out of Chicago. Epstein said, Eddie's our friend. Sure, Lou. Sure he is, but show business is show business. You know the first rule—the show must go on. And Jolie ain't the one to break it. But Al, you're a very sick boy. I should call a doctor right now. In fact, you're getting paler by the minute. You'll collapse on stage in the middle of your song—you want that?

There was no holding Al down. Epstein realized it soon enough. The show would go on, with a sick Jolson singing his numbers. Al did feel wobbly. He wanted very much to lie down. Then he thought of Cantor giving his performance in *Kid Boots*, and he put on the burnt cork. When his cue came, he was ready. His head ached, his breath was labored; there was an incipient cough developing which he tried to repress. The perspiration stood out on his blackened forehead.

Epstein put his hand on Jolson's arm to steady him. Al, do me this one favor, I beg you. Let me announce that the show can't go on. We'll refund their money or give them a raincheck.

Al rose to his full height. He felt a nauseous sensation in the pit of his stomach, his legs felt weak—but he pushed Epstein aside. As long as Eddie goes on, I go on. Nobody's goin' to say that Jolie's giving a clear field to Cantor. *Bombo* has as much right to an audience as *Kid Boots* and anybody knows that *Bombo* is a better show. Epstein shrugged. I'd like to catch the guy that invented this malarkey that "the show must go on." A man is dying but he's got to go out there and make the customers laugh. An actress is about to give birth to a bouncing baby boy, but she's got to go on and give the bald heads in the front row their money's worth. I tell you it's crazy, and the people in show business likewise. And especially one guy with a blacked-up face. And me? I'm crazier than all the rest, just for being his manager.

Bombo went on that night.

After the closing curtain Al, in his dressing room removing his makeup, received a report that *Kid Boots* had not played that night. Eddie Cantor had come down with an attack of pleurisy and was in a hospital.

Al looked weakly at Epstein, forgetting to finish cleaning his smudged face. That Cantor—he even beat me to the hospital. Lou, I feel awfully sick. Al slumped over. At once Epstein phoned for an ambulance. Jolson was taken to a hospital.

Epstein made sure that Al was comfortable in his private room. Now you don't have to worry about Eddie Cantor. You're both even. Two hospital cases. I still would like to get my hands on the guy who invented the eleventh commandment—"the show must go on." One thing I can guarantee you. There would be a third hospital case.

Al grinned faintly. Give my best to Eddie and Ida. Phone Alma in Scarsdale. Thanks, Lou. You're a dog.

Al dropped off into a fever-wracked sleep.

The Apollo and Wood theaters were darkened, and their respective hit shows, *Bombo* and *Kid Boots*, did not go on— much to Epstein's inward glee.

2

Al was always afraid of the movies, so far as being a screen actor was concerned. He knew the popular stars of the time were primarily handsome, dashing young men, and he was sure that for this category he did not qualify. Besides he was sailing full steam ahead in his stage career and he was not anxious to stop at this point. He was fully aware of the impact he was creating upon the nation's theatergoers and phonograph listeners and he was satisfied to keep on that way.

But he did have offers from Hollywood, especially during that year 1923 when *Bombo* was on the road. The film capital had had its eye on him ever since he had hit the limelight at the Winter Garden.

Finally, when *Bombo* reached the West Coast, the great director, David Wark Griffith, succeeded in convincing Al to take a screen test in Hollywood. Griffith announced he had a sure-fire story for Al. It would be titled *Mammy's Boy*. Griffith prophesied it would sweep the country. He promised to make Al a top picture star, if Al would put himself into his hands. The contract was prepared. All Jolson had to do was to sign it. The screen test was a mere formality.

Al was impressed by the importance of the famed director with his past record of achievement, his creation of such masterpieces as *The Birth of a Nation* and *Intolerance*. Al could see the opportunity, through the medium of the films, of reaching millions of people who had never seen him before. The offer was irresistible, so Al signed on the dotted line, then took his screen test. When he saw the rushes in the studio projection room, he threw up his hands in disgust. He told Griffith the screen test stunk. He could see himself as the screen's biggest ham and prize boob. The people would laugh him out of the theaters and the studio would go bankrupt.

Al walked out, and kept walking—as far away from Hollywood as he could go.

Later, Griffith's long distance telephone calls, his letters, then his attorney's letters had no effect on Al's decision. He was through with the movies—even before he had started. His place was on the stage, where he could face an audience and sense their reaction on the instant. Let the pretty boys act in the films—that's not for Jolie.

After that it would be three years before he would hear from Griffith again, and in a different temper.

3

After the closing of *Bombo*, with a record of 219 performances, during the late summer of 1924, Al joined his wife on their recently purchased estate at Scarsdale, New York.

It was the home Alma had dreamed about and the one he had promised her after they were married. Though part of that dream had been realized, there had been one disturbing factor that grew more intense as the days wore on—her loneliness.

Al had been on the road with *Bombo* for two years and during a good part of that period Alma had lived on the estate alone. Life had become for her a process of waiting—waiting for her husband to come home. He did pay her flying visits—"one night stands"—then was on his way again. Alma walked about the estate. To keep her occupied and amused Al had installed various animals that were to be her pets—horses that she could ride, dogs of sundry ancestry, cats; and in the house there were canaries, and even a huge parrot.

In feeding and taking care of this livestock, Alma should have had her days occupied, besides directing the maid, the cook, and the hired hands. But this was not what she had anticipated. The loneliness grew upon her and she was always looking up the driveway for the appearance of an automobile that would bring Al.

She read the notices in the newspapers as *Bombo* moved from city to city. Thousands watched and listened to her husband—except herself.

She would stand in the yard and gaze in the general direction of New York where she had left her life behind. It had been a gay, an exciting life. Once she had dreamed of a great career on the stage and she had had her first break in the *Scandals*; then along had come Al, the blackfaced singer. She tried to understand why she had fallen for him. He was not what she would call handsome; he was brash, he was not an interesting conversationalist; at times, after they had been together for a while, he could, in fact, become quite boring. And if she tried to discuss something besides show business, he seemed to be at a loss. And yet, there had been a quality about him that had charmed her into becoming his wife.

She remembered now that his first marriage had ended in a divorce—after thirteen years. And there had been no children. She dwelt, with some concentration, on this point—no children. And now it was the same with her after being married to him for two years. She wondered whether there might be a chance of Al fathering children later on. How much of a chance? She knew that was the key to fulfillment for her. Children would solidify the marriage, make it complete. As it was, she seemed to be perched on an unbalanced see-saw, with Al at the other end and herself way up in the air.

And so after *Bombo*'s final performance, when Al came home, embraced his wife, kissed her like a college boy saying hello to his sweetheart after a separation, she confessed to him of being lonely.

Al promised her he had had enough of show biz. He had come home to roost. They would take a vacation and see the world. Look, Baby, never feel lonely again. This is the home you dreamed about, remember? Besides, you've got horses, cats, dogs. . . . She pouted. Yes, I know. But it's you I want. If you had a regular business or a job—maybe a producer with regular hours. . . . Honey, the only thing I can do is sing, and that's all the public wants from Jolie.

He put his arm about her and she nestled close against him as they walked slowly into the house. The cook prepared a snack for Al. After he had finished a sandwich and coffee, they talked some more, and then went out into the graying twilight of the countryside. Al inspected the livestock, stroked the horses. You know, Sugar, maybe I should become a regular breeder of thoroughbreds for the track. Sometimes I think about it.

Darling Al, if only we had a baby. She glanced at him quickly.

Al always had been afraid of this one subject. It stymied him. He said, you know I want a child as much as you. Al, it's over two years now. I know, Sugar, I know.

Al, it would be wonderful if we could adopt a child.

Jolson was silent for a brief moment.

He had never dreamed it would come to this. It had a familiar ring—something he had heard before, not too long ago.

Honey Lamb—he tightened his arm about her—you can have your baby as soon as the adoption proceedings go through. But before we begin I'd like to ask you a favor. Would you give it another year's try for one of our own? Al's voice was hopeful.

You don't want to adopt one, do you, Al?

Now, Sugar, I didn't say that. I'm asking for a year—just in case.

Al, a year is a long time. If I had a baby to take care of I wouldn't feel so useless. Sometimes I get the feeling that I'd like to go back on the stage.

Okay. It's settled. We'll adopt a baby. It may not be so easy.

So the matter rested until Al's next move to put into action what he had promised.

4

That first feeling of warmth between them, that crystal-clear relationship they had had before, seemed to be clouded now with shadows of doubt. A feeling of strain began to manifest itself between them, as though they detected in each other a disturbing flaw.

That night they lay upon their bed almost like two strangers. Al was wondering, was it his pride that was hurt? He tried to tell himself, as he lay there in the darkness, that she had not meant to belittle him in any way; she had simply stated the truth. Yet he did feel a resentment. He bit his lip and buried his face in the pillow.

He was afraid, he told himself, to confront the truth. He turned on his back, looked straight up at the darkness of the ceiling.

Thirteen years of marriage to Henrietta and no children. Now over two years with Alma.

A soft late summer breeze fanned in through the open window, sweet with the scent of honeysuckle and wild rose. It was wonderful here, and they could be so happy. He clenched his hands until his nails bit into the palms. I've got to be nice to her. She's only a kid but smarter than me.

In the morning he found her nestling in his arms. Her eyes were misty. Al, I'm sorry. I've hurt you. I know I have.

He smiled at her, kissed her tearful eyes. Now hush up, Honey Chile. How can you ever hurt anybody?

Al, I don't want anyone's baby except our own.

Look, Sugar, I've made up my mind, so there's nothing you can do. We're goin' to adopt a baby and that's that.

Al and his wife made formal application at the New York State Charity Association for the adoption of a child, with the proviso that it be under three years of age. They didn't care whether it would be a boy or a girl. The papers were duly filed and now it was a matter of waiting while the necessary investigation and preliminary survey were made. As Al had predicted, Alma discovered at once that it was not going to be easy.

But she was willing to wait.

5

With free time on his hands, Al couldn't stay put.

He found temporary balm in campaigning for Calvin Coolidge during that fall of 1924. The excitement of the election, the singing of campaign ditties and his impromptu "political" speeches to applauding coteries of constituents gave him a feeling of importance.

He fancied himself a politician. Maybe he'd run for office. Become a Congressman. Alma would sure respect him.

When he realized that he was neglecting his wife in this new venture, he made a beeline for Scarsdale.

19

1

As the summer drew to its close, the inactivity on the part of Al
Jolson was killing him. He grew restless, fidgety, almost morose.
His usual ebullient nature and happy-go-lucky attitude were
being erased by the monotony of his present existence. It was not
the fault of Alma in any way, but was entirely within himself. He
had been used to riding on the crest of achievement and acclaim,
and this sudden cessation left his spirits sagging. Before long he
took to making excuses to Alma about running over to New York
on certain financial matters, but while in New York he would drop
in to see his friends, and he began to join them in pinochle games
with promises to repeat.

He visited the track at Saratoga. He bet more and more heavily
on the nags, losing considerable sums. Coming home one night
near dawn he went through a familiar scene, only this time it was
with a wife with a different name. When the argument was over
he raged at himself for not being fair to Alma.

But at breakfast he was almost curt with her.

Well, hear anything from the adoption board? he asked her.

Nothing.

He grumbled. They take their good old time.

Maybe they should, Al.

You mean, they're finding out things?

What things, Al?

About me. I gamble. I play the ponies. I stay out late.

Al, while we're on the subject—don't you like being with me?

Of course I do, Honey. You ask the most foolish questions. It's about time you realized that we can't go on cooing to each other forever like a couple of lovebirds. We're adults. We shouldn't doubt each other.

Al, am I nagging you? Lately, you've been running off a lot. You can't sit still a minute. Once you said you'd like to raise horses.

I will—some day soon.

He rose, paced the floor of the spacious kitchen. He looked out at the November grayness of the fields. Honey, I'll level with you. I've got to get back to work.

Alma's face paled. She looked at Al, her eyes hurt.

Al, you promised you'd stay away from the theater for a while. . . .

Well, I've kept my promise, Sugar. The "while" is up.

But Al, I thought you'd stay away from the grind for at least a year. If they give us a child you'd have time to get acquainted.

If I stay here much longer doin' nothin', I'll go nuts.

Al, I thought you'd like it—the two of us together—alone—that was your plan.

A man just can't play around—no reflection on you, Sugar.

The silence returned between them.

The subject was not discussed for several weeks.

2

Al came and went. Somehow he couldn't remain stationary.

That New Year's Eve they celebrated in New York at a party held in the roomy backstage of the Jolson 59th Street Theater.

Alma seemed to be her old self. She laughed, she drank her share of the champagne, and she danced the Charleston, the collegiate, and the dreamy waltzes—but mostly with the younger men, who were only too willing and eager to oblige so ravishing a beauty. Al slumped in a chair, looking on, and he felt himself growing lonelier, older, and more resentful by the minute.

At the stroke of midnight, as the New Year, 1925, was ushered in, he was saved from doing something reckless by Alma herself, who put her arms about him and kissed him.

When the new year was hardly an hour old the revelers turned at last to Jolson and the requests came for a "few songs from good old Al." Alma, her face flushed with the excitement of dancing, had taken her place beside Al, sitting on the arm of his chair. She realized there was only one thing to do—give him the word to go ahead full steam. Al became alive again, gave Alma a grateful smile. His eyes shone as he rose and the crowd about him formed into a listening audience. They were waiting for him to begin. They wanted him to sing his favorite tunes and he obliged.

He was in his stride once more. This was the Al Jolson the world knew—alert and bouncing, every nerve tingling. With great zest he sang "Swanee," "Rock-a-Bye Your Baby With a Dixie Melody," "April Showers," the ever-enchanting "My Mammy," followed by request numbers.

For the rest of the celebration it was, as on previous occasions, Al Jolson all the way through.

That night Al and Alma stayed at a hotel.

The next day they motored to Scarsdale. The deep silence came back between them.

In their home Al seemed to wake up to the critical state of affairs, and he came to her as she was sitting in the living room, looking through a home furnishing magazine. Al told her, Honey, I feel like an ogre in a fairy tale, only this is no fairy tale.

Al, what do you want me to say?

That you love me, the way I love you.

It's one thing to say it and quite another to prove it.

I admit I've been terrible. I've acted like a spoiled brat, but that's over with. I've made a New Year's resolution and here it is . . . we're taking a long vacation. Suddenly at that party in New York, when I watched you dancing with those young chaps, it kinda woke me up. Jolie, I told myself, stop short-changing Alma—if you want to hold on to her.

Al, do you really mean it? About taking a long vacation?

Sure. I'll find something to do. Maybe I'll breed those horses after all.

Al, I do want to believe you.

He was near to her now, and she was in his arms.

Honey, I know it now—ol' Jolie needs you bad.

Oh, Al, we'll get the baby from the Charity Association and we'll have a real home.

Sure, Honey, sure.

On the following day he received a call from Lou Epstein, his manager. The Shuberts had a new revue about to go into rehearsal, *Big Boy*. Lou sounded very anxious on the phone and Al ended the conversation with, Okay, Lou, I'll do my best to arrange it. Al replaced the phone on its cradle. He slowly turned to face an inquiring Alma.

I heard you on the phone, Al. That was Epstein. There's a new show coming up.

Honey, you're a mind reader.

I've got good ears. She came near him. Al, you're not doing it, are you?

Al groped for the proper words. A new show—*Big Boy*—probably the best thing he would ever do. All those audiences waiting for another Jolson smash. Never before had he let his public down. He took Alma's hand in his own.

I know I'm a brute but I'm going to lay my cards on the table—face up. Listen to me, Honey, I'm going to ask a big favor of you. It's the biggest favor I could ever ask you and if you grant me that, then I'm telling you the whole world is yours. I'll put it right in your lap.

Al, I don't want the whole world. All I want is you—and this home.

Now, look, Honey. Let me explain it—

Al, you don't have to try so hard. I know all about it. You're going to do the show. You've already told Epstein.

That public out there—they were good to me all these years. They gave me everything—even you. You wouldn't want me to let them down, would you, Sugar?

Of course not, Al. Go ahead and do the show.

You mean you don't care?

Of course I don't care. You want to do the show—then you do it.

Al peered at her closely. You don't sound right to me.

Don't be silly. You asked me and I said go ahead as planned.

You're a doll. I'm crazy about you more than ever. He put his arms about her, but she drew back. Al said, Ah, you're tired.

Well, I'll let you take it easy.

There was silence—strained, bristling. Al broke it. After this show—which, by the way, is positively my last one—we're going to live right here like a real settled-down married couple—and I'm not forgetting the children.

That will be very nice, Al.

That night Alma was aloof, cool. Al felt frozen out. He was filled with anxiety. If only she would converse with him, so that they could discuss the subject as man and wife. But the frigid wall that had risen between them, remained.

In the darkness, lying there beside her, but out of reach, Al said, Honey, you're angry.

Al, don't be silly. Why don't you go to sleep? You'll need your strength for rehearsals.

A brief silence, then from Al, Honey, I've decided to call Epstein tomorrow and cancel my engagement. I won't do the show and that's final.

Al, you know you don't mean that.

All right, we'll see about that.

Al, if I could only believe you—

You can, Sugar, you can. I'm telling you—no show, so help me.

Oh, Al—

The next moment they were in each other's arms as though they had just found themselves—after a long and painful groping.

Next day Jolson left for New York to start rehearsals on *Big Boy*.

3

Al became immersed in *Big Boy* rehearsals.

When the show opened at the Jolson 59th Street Theater it was with the usual fanfare and first night hullabaloo, and Al took hold, as usual, with a master hand. He belted out his songs, interpolating any song that was in demand or that he thought would be welcomed by the audience.

But there was a note of difference about this revue from those that had preceded it. For the first time since the Winter Garden shows had begun in 1911 with Al Jolson, there was an evident, though not an alarming, decrease in the enthusiasm of the audience.

Al caught the reviews in the morning after the opening and, strangely enough, he was not too surprised at the opinions of the critics that the present show lacked the freshness, the verve, the sparkle of *Robinson Crusoe, Jr., Sinbad,* or that last record-breaker, *Bombo.* Jolson read the papers in his hotel room and leaned back on the divan. He was tired. He had never before felt weariness during the run of a show, but now, for the first time, he wanted to rest.

His manager, Epstein, sensed Al's despondency.

Cheer up, Al, this is only the beginning. You'll pack them in, like you did before.

Al shook his head. He grinned at Epstein. Thanks, Lou. You make me feel more confident than I am.

Al, it's not like you, talking like an old man.

I'm forty, if you care to know.

That's a good age. You've got plenty to deliver yet.

Al was thinking of Alma. The last few times he had gone up to Scarsdale she had not been at home. The servants had told him she had sailed for Paris.

Al stood up, walked to the window, and looked out at the street twenty stories down. So it had finally come to the inevitable end. Alma had, in fact, left him. Al wondered whatever had happened to the proceedings for the adoption of a baby. No doubt the Charity Association, not hearing from them, had pigeonholed the application indefinitely. Another dream had disintegrated.

He felt suddenly alone in the world. At the time when men of his age were usually established in life's journey with home and family, with him it was a process of slipping back to where he had been in the beginning—alone and homeless.

During the months that followed, Al tried to forget his personal misfortunes in his preoccupation with the show, but he could not drive from his mind the memories of those happy moments with Alma. He could have held on to those moments—she had offered them to him on a silver platter, pleading with him to accept them, but he had turned his back. He had indeed walked out on her that morning, breaking his final promise to her. Now his world began to crumble once more when he received notice from her attorney that she was establishing residence in Paris and that divorce proceedings had started against him; but Al would make no protest, no contest.

He tried reconciliation. He wrote letters, saying that he would change. But when she did answer him, her letters were cool, formal, offering no hope of a future resumption of their life together.

Big Boy closed after several trying months of lukewarm reception; it seemed that to a perceptible degree Jolson's performances lacked their customary powerhouse delivery.

In October of 1926 he received formal notification of a divorce granted to Alma in Paris on the grounds of desertion and, so far as he was concerned, Alma was again a beautiful stranger, taking away with her another lost ecstasy.

He had never felt so alone.

4

During that year of 1926, in addition to his marital troubles, Al received a summons to appear in Federal Court in New York as the defendant in a suit brought against him by David Wark Griffith.

Griffith had filed the suit for $571,696 in damages, the amount he estimated he had lost due to the breach of a contract Jolson had duly and legally signed in 1923 to appear in the picture *Mammy's Boy*.

The judge peered over his spectacles at the defendant. Jolson, what have you to say?

Jolson gave a real performance right then and there in the Federal Court. Your Honor, I'll say this, this man Griffith made me some promises. Tried to fool me into believing that I'm a natural-born movie actor. Talked me into signing a contract which I didn't want to sign in the first place—not until I saw the screen-test film. Well, your honor, I finally did see that film—and what a clown I was in it—why, I was not only terrible as an actor, but looked like I had just spent ten nights in a barroom.

The hearing dragged on for a while, then the judge, wishing to end the affair, awarded Griffith a moral victory by fixing the damages at $2,600.

Jolson walked out of the courtroom, swearing oaths against that particular director and against the movie industry in general.

If I can help it, he told his manager, ol' Jolie is goin' to keep his distance from Hollywood.

5

For the first time in his comet-like career, Al Jolson saw the tide beginning to turn against him. It was no longer a matter of soaring upon the crest of the great wave of universal success and popularity that had swept him along through show after show and made of him the king of entertainers.

Suddenly the applause was beginning to subside, and now in 1926 after *Big Boy* he found no frantic rush on the part of producers to star him in another show. It was then that the William Morris Theatrical Agency held out a rescuing hand.

Another winter in California without work had made Al restless. William Morris had a long talk with Jolson and Epstein about a one-man theatrical tour, a series of concert engagements across the continent. Al was skeptical. Solo performances were limited to great singers like John McCormack or dancers like Mary Wigman, but no Broadway entertainer had ever taken to the road to do a one-man show. The one and only Sir Harry Lauder had given a two-hour sabbath evening program in his kilt, but for Lauder's coast-to-coast "annual farewell" tours he was supplied with five or six outstanding vaudeville turns.

Morris was aware that, in spite of Jolson's ability to stay on the stage of the Winter Garden for over an hour and a half as a solo performer, he was still gun-shy about being billed as a solo entertainer and taking on such a tour. Morris kept prodding him without result, but later, as Morris sat in the springtime sun at his mountain home, Camp Intermission, at Saranac Lake, New York, up drove a touring car, and in it were Jolson and Eddie Elkins, the well-known jazz bandleader. Jolson and Elkins had put up at Paul Smith's, a famous resort nearby, after a motor trip across the United States. Morris welcomed his guests and in a short while seized the opportunity to drive Al and Eddie to the Saranac Lake Day Nursery, ten minutes away, to meet some children. It was these beautiful children who supplied the needed inspiration. The magic worked. Jolson promised to go back to the coast and work up a program. In early fall he came to Saranac Lake with his accompanist, Harry Akst, and gave a benefit performance for the Saranac Lake Day Nursery at the local Pontiac Theater. The success of this performance led to a tour of more than six weeks of gruelling concert dates under William Morris's direction. This was the tour that set the precedent in America for all the one-man shows to follow.

The tour ended, and once again Al was an unemployed performer. Idleness drove him into a state of despondency. The audiences that had loved him so much—had they forsaken him?

6

Since radio broadcasting had begun to establish itself as an indispensable adjunct of the American scene, motion pictures had taken a hard right to the chin. Soon there was moaning and groaning in the fabulous Baghdad of California, Hollywood. Production of films was curtailed, actors and technicians were laid off by the hundreds, and simultaneously over the land scores of movie theaters, from the magnificent metropolitan palaces to the modest village film houses, were compelled to turn off their marquee lights and close their doors.

But there were pioneers—as always in the history of new advances—experimenting with something that would instill new lifeblood into the tottering movie empire. Frowned upon by other film producers as a novelty and curious toy, the "talking picture" was considered in a serious manner by one studio, Warner Brothers, which was on the verge of closing its doors in bankruptcy. Toward the latter part of 1926 and early 1927 they made their last all-out gamble with the production of short one- and two-reel talking picture featurettes of vaudeville acts, with the process known as "Vitaphone," a synchronization of a phonograph record with the film itself. Immediate reports from the exhibitors came as a revelation to Warners. Box-office figures leaped upward wherever Vitaphone pictures were shown. At once the forward-looking producers contemplated the production of a full-length talking picture, preferably with music and song, which they felt sure would take the country by storm.

BOOK FOUR

Hollywood Years
1927–1942

First Talkies and Radio

20

1

There was a play running on Broadway, *The Jazz Singer*, starring George Jessel, which was packing them in nightly, and the Warner Brothers organization figured that this would lend itself perfectly to adaptation as the feature talking picture they had in mind. Also, to launch the production with maximum thrust, they planned to star Jessel.

Jessel, however, refused to do the film because the script had a different ending from that of the play. In the play the jazz singer leaves the stage and returns home for good to be a cantor in the synagogue. In the movie version, after a visit home, he returns to the Broadway stage. Warners refused to change the script. Jessel stood pat. An impasse.

Then an idea struck Jack Warner. Why not obtain the services of the original jazz singer himself, the greatest entertainer of the time—the man who had enchanted a nation with his singing for many years—Al Jolson. Without delay they dispatched their agent to interview Jolson. Al, of course, was doubtful. He had never thought of himself as any kind of movie actor. He had always had the impression that the prime requisite was personal handsomeness, an attribute not high on his list of qualifications.

He recalled only too vividly his failure in 1923 when he had taken a screen test for Griffith, and the resultant court action. He remembered, also, his vow—that he would have nothing more to do with the movies.

But now there was a new consideration—the movies were

beginning to talk—the audiences would hear him sing, and that truly would be like the stage. The idea of having people hear him speak and sing on the screen seemed to him a fantastic and unbelievable fairy tale, but Al was always willing to gamble, whether it be on horses, cards, or some newfangled idea.

Epstein, his manager, spread his hands and shrugged, What can you lose?

Al's friends and acquaintances in the Broadway theatrical firmament shook their heads and advised Al against the venture. They warned him that the whole project might become a fiasco and make Al the laughing stock of the show-biz world. Such an event would be a catastrophe that might wreck his career.

But Al could not very well turn down the offer by Warner Brothers, which was accompanied by a $200,000 cash guarantee.

And so he set off to Hollywood, signed the necessary papers, and reported to the makeup department.

There was a slight hitch in the proceedings. George Jessel, star of the *Jazz Singer* on Broadway, had made the play a hit with his "socko" performance. George felt that by natural right of priority and his relation with the play, he should have been the one to play the role in the film. He presented his protest and argument to Warner Brothers that they reconsider and use the play's ending, but to no avail. They would take a chance on Jolson, feeling that

Al was the one for the part, anyway, since the play itself, by Samson Raphaelson, was a dramatization of Jolson's own life and career.

The cameras began to grind on the Warner lot with Jolson as the star.

Performing for the studio was a new experience for Al. A battery of multilensed cameras, sound equipment, cables, lights of varying intensities, and the personnel of the studio—directors, assistant directors, script people, electricians, carpenters, and a host of others busying themselves about him like bees in a hive—made this an absorbing and sometimes distracting ordeal. In one way this was beneficial to Al—he had to keep his mind on his work, steering his thoughts away from his own personal life and its disappointments.

But even in the midst of all this frenzy he found time, when alone in his apartment, to write his weekly letter to his mother and tell her what was going on.

"And now, Momma, believe it or not, your son Asa is a movie actor. Maybe some day I'll be another Rudy Valentino. Who knows? Looks like anything can happen in this place called Hollywood. Give Poppa my best."

During the days they were not shooting scenes he would run down to the track and place his bets on the nags. Usually he bet heavily, lost two or three thousand dollars at a clip, but took this in stride. Besides, he could well afford it. His investments were earning favorably for him and he knew that his net worth hovered about the seven-figure mark.

There were some Hollywood parties he attended, came to know personally the stars of the silent screen about to face the challenge of the talkies—Lon Chaney, Thomas Meighan, Florence Vidor, Lillian and Dorothy Gish, Monte Blue, Claire Windsor, Norma Talmadge. Invariably, of course, he was asked to sing at these hoedowns, and Al Jolson was never the man to say "no." When it came to performing for audiences or conclaves of friends, he was "Johnny-on-the-Spot."

It was only when he was by himself, in his own apartment or driving his newly acquired car, that memories came back to him of his life with Alma, and in his imagination he lived again those golden moments.

TS 109.

2

Sometimes a great restlessness came over him. There was an undeniable monotony here in the long stretches of sunshiny days with hardly any changes in temperature or humidity. Al was not one to interpret the natural beauty of California, to analyze the lush greenery of forests, vineyards, vegetable farms, the majestic grandeur of the mountains rising on the horizon, the blue waters of the lakes. He enjoyed these charms without probing.

This state was tied in with his life. Here he had found his first real taste of show business on Frisco's Barbary Coast. Here he had found Henrietta, and here he had lost her.

But he could not repress his growing impatience with the process of performing for unresponsive mechanical equipment amid a tangle of electrical cable. More and more he felt a need for audiences that he could look at and sing to, as in a legit theater.

In that year of 1927 there were two events that were turning points in the life of the nation. The first one was the lone flight of Charles A. Lindbergh, an unknown young airmail pilot, in a single-motored plane called the *Spirit of St. Louis*, across the Atlantic to land thirty-three hours later at Le Bourget Field in Paris.

With the June issue of *Movietone News,* Fox released the first sound newsreel, showing Lindy's triumphant receptions, and fascinated audiences listened to the hero's own voice telling them about his history-making flight.

The second event was the premiere of *The Jazz Singer* at the Warner Theater in New York on October 6, with Al Jolson in the title role. Notables from the political and industrial worlds, celebrities of Broadway and Hollywood, drama critics, socialites, all stormed the theater from which hundreds of others seeking admission had been turned away.

It was a critical, a discerning audience, come to applaud or to scorn, as the case might be. It was a climactic moment for the motion picture industry and for the future of talking pictures. It was also the moment of truth in the reckless plunge by Warner Brothers. And for Al Jolson himself it was the moment of judgment. Would this performance bring ridicule from his former admirers? Would this summarily chop off his career?

Those final seconds preceding the raising of the curtain that shielded the screen were painfully long.

But the waiting period ended, the curtain rolled up, and the screen, a rectangle of gray, was about to exhibit for all to see the success or the failure of a great gamble.

Al himself, with Lou Epstein next to him, was sitting in the gallery, wondering what the reaction of the audience would be.

3

The house lights went out. There was a preliminary organ recital of a medley of Hebrew melodies, ranging from the sorrowful songs of the ghetto to the gayety of the *kasatchka* dances, music that put people into the mood for what was to follow. Then suddenly the screen became alive with the first feature talking picture. The credits on the screen informed the audience that Al Jolson was Jakie Rabinowitz, later calling himself Jack Robbins, the "Jazz Singer" himself; Warner Oland, the cantor father; Mae McAvoy, the leading lady. The locale was the lower East Side of New York, then it shifted to San Francisco, then back to New York and Broadway.

Again, as in all the stage revues in which Al had starred, it was not the story that mattered so much to the audience as Al Jolson himself. Inevitably he became the substance, the purpose, and indeed the whole show before the performance was many minutes old. And so it was with the motion picture, *The Jazz Singer*. The film was all Al Jolson—even the story was a reflection of his own life. From the very beginning, when it portrayed him as a small boy in a lower East Side cafe giving his first "jazz" rendition of a song, to the mature singer who swept along from honky-tonk to vaudeville, to musical comedy, the audience in that darkened theater was held spellbound by the impact of his singing personality. Surprising to many, even his acting was commendable as he interpreted the gamut of human emotions.

It was Al's story. Jakie's father, Cantor Rabinowitz, wanted his son to follow the family tradition and become a cantor in the synagogue. Jakie wanted to sing on the stage. The cantor caught him performing in a cheap cafe, and pappa's belt collided with Jakie's backside. His pride hurt, Jakie said a tearful good-bye to his mom, skipped out, and sang his way through life in honky-tonks and burlesque shows, simultaneously achieving young manhood on the Frisco Barbary Coast. There in a cafe he sang the number, "Dirty Hands, Dirty Face."

The miracle was happening right in front of the audience. Al Jolson on the screen could be heard just as clearly and distinctly as though he were standing there and singing in person—as big as life.

And as Jakie Rabinowitz on the screen, at the end of the number, hearing the enthusiastic outburst of applause, he held up his hands and assured them, "Wait a minute! Wait a minute! You ain't heard nothin' yet!"

Actually, Jolson had spoken those words spontaneously during filming. They were not in the script. This had been his pet admonition during the Winter Garden days, and Warners had decided, when the film was edited, to leave in this bit which added greatly to the realism.

Jakie then sang "Toot-Toot-Tootsie" and the girl of the story, Mae McAvoy, an actress, called him to her table and introduced herself. Through her influence he obtained a vaudeville booking, and his career advanced rapidly. His ringing performances won for him a role in a Broadway show in which she played the leading lady. The highlights of the movie were his portrayal of his love for the theater and the show girl, clashing with his love for his parents and the synagogue; the reunion with his mother, when he sang "Blue Skies" for her in straight melody, then in a snappy "jazz" version; and his efforts to win over his father, who had insisted on disowning him for having turned away from the synagogue to be a jazz singer. The climax was the deathbed scene which took place on the Day of Atonement, when his dying father forgave Jakie, and asked him to sing the "Kol Nidre" in the cantor's place in the synagogue. The jazz singer had become, for the time, a cantor himself, singing the "Kol Nidre" with a feeling and reverence that justified the dying father's faith in his son. But Jakie left the synagogue and returned to Broadway.

The picture ended with Jakie—in blackface—singing "My Mammy" in the best Jolson tradition, while his mother sat in the audience and proudly watched her son. Then came the final scene, with Jakie imploring, on his knee, "Mammy, I hope I'm not too late—Mammy—I'm coming—" and the culminating impact of the assertion, "I'd walk a million miles for one of your smiles, My Mammy—"

Fadeout, and the picture that had brought Jolson and his voice to that amazed audience was over; the house lights went on, bringing the people back to themselves. After a brief recuperative silence, the applause broke out. It was a thunderous ovation for the screen play and for Al Jolson who, through the magic of the talking picture, had started on a new and fresh career to reach the thousands who had not yet seen him perform.

4

The picture had musical and sound effects in Vitaphone, as well as all the songs Jolson sang, and bits of dialogue at certain points of the film. But the clarity, the lifelike enunciation, and the perfect synchronization of sound to visual movement was enough to establish the far-reaching potentialities of the talking picture.

Al could not escape the theater unnoticed despite the efforts of Epstein. They were surrounded by well-wishers, reporters, critics. Al was feted, and hailed as the lone pioneer, the "Lindbergh" of the talkies, who had ushered in a new form of screen entertainment, and for himself the beginning of a spectacular new phase of his career.

And perhaps this happened just in time, for his stage predominance had been showing the first signs of a decline.

Once more Jolson rode the crest of the wave—a new wave and a much bigger one. His screen personality reached out to the four corners of the world. He became the highest paid and greatest drawing card during the early years of the talkies.

He himself was surprised at the degree of his acting ability. He had been afraid, during the shooting of the film, that his interpretation of the more emotional scenes would emerge, when screened, as the ludicrous antics of a clown, but his acting was plausible and in good taste. He had not overacted. As the script intended, he was just himself.

And so Al, at last, was not only a singer but also an actor.

The Jazz Singer, was to earn three million dollars for Warners, a record for a low-budget picture.

Jolson was immediately signed for another picture which would prove to be a record money-maker in the industry to the tune of ten million dollars gross, and elevate Jolson to the pinnacle, the purple heights, where he would reign supreme for a period of three tumultuous years.

In The Singing Fool, Jolson sang "Sonny Boy" with child actor Davey Lee upon his knee and, at once, the song sold in sheet music and records more than a million copies each. The picture itself further emphasized the acting ability of Al Jolson, who was even more surprised than the critics at his own hitherto untapped talent. In the role of an abused husband with a hard, scornful wife he brought forth an emotional deluge that overwhelmed audiences wherever the film was exhibited. There was hardly a dry eye in the theater by the time the picture had run its course.

Jolson was at the top of the heap in the film industry, the

hottest box-office name of the time, and Warner Brothers flourished with their unexpected windfall and blossomed into one of the most powerful producing companies in Hollywood.

The successes of *The Jazz Singer* and *The Singing Fool* were all the impetus the talking pictures required. Within the year 1928 other film companies began the production of "talkies" with the development of other processes, such as Fox Movietone, a sound track on the film itself instead of the Vitaphone system which required the use of synchronized records.

Al Jolson found himself the most popular and sought-after actor and singer in America during that year when *The Singing Fool* hit the movie theaters that had been hastily wired for sound.

21

1

The sound films were to play havoc with many of the favorite stars of the silents.

For the actresses, it was not too alarming a situation. As long as they remained visually appetizing, the fact that their voices were weaker than expected did not matter much, since the public could accept this as the gentle trait of a lady. This, however, did not in any way reduce the invasion of actresses from the legit theater into the newly discovered gold fields of Hollywood.

With the male contingent, unfortunately, the story was quite different. Audiences expected to hear their male idols speak with manly voices, and those who lacked such voices were to be banished without mercy from the scene of their recent triumphs. Buster Keaton, Harold Lloyd, Harry Langdon, Raymond Griffith, John Gilbert—these would be among the victims. In their place would come actors from the vaude and legit stages who could talk or sing or do both—the Marx Brothers, Ed Wynn, Lou Holtz, Eddie Cantor, Jimmy Durante, W. C. Fields, Will Rogers, John Barrymore, and a continuing host, all following the path worked out by Al Jolson, blackfaced singer.

Jolson now had everything that a man could possibly want— fame, fortune, and popularity. But within himself he felt a growing sense of loneliness. No matter how many people were close about him—his aides, his publicity staff, his advisors, the usual group of hangers-on—he still seemed to be missing someone. He was a man who could never find peace or a feeling of self-sufficiency within his own being. Always he had to have people around him—otherwise he felt bewildered and uneasy.

He had, these days, an intimation that life was beginning to pass him by with accelerated speed. He was past the forty mark in years, and though he had already obtained from life more of the material things than most men could ever hope to garner, yet the sight of a man and wife arm in arm on the street, or sitting and chatting quietly in a restaurant, filled him with envy and a realization of his own inadequacy. And if he dwelt further on the matter, he began to visualize the kind of homelife these people enjoyed, with families, with children. It was then that an awareness of his own lack came full upon him and left him more despondent than ever.

2

He had asked Warners for a leave of absence, and he had come back to New York in the summer of 1928. His two pictures were going strong in the movie theaters and he began to feel the urge to visit his old Broadway haunts. He caught the shows at the various legit houses. He visited the night spots, spoke to the old-timers.

Al was impressed by a tap dancer at Texas Guinan's night club. Her nimble-footed routine, her youthful exuberance, her laughing eyes charmed him. Texas agreed to the favor of an introduction to Ruby Keeler.

Al talked to the girl, danced with her.

Three weeks later he rediscovered her on a somewhat higher show-biz plane.

While attending George M. Cohan's *Rise of Rosie O'Reilly*, he recognized the strikingly beautiful tap dancer whose youthful charm had left him "hanging on the ropes." He came back several times to watch her perform, to enjoy the thrill of her personality which pervaded the entire theater. Of course, he was not the only one who admired her. Night after night the audience reveled in her impish beauty, her twinkling, tapping feet, and that gay, winsome smile.

Al forgot his own age, his own successes, his own problems— he knew only one thing at this time—to enjoy the presence of that girl on the stage.

He knew he had to meet her again.

He went to see her perform in *Show Girl*, a Ziegfeld production, and endured with her the first breathless moments of her specialty, the singing of "Liza." The audience, a typical furred and bejeweled Ziegfeld house, enjoyed her young verve and her rapid-fire tap dancing, but when she started her song there was an apparent waver in her voice. Al, sitting in the audience, could not control himself; his sympathy for the girl prompted him to rise and sing along with her. Ruby, recognizing him, smiled gratefully and went into her number with newly discovered confidence, her voice stronger, steadier. The duet of Ruby Keeler and Al Jolson was a smash hit. The instant they finished, the theater resounded with the impact of the applause.

Florenz Ziegfeld asked Al to come back for each performance and, from his seat in the audience, sing "Liza" along with Ruby. Name your own price, said Ziegfeld. Al was only too glad to do this and Ruby Keeler became a star attraction. She was overwhelmed by Jolson's participation. She regarded him as the most exciting person she had ever met, and the kindest for helping her.

As for Al, his fascination was complete. Perhaps it was her clear innocent eyes. Or was it something about the magnetism of youth that Al could never ignore or resist? Of this quality Ruby Keeler had full measure. And then there was her talent—to dance, to sing, to act—which was to make of her within a brief period one of the most loved and admired stage and film stars in the country.

The first night she went out with him Al wondered, as she looked at him at close range, what did she really see? Was it a middle-aged man making a bid for a romantic fling that was the prerogative of youth? Or did she admire him merely for his successes, his prestige, his wealth? Or was it possible she saw in him a quality that would spur her interest in Al Jolson as a person?

For the rest of the night they dined and danced at one of his favorite haunts, Rector's.

Dancing with her in his somewhat outmoded style, a self-consciousness seized Al which was quite foreign to him. He felt uneasy at times about monopolizing her attention, preventing her, perhaps, from flying into the arms of some young energetic Romeo, which was her natural right.

But he knew he could not let her go.

After he left her at her apartment door some time past midnight, he congratulated himself as he walked to his car. Jolie, you're in clover again.

3

Epstein had dropped in to see Al Jolson at the latter's apartment. Lou seemed worried. He settled himself in a comfortable armchair near the open window. The rays of the setting sun streaked in through the apertures of the Venetian blind.

Al was just coming out of the shower, preparatory to dressing for the evening's date with Ruby Keeler.

Al—Epstein's voice was gentle, almost fatherly—that girl—Miss Keeler—I read an item in the paper about you and her. You're not serious about her, are you?

Lou, I'm goin' to tell you a secret. I'm nuts about the kid.

Kid is right. When you're together, you know what people will call you? Cradle snatcher.

Lou, I'm nuts about her and I'm ready to marry her, if she'll have me.

Epstein lit a fresh cigar.

Al, I don't blame you for taking her out. She's a cute little *shiksa* with plenty of talent. But she's too young to know the score. She sees in you a great man. After all, not every young flapper can have dates with Al Jolson. Al, why don't you be sensible? For your own good—and God knows, for hers—have your fun with her, then let her go. She needs a young sheik her own age—who can go dancing with her all night.

Lou, I love you like a brother, you know that. But you're an old-fashioned guy with old-fashioned ideas. I believe in living young and with young people. Who wants to settle down? When a man settles down, he becomes a vegetable. I want to be wide-awake, take it all in. This gal Ruby—she can show me the way.

So you are serious about her.

Eppy, if that gal says yes to me, she's the next Mrs. Jolson.

Epstein rose. He put out his cigar in the ashtray and took his hat. Al, I still think the best thing for you would be a nice Jewish home girl.

4

During the months of July and August the heat was merciless. New York was a boiling cauldron of high humidity and high temperature.

But for Jolson it didn't seem to matter whether it was hot or cool. He knew only that he wanted to be with his newly discovered dream girl as much as possible. He even hoped that her show would close, and in August it did close, and that was a break for Al.

He escorted Ruby to all the important night spots. They visited the racetracks together; they caught all the shows on Broadway. He showered her with expensive gifts of jewelry. It was a mad, happy merry-go-round, and always Ruby's dimpled smile, her enchanting voice, her arresting beauty filled Al's mind and heart. He had no urge to resume his career on the stage or to make more pictures in Hollywood for the time being. He could not afford to let Ruby out of his sight. She was like a peach, luscious, ripe, and there were many wolves who would not hesitate to reach out for her.

Yet he did not want to appear too anxious. He had learned that young girls had little use, romantically, for any man who betrayed

himself as an eager-beaver. He must assume an air of indifference, a sort of casual man-of-the-world attitude, the best gimmick
for an older man to attract and hold the attention of a young
chick.

But he forgot all about this philosophy when he was with her.

The round of entertainment to keep Ruby happy and at his side
was beginning to tell on Al's nervous system. He felt that this
courtship, though brief, must have its culmination very soon; he
had much to do in his career, and this playing around could go on
indefinitely. After all, Ruby was just starting out in life, and to her
time would not have that stress of urgency that it did to Jolson.

In a night club one evening a former beau of Ruby's greeted her
and asked her to dance. Jolson nodded assent and watched the
two start off on the crowded floor. It was a hot, fast collegiate
number, and Al felt frustrated and suddenly old as he watched
the young couple romp through the intricate lightning-like steps
with ease and seemingly without effort. Al bit his lip, tried to hide
his resentment. Why hadn't he met a girl like her twenty years
ago? Then he would have shown a young punk like this a thing or
two.

Al sat at the table, studying Ruby and the young fellow as they
danced their way around and around. She was smiling up at her
partner who was saying something to her—Al wondered what.
Jolson wished he was a drinking man. He would have gone the
limit—the way he felt.

If only he could get her away from all this, the nerve-twanging
merry-go-round of bistros and those dancing gigolos.

Maybe, he told himself, Epstein was right. What was he doing
with a nineteen-year-old beauty? Was it going to be like this with
her all the time? He knew he was jealous, but he couldn't help it.
He knew he would feel jealous every time a younger man looked
at her.

Finally the young man was returning her to the table. He
grinned at Al. That kid was disgustingly handsome.

Thanks, Mr. Jolson. Ruby's one crackerjack of a dancer. You
won't mind if I come back for an encore?

Jolson tried hard to control his temper. He said, Whatever the
lady wants, kiddo.

The young fellow grinned again, shrugged, gave Ruby a knowing wink. Al looked at Ruby, asked, Now what was that for?

He's just kidding. He was one of the chorus boys in *Rosie O'Reilly*. He took me out a few times. Just friends, Al.

A moment later, Al, dancing with Ruby, felt better, but he also realized that, compared to her former partner, he must have seemed quite a drag. The warning words of Epstein kept recurring: Have your fun with her, then let her go.

Perhaps he should do just that—before it was too late.

But the next moment he knew there was no escape.

If he let her go, he'd be dead.

There were other moments of frustration and disappointment.

It was Ruby herself who finally said to him one night when he had brought her home and was about to leave, Al, dear, you like me a lot, don't you?

Like you? Baby Doll, I'll say I'm crazy about you.

You really sure you love me?

Love you so much I can't see straight. What am I going to do?

Ruby nestled in his arms. Al, honey, if I were a man I'd know what to do.

He kissed her; he had never kissed any woman like that. It was as though she were his first love—and perhaps she was.

You want to ask me something, Al, honey?

Yes, but I'm afraid you might give me the wrong answer and that would kill your ol' Uncle Jolie.

Try me.

You mean—you'll marry me?

She nodded. The dimples twinkled into sight as she smiled.

And that, in reality, was the most ecstatic moment in the life of Al Jolson.

It was a moment that came once in a man's lifetime—and then it could only be remembered.

When Al left her that night, he was filled with the wonder of it— a slip of a girl who had barely begun to live, awakening within him such wondrous emotions and making him forget everything else.

The next Mrs. Al Jolson, the real Mrs. Al Jolson.

As he entered his own apartment, he was twenty feet tall and twenty years young.

1

Al and Ruby were secretly married on September 21, 1928, in Port Chester, New York. Al reserved the Prince of Wales suite on the White Star liner, S. S. *Olympic*, and before long they were on the high seas bound for a honeymoon tour of Europe.

On a moonlit night they strolled along the deck and finally were leaning against the rail, watching the moon-dappled rollers caressing the ship's side. There was a tranquility here that Al had not experienced for many years in the hectic scramble of his career. He was trying to recall another voyage he had taken a long time ago, but in the direction of America, the Promised Land. He did remember, though faintly, flashes of impressions of that journey; the whitecaps on the waves, the heaving of the ship in a storm—a ship that was much smaller than this present liner—the other immigrants with him in the steerage. He remembered the landing, the towers of a great city; he remembered the lighted windows of a train in the night that bore them to Washington and their new home.

And now here he was going back to Europe, having found the fabled gold in the streets of America, and this girl beside him—his wife—was another precious gift of that wondrous country.

When she asked him what he was thinking about he told her he was trying to remember another Atlantic crossing—the opposite way. He told her of his family coming to America; about his cantor father and of Al's own struggle to break away from the family tradition of cantorship. Ruby was fascinated. He told her of his first painful steps up the ladder of fame. She said, Now you are Al Jolson, the greatest name in show business, with millions of fans, including little me.

She took his arm and leaned against him; the pressure of her body felt warm, reassuring. She told Al they would teach the Broadway wise guys the meaning of a successful marriage. He admitted he had made mistakes. But from now on things would be different.

Ruby was quiet for a moment as she looked out over the moonlit expanse and listened to the low pulsation of the ship's engines as the great steamer glided ever eastward.

Al, honey, when we return from our honeymoon I'm not going back on the stage. I'm going to be a real housewife, take care of our home, and see that you have the proper attention.

He learned from Ruby that she came from a family that had known extreme poverty when she had been in her early teens. Times were so bad for us, she told him, my poor mother had to accept baskets from the Salvation Army and, believe me, she was a proud woman, so it must have hurt her plenty. But what could she do? We were hungry.

She looked up at him. And Al, honey, we'll have children, lots of them.

He glanced at her quickly. For a moment he floundered in quiet panic, then struggled to find his voice. Of course, Ruby, children. What's a home without a few kids playin' about?

They remained silent, their arms about each other.

For Al this was fulfillment. Surely, he could want for nothing else. But her mention of children had brought back his feeling of guilt. She stirred presently, and Al was surprised when she asked him to sing for her—very low—almost a whisper—so that no one might hear.

Sure, Baby. What's your pleasure?

"Rock-a-Bye"—you know the one, she said.

He winked at her. Then he bowed and sang:

Rock-a-bye your baby with a Dixie melody—
    When you croon, croon a tune
    From the heart of Dixie—

Just hang my cradle, Mammy mine,
Right on that Mason-Dixon line
And swing it from Virginia to Tennessee . . .

He knelt down on one knee and extended his hands toward
Ruby, whose eyes shone with the excitement of this unexpected

performance to an audience of one—herself. Al climaxed the
song with his customary sweep, but softly:

Rock-a-bye your rock-a-bye baby with a Dix-ie me-lo-dy.

Her eyes closed in rapture as she listened to his voice. When
he finished she sighed. Al, honey, I'm sleepy.
Come along, woman.
Arm in arm they left the rail and moved along toward their
suite.

2

In their tour of London, Paris, and Rome, Al's interest in the history and customs of the people did not reach the point of analyzing or studying them. The sights and sounds did impress his normal curiosity, but Al was not one to probe too deeply into the whys and wherefores.

He did, however, take a genuine interest in what the European theater had to offer in the way of legit and musical shows. Ruby showed a greater absorption in the old-world scene—the medieval palaces, the museums, the age-old streets and ancient houses of the cities, the people themselves, their languages, their clothes, their daily living—all this fascinated her, and she felt like Alice in Wonderland as she hung onto Al's arm as they made their way about.

For the first two weeks all thoughts of their careers back home were forgotten in their mutual awareness. With Ruby, Al found a happiness he had never suspected could exist for any man. But as the days went by and they journeyed about Europe, almost imperceptibly the old restlessness gradually began to manifest itself. He found himself wondering what his next move would be. He had left a tremendous audience back in the States, and no doubt they were waiting for his return, to entertain them once more as in the past.

He began to read the New York newspapers wherever he could find them—at newsstands, or in the hotel lobbies.

In the hotel at Rome he noticed an item in a New York gossip column that halted him in his tracks. He read it slowly, unbelievingly, but there it was, leering at him from the newsprint. The impact left him chilled.

"Sounds in the night. The grapevine has it that a Mammy singer gifted a certain teen tap dancer to the tune of a cool million as a little wedding present."

This was the first time that an item in a newspaper had hit him below the belt.

Al hurried up to their apartment where Ruby was dressing for the evening. She noticed Al's livid face at once. Al, what is it?

Plenty. He was furious.

He held up the newspaper. He pointed to the paragraph. Ruby took the paper curiously. She read the item. Then she looked up at Al, her eyes hurt.

Oh, Al, how ever did such a rumor start?

Some scandal monger whipped up a fast buck. But he won't get away with this. I'll sue the mug for libel—and clear this thing up with the public. That's a helluva thing to print.

Ruby went up to him, put her hands on his shoulders. Al, honey, don't let it upset you. We're on our honeymoon, so let's forget everything else.

Forget? Look, Ruby, this ain't goin' to do you any good. People might even believe you sold yourself—for a million bucks.

Al, if they want to believe that, then I don't care. Promise me you'll try to forget it.

Ruby, I promise it won't interfere with our honeymoon, but when we get back I'm goin' to demand a retraction and an apology.

3

For the next two weeks their stay in Europe was not as carefree as it had started out to be. Suddenly, Al walked with a heavy step. There was more of a frown upon his face than a smile. The thought of that item in the New York newspaper rankled in his mind, filling him with uneasiness. Did some smart aleck figure that the only way he could win a pretty young girl like Ruby was to buy her? He fumed inwardly when he thought of this. But he did make a great effort to be pleasant in Ruby's company, to make her laugh. Poor kid—married to him only a couple of weeks and already faced with her first painful disparagement.

In Paris, on their way back from Rome, they visited the Cafe L'Anglaise. Al was instantly recognized by some of the patrons and by the manager who greeted him profusely, introducing himself as a long-time admirer. Inevitably, Jolson was soon urged to sing.

Ruby pressed Al's hand. Go on, she said, it's good for international relations.

You should have been a diplomat, said Al. He nodded and grinned at the patrons. At once a respectful silence ensued. Al rose and raised his hand for their attention. Ruby smiled at him proudly. That was her Al, all right.

He beamed at his new audience. He was in his element once more. That was his real joy.

He broke into his number, "Swanee," and the patrons were in ecstasy as they listened. They had never heard anyone—certainly not in Paris—sing like that—*tres bon, tres magnifique.*

He received a sincere ovation and of course he had to oblige with an encore, so he gave them his favorite Stephen Foster ditty, "Camptown Races." Again, a great flurry of applause and cries of *"Viva le Jolson! Viva le Jolson! Merci, M'sieu Al!"*

One young Parisian doll sang out, *"Je t'aime! Je t'aime, M'sieu Jolson."* Ruby chuckled, and her eyes twinkled as she looked at Al.

Heart breaker, she said.

That's your Jolie.

What am I going to do with you, Mr. Jolson? Women are always going to make eyes at you.

I'm a one-woman man. Remember that.

Again Ruby's eyes were twinkling. She smiled impishly. Sure, Al, one woman at a time.

They looked at each other and laughed.

4

And so the pain of that newspaper item was assuaged and laughter came back to them during those last few days of their honeymoon.

But, like all things good or bad, their European romp came to an end and they sailed for the States. They arrived in New York the first week of November.

Al was not the man to hold a grudge or keep alive a vendetta for any length of time. He did have a temper that flared up when provoked like a Fourth of July rocket, then fizzled out. He had already dismissed from his attention the "million dollar" item he had discovered in a New York paper in Rome.

Jolson was anxious to get back to work. He had grown more and more impatient with the passage of days. Primarily he was a man of action. He was not one to sit in a rocking chair and meditate upon the follies of his fellow men, including himself, though he could have retired and lived a life of ease and luxury. There was only one thing that could keep him happy, and that was work—his kind of work—singing to an audience, from the screen or the stage—but, of course, preferably from the stage.

He noticed, on his return to New York, that there were strange happenings on Wall Street. The stock market was climbing with sudden aberrations that culminated in quick-selling splurges. People were buying stock on reckless margin in the hopes of quick clean-ups. Paper profits expanded like overinflated balloons—into the millions. Everybody got into the act—office clerks, stenographers, bricklayers, factory workers, domestics, street cleaners, and even the cop on the beat. All were talking the lingo of the stock market—bulls, bears, selling short, buying on margin, bucket shops, points of change, and being "wiped out." It was a mad scramble, a crazy free-for-all that mystified the wondering Al Jolson.

He received calls from his brokers, asking him whether he wanted to reap some quick profits by smart speculation, but the shrewd Jolson could see no reason for that, and just held on to his solid securities, neither selling nor buying. He stood pat, confining his gambling operations to the nags and pinochle.

His interest was in getting back to California and Hollywood as fast as possible so that he could resume his work in pictures. Warners were preparing the ground for the start of a new film, *Say It with Songs*, and Al could see no reason for delay. However, there was some shopping Ruby wanted to complete for Christmas and Al agreed to wait a few weeks.

He met his old Broadway cronies again and there were the familiar pinochle games. Ruby realized a man had to do something besides entertaining his wife through every minute of the day, so on her part there was no complaint.

On a December day, with the first snowfall settling down upon the metropolis, Mr. and Mrs. Jolson were in their apartment, looking out at the white cascade sifting down upon the stone and steel battlements that was Manhattan.

Al, honey, you haven't grown tired of me yet, have you?

You're pretty and young—otherwise, who knows?

Al, are you going to ask me whether I'm tired of you?

Nobody gets tired of Jolie.

Al took her in his arms. It was very easy and such a satisfying thing to do. Sugar, when we reach Hollywood, we'll settle down. California is my favorite state. I even helped write a song about it, and I know you'll love it out there. Warners has a whole new schedule lined up for me.

I'll keep house for you, Al. I'll set a good example for Hollywood wives.

A brief silence.

Al, honey—

I'm listening, baby.

Mr. Cohan phoned me.

What did ol' Georgie want?

He said something about a part for me in his next show.

Al glanced at her closely. There was the shadow of concern in his eyes.

I wouldn't consider it, Al. I told him I was through with show business.

Ruby, tonight I'm cutting the pinochle game and taking you out on the town.

I'll get dressed right away, she said. I just love going out in the snow. Do you think we'll have a white Christmas?

They did go out that night, in an increasing snowstorm. They slowly made their way on the street, found it impossible to spot a cab, so they rode the subways.

Al felt elated that evening. Baby, pretty soon we're going to Washington. There's an extra-special sweetheart of mine I want you to meet. I've written her about you and she's kinda anxious to see what an angel looks like.

That's your Momma. Do you think she'll like me?

They dined, they danced, they laughed through a flawless evening.

Several young men who knew Ruby danced with her— something that Al now took for granted and would lose no sleep over. He knew where he stood with Ruby. And he was right. At the end of it, she came into his arms and pleaded, Al, honey, let's go home.

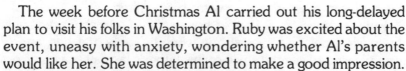

23

1

The week before Christmas Al carried out his long-delayed plan to visit his folks in Washington. Ruby was excited about the event, uneasy with anxiety, wondering whether Al's parents would like her. She was determined to make a good impression.

Al, I'm worried. Maybe your mother won't take to me.

Baby, take a good look at yourself in the mirror. Did you ever see a more innocent-looking doll?

Ruby gave Al an amused glance, but a half-pout still lingered on her face. Al, dear, we're of different faiths, and what's that name you sometimes call me?

Shiksa. Prettiest word in the Yiddish language, believe me. What's more, Momma's used to it.

So the matter was settled.

When they arrived at the Yoelson home in Washington there was a warm greeting for both of them.

Once more Al felt he had come home—to his real home. The street was covered with fresh snow and there was a holiday spirit hovering over the capital city.

Mrs. Yoelson and the cantor received Al and his bride like long-lost children. When the welcoming was over and while Ruby was upstairs in the bathroom, freshening up, Mrs. Yoelson cornered her son. Asa, another *shiksa*?

Momma, this is the best of the lot. Tell me honestly, ain't she beautiful?

Beautiful she is, Asa. But when it comes to cooking?

Momma, she's goin' to be the best cook in Hollywood.

Asa, tell me one thing, you will keep her and settle down?

When we get back to Hollywood, we'll look for a home. No more jumping around. By the way, Momma, need anything? New furniture maybe?

Asa, three times you bought us new furniture. Already we have everything. Thanks.

Al put his arm about his mother, beamed down at her. Momma, do you really like her?

Maybe she could be a little older. Mrs. Yoelson sighed. Anyhow, keep her in good health.

When Ruby came down she conversed with Cantor Yoelson. The cantor was not too well; he was under the doctor's care and his duties in the synagogue were now limited.

Ruby seemed to fill the old house with a refreshing radiance. Even Mr. Yoelson's eyes shone when he looked at her, and Al was pleased to see the smile on his father's face after a kiss from the new daughter-in-law.

2

The stay at the Yoelsons was a pleasant one.

Al was jolly at dinner, enjoying as always his mother's tasty Lithuanian dishes. To Ruby the meal was quite an adventure— the gefilte fish and the *chain* (ground horseradish) that went with it, the golden chicken soup and the potato *kugel* that tasted so good on a cold day.

After the dishes were cleared, Al talked about the humorous incidents of his boyhood days here in Washington and Ruby laughed till the tears came to her eyes, but she winced when Al described the whippings his father had given him with the all-too-efficient trouser belt.

There was only one hitch, said Al. Poppa had a heck of a time keeping his pants up while swingin' that strap.

It was a gay family reunion. Al's half-brother, George, had come in but, as usual, Harry was on the road and would be home at a later date.

The snow had started falling again, and that night Al and his wife slept in his old bed in his old room which was always ready for him.

They could hear the north wind howling against the side of the house, the rattling of the windows, and the soughing of the naked boughs of the maples. It was a mournful dirge and brought Al back to his boyhood when he had hidden under the covers in this very bed and listened to the madcap wind. Now it was the same, and yet not the same. Now there was a young girl tight against him in his arms, her hair lying over his shoulder, her softness, her warmth lulling him into a blissful sea of forgetfulness.

The following day, though it had stopped snowing, the fresh white depths blanketed the entire city. There were no automobiles moving and men were clearing the snow off the trolley car tracks.

It was almost like being snowbound, but Al didn't mind.

With a girl like Ruby near him he didn't care how long they'd be marooned.

3

The Jolsons moved to Hollywood and Al started on his next picture, *Say It with Songs*. Al had grown somewhat accustomed to the monotonous grind of working in films, but what disappointed him more than anything else in this type of work was the absence of an audience to which he could appeal. The lens of a camera was a poor substitute as far as he was concerned, and he walked about with dreams in his mind of an early return to the Broadway stage.

He could not drive from his memory the old Winter Garden days, the salvos of applause after each of his performances, the thrills of introducing new hit songs.

In the wake of his talking picture splurge, realizing that his older brother was through with the vaude stage, Al, in a burst of enthusiasm—as was his way—announced to Harry: From now on you're my agent. You will take care of my future bookings.

Harry drew back, half in fear, half in doubt.

But, Al, I have no experience, and you're the biggest name in show business.

All you need is confidence. You know the show-biz game better than most. You came up from the old days.

Yes, I suppose so, but as an agent—Al, let me talk it over with Lillian. The responsibility scares me.

Take all the time you want, Harry. You work the thing right and you'll make a million.

In the light of Al's glowing promises Harry could see the elusive rainbow of success. No more grubbing for a paltry subsistence, subjecting his wife to a string of hardships. He must remember at all times that his Lillian was not in good health. She was delicate, growing more so with the years, and he must take care of her.

To Harry, suddenly, Al became a sort of god—a messiah, no less.

Lillian did not hesitate to give her approval. She told Harry, I know you will do a good job. Never underrate your abilities.

At once Harry started his new career.

He had, with the consent of Al, opened a comfortably furnished office in Hollywood; he would direct his operations from this point. He did obtain bookings, not only for Al but for Ruby Keeler as well. He got them a spot on the Lux radio program. They did a show called *Burlesque*. It seemed at the end of the year that Harry had finally mastered the art of being a bona fide agent.

Then out of a clear sky, without any hint or notice, this item in *Variety* almost floored him:

We are proud to announce
that Al Jolson has exclusively authorized us
to represent him as agents for the negotiations
of radio and theater engagements.
Any other person or persons purporting to represent Al Jolson
in this connection
do so without his authority.

This declaration was signed by the William Morris Agency. Harry was stunned.

Al called him on the phone, tried to explain, but Harry was too upset to understand Al's reasons.

Finally Al arrived in Hollywood and spoke to his brother in person: Harry, believe me, the Broadway and radio network producers were complaining about your methods, your decisions. They thought you were not flexible enough. Maybe your lack of experience. After all, Harry, you yourself were doubtful in the first place. It was my mistake for insisting you take the job. Maybe you are not cut out to be an agent. It's a messy, finagling business. But there are other things you can do. You can still run this office and work along with the new agency. Your experience in the theater will come in handy. In time you'll know the game and it's all yours. Now, what do you say to that, Harry? Your salary will remain the same. You can work together with Eppy. How about it, Harry? Look, don't be sore.

Harry was a deeply sensitive person. There was no use denying it—he was hurt, plenty hurt.

Al, at least you could have talked to me first.

But you weren't handy. Besides, I figured you'd understand.

Understand? When you knock the ground from under a guy's feet? Al, I'm burned up about this, I'll have you know.

Harry, listen to me. We've worked together in the old days. I owe a lot to you. You showed me the way. Don't walk out on me now.

I'm not only walking out, but I'm going to see my lawyer. We have a contract and you broke it.

It was Al's turn to be stunned. He stared at his brother.

Harry, you don't mean that?

Wait and see.

Now look, Harry, I'm going to take care of you and Lillian.

By making a dumb jackass out of me. The laughing stock of show biz. You insult me and my wife by offering to keep us as one of your pet charities.

Charity, hell. You'll work for whatever you get.

Who you kidding, Al? Some brother you turned out to be. No wonder Poppa hates your guts.

Now wait a minute, Harry. Poppa and me understand each other.

Harry was packing his briefcase. Al stood in one corner of the office, watching his brother. The silence bristled.

But Al was thinking of Lillian, frail, ailing, with that slight hack of a cough, her shoulders somewhat stooped by the burden of survival. Al knew also that it was wiser not to say anything more.

Harry walked out of the office, into the sun-bathed street. Al was alone.

He slumped down in the chair behind the glass-topped desk.

What was a man supposed to do when the brother he wants to help whiplashes him in the face?

After that Harry went his own way, venturing into various types of businesses, with his wife doing her share of work, trying always to establish themselves.

Their wonderful home in Hollywood that they had built with such sacrifice was now in imminent danger of being lost.

While Al went on to new triumphs, Harry became more and more enveloped in the shadow of oblivion.

Somehow he and Lillian managed to eke out an existence.

The suit he had started against Al for $75,000 damages was thrown out of the New York courts. Harry himself, after his first burst of anger, had decided to drop the whole matter, though friends advised that he would have won the case if he had brought suit in the state of California.

4

Al Jolson found Ruby a patient and inspiring partner. As she had promised him back east, she took care of their temporary quarters in a house in Beverly Hills. Al still had his dream of a home somewhat removed from the Hollywood scene, where he could live freely and have space to stretch out and enjoy the California climate. He had seen some of the nearby estates, and they had appealed to him.

Warners did not show as much enthusiasm for Al's work as they had done in the first two pictures—*The Jazz Singer* and *The Singing Fool*. Apparently Jolson had given his all in those two productions and now it seemed in good part a matter of resting on his laurels.

At this point a new medium—radio—attracted him.

Radio, in the period of 1928 to 1930, also attracted such luminaries of the show firmament as John Barrymore, Paul Whiteman, Douglas Fairbanks, Charlie Chaplin, Norma Talmadge, Eddie Cantor, Will Rogers, and even the durable Scot, Harry Lauder, who blithely accepted $15,000 for three songs (including "Roamin' Through the Gloamin'") and, it being Sunday, Lauder ignored his Scotch heritage and threw in a hymn free of charge. Walter Winchell adventured into radio, doing his machine-gun patter on the air for the first time on January 18, 1929, over a forty-two station network. Also falling into line in this new medium was Maurice Chevalier, over station WABC for a five-grand token of appreciation. And 1929 marked the beginning of Amos 'n' Andy's radio reign with a fifty-two week NBC opening contract, six days a week.

Variety predicted, "Radio is here to stay, but what comes next?" Television was still in embryo.

And Jolson, too, found himself enmeshed in the networks as an aftermath of his first two talking-picture smashes.

As was the custom, Al and Ruby attended some of the Hollywood parties, met other stars of the screen. Al learned how to play golf. With Ruby he took motor trips about the highways and byways of this section of California. But in all these activities there still remained with him a feeling of unrest, a slow-burning discontent, as though he were being kept away against his will from something that had become part of him—the lights of Broadway.

Ruby sensed this in him, but she did not bring the subject forward. Quietly and patiently she waited for Al to grow accustomed to his new mode of life.

When *Say It with Songs* and *Mammy* were released that summer, the impression they made upon the public was well below the impact of his first two film productions. There was no rush on the part of moviegoers to crowd into the theaters to view the films. The financial reports in the studio front office indicated a break-even proposition.

Ruby found Al standing at the window of the living room, gazing disconsolately at a distant ridge of hills. Of late he had grown less and less communicative. Ruby began to worry. She had never realized that her husband could be in any other but a favorable mood; this despondency on his part was a phase she was now discovering:

Al, honey, anything wrong?

Nothing serious, except my pictures are not doing so hot.

Don't worry. People still want to see Al Jolson.

Maybe, but that's not enough for me. I used to pack them in solid.

And you will again, Al.

Thanks, Ruby. You're a pal.

We're invited to a gathering at Gloria Swanson's. Shall we go?

Do you want to?

Yes, said Ruby.

At the party that night there was no request from anyone to hear Jolson sing. In the beginning it had been otherwise—they had never overlooked him at any assemblage.

5

During these days there were other things happening. Back in New York, on Wall Street, all hell broke loose. The stock market had gone completely haywire. Additional payments to cover margins on stock were being called in, in ever-increasing amounts, and thousands of investors were being wiped out. On October 29, 1929, the bottom fell out and the financial structure of the country was shaken to its foundations. Frantic stockholders struggled to unload, but there were not enough takers, and shares fell to a drastically low level of value or became entirely worthless. Men of wealth and position were reduced to paupers. Frenzied bankrupts jumped out of skyscrapers' windows. The national economy trembled on the brink.

The aftermath was even worse. Banks closed their doors after overwhelming "runs" on the part of depositors that wiped out the cash reserves and caused bank failures that swallowed up the life savings of millions of working people.

Variety, the show biz journal, headlined its October 30, 1929, issue, "Wall Street Lays an Egg."

Jolson received word that his friend, Eddie Cantor, had been virtually ruined in the crash. Al forgot his own problems. He phoned Eddie at once. Listen to me, Eddie. I heard about your losses. Look, sonny boy, sometimes we bumped into each other trying to make the biggest splash. Remember that time in Chicago? You in *Kid Boots* and me in *Bombo*. We had a battle then, but let's forget about that. Eddie, this is your pal, Jolie. Maybe you need a little cash to tide you over. Say the word, Eddie, and it's yours.

6

For Al, life with Ruby was complete and fulfilling. If only he could control that recurring restlessness that seemed to come over him. He tried to live a quiet life of contentment, going to the studio in the morning and returning in the afternoon or evening, as the shooting schedule permitted. He tried to enjoy the weekends, taking Ruby out on long drives, or stopping in Los Angeles to take in a show. Sometimes they would go sailing in a boat he had purchased.

But Ruby often found him alone and brooding, probably thinking about his past glories. In 1930 he completed another picture for Warners, *Big Boy*, which was adapted from his last stage show of the same name. But this opus met with no greater success than *Say It with Songs* and *Mammy*. The fact was, the picture grossed less than the previous one, and Warner Brothers began to look upon Al Jolson with some perplexity. It was difficult to comprehend that so sensational a star of stage and screen could be losing his box-office appeal.

Jolson himself felt discouraged with the motion-picture industry. It was difficult for him, also, to accept the change in the public's regard.

He tried to ignore it but the feeling of inadequacy, of losing ground, persisted.

He began to lose, also, that familiar Jolsonesque buoyancy and flippancy that had so charmed Ruby. She started to regard him with compassion. If only she could do something to pull him out of this state, but what? Sometimes, when she mentioned the idea of Al stepping aside for the time being and letting others take over, he snapped at her and told her she was crazy for even suggesting such a thing.

Ruby, get one thing straight. Jolie ain't quittin'—not now, not ever. I made up my mind some time ago that I wasn't goin' to quit.

Instead of busying himself with another movie, Jolson was struck with an idea. Perhaps the films were not his destiny after all. Intrinsically, he was a stage performer. The smash hits of the past proved that. His mind was made up. His next venture would be another musical in the tradition of *Sinbad* or *Bombo*. He would contact the Shuberts. He would at once dispatch his manager Epstein to New York to arrange preliminaries.

Strange that he should not have thought of this before. This time he would be his old self—the Jolson Broadway had known.

His comeback would make show-biz history.

Epstein did travel to New York and he had his conference with the Shuberts who were willing to take a chance, though they themselves were in bad shape financially. Their string of theaters had dwindled to two or three, as the banks had taken them over in satisfaction of unpaid mortgages. Perhaps this was what they needed—the old combination with Al Jolson in another smash. The writers, composers, choreographers, and cast were assembled. A new show, *Wonderbar*, went into rehearsal and the Jolsons came back to New York. Al felt like his old self. Once more he laughed, clowned around, and quipped with the show's personnel. He told Ruby that the world was theirs again.

24

1

Ruby was glad, of course, that this had happened. She smiled happily as Al romped through the rehearsal sessions. His voice seemed as powerful and vibrant as it had ever been in his younger days. Those oncoming gray wisps at his temples had not marred the quality of his vocal performance.

On opening night Jolson was in his element. There was a good house and he sang with all his energy. It was a plea, in fact, to the people, sitting there in judgment, asking whether he could sing his songs to them again.

Once more the sound of that applause.

It was the same as before . . . he assured himself. . . .

Backstage, after the opening, Al embraced his friend and manager, Epstein. What did I tell you, Eppy? I wowed them, didn't I? I'm the same ol' Al Jolson. I didn't want to be a screen actor in the first place. This is where I belong—Broadway.

It was a gala occasion that night. He took Ruby to Maxim's. They danced and he received a request to sing a number, which he did. When he finished he told them: Folks, you ain't heard nothin' yet. Buy tickets for *Wonderbar*.

Al, honey, you did it, said Ruby on their way home in a cab.

Thanks, baby. Now I know. Broadway is my territory and no one can take that away from me.

The next morning, at the breakfast table in their apartment, he looked at the reviews in the newspapers. He was all set to enjoy the tributes and accolades hailing his return.

But the reviews seemed to indicate a common theme. "Last night the great Al Jolson was back on Broadway, belting out his songs in the best 'Mammy' tradition. But the world changes and the tastes of the people comprising this world change likewise." "The same style of delivery with the bended knee, the extended hands, the same old Jolson—perhaps, too much the same— except—regretfully—minus the blackface." "Sometimes it is a pity that we cannot go along without changing, without developing new ideas and new attitudes, so that we can look upon something out of the fond past without regarding it as an anachronism." "Last night we caught a glimpse of how it used to be. The corn was green. Jolson and nostalgia, synonymous."

Al looked across the table at Ruby. His food remained untouched. She rose, moved around to take her place behind his chair. She leaned over him, placing her arms over his shoulders. Al, honey, I wouldn't take those reviews too seriously. You had a full house last night and that audience really liked you. *Wonderbar* is a hit, believe me.

Baby, I sang my best to them. You're right, Ruby. Those smart alecks can write their heads off—from now on, kiddo, I don't pay them no mind. I'm goin' to give them a real surprise. *Wonderbar* is goin' to be one of the biggest hits on Broadway.

That's my Al.

Ruby, you really believe in your ol' Jolie, don't you?

Of course, honey. You're the greatest and always will be. So now finish your breakfast and we'll take a nice walk on the avenue and get some fresh air. We both can use it.

That night Al went all out on the stage. He put into his performance every ounce of energy at his command.

But he could see, easily enough, that there were quite a number of vacant seats. The applause was generous but did not have the gusto and spirit of the old Winter Garden ovations.

He did not speak about the show when he met Ruby backstage, and they went home.

Epstein seemed worried when he presented himself at the Jolson apartment the following morning while Al was still in bed. Ruby was up and about.

What do you think, Lou? asked Ruby.

I don't know. Epstein shook his head. Maybe Al should have remained in Hollywood. At least he had steady work.

About *Wonderbar*, Lou. It's okay, isn't it? Ruby's voice was low.

The show will run for a while. There are plenty of Jolson fans running loose—but they're on the older side. The younger people go for Rudy Vallee. You know, it's hard to believe. They go berserk just looking at that young college crooner. And he uses a megaphone to make himself heard. What do they see in him? Ask me, and I'll tell you I don't know. It's crazy.

If *Wonderbar* closes too soon, it will break Al's heart, said Ruby.

Miracles are happening all the time. Maybe it will run for a few weeks. I hope so.

Lou, do me a favor.

Sure, Ruby. Anything.

Build him up. Tell him the show's great. Tell him his performances are wowing the audiences.

Ruby, tell me to jump off the Brooklyn Bridge—for you, I'd do that too.

Lou, you're a doll.

Ruby, this I must say. You have a great husband, even though he drives me—and maybe sometimes you too—absolutely crazy. If I ever tell you all the people he has helped, all the money he has given to different charities—well, maybe you already know about that.

Yes, I know.

2

In the days that followed, *Wonderbar* began to slow down.

The audiences grew smaller and smaller. The critics didn't even mention it any more in their columns.

Meanwhile in that year of 1931 the great depression was in full swing. Unemployment across the nation rose to an appalling fourteen million. In consequence, theater attendance suffered. Epstein used this fact to explain *Wonderbar*'s dying throes. Jolson would have liked to believe this, but he saw no sense in kidding himself. Why were certain other shows on Broadway playing to packed houses, week after week?

Wonderbar closed after 76 try-hard performances that just about pulled the show through without plunging it into the category of a total flop.

Al had made his return to Broadway and the street had brushed him off. It was as if it had said to him, "You've read the reviews and what they've said was the truth."

Yes, the world was changing. Jolson realized now that he had not changed along with it. He saw now that his own show, alongside the others on the stem, was unquestionably antiquated. For the first time he had come across the word "corny" in a reference to his own performance.

It was hard for Jolson to take.

He turned to Ruby after the show had folded. You could have told me the show stunk, he said.

Ruby was combing her hair at her dresser, preparatory to bed.

Now, Al, even if I did think so, you know I wouldn't tell you that.

You might have saved a lot of trouble and expense.

Al, may I say something to you, a little on the hard side?

Now you're goin' to tell me that show biz is through with me.

Something like that. Al, why don't you wake up to it? Are you afraid?

You know better than that.

Well, are you?

Look, Honey Chile, I'm afraid of nothin'.

Including failure?

Why failure? I was a smash hit for years.

There comes a time, Al, when we must face up to it.

Not Jolie.

Jolie, too.

Ruby, I know what I can do. I admit I was only good for two pictures in the movies. But I won't admit I'm through on the stage. Give me an audience and—

Al, honey, you *had* an audience.

Al looked at her for a long moment, then he slumped into a chair and covered his face with his hands. For the first time Ruby saw her husband like this. She put her arms about him. Al, dear, who cares about hit shows? There are so many things we can do. Show business isn't the whole world.

Ruby, I wanted you to be proud of me. I wanted you to see me as I used to be—knockin' 'em dead.

Ruby dimpled and smiled at him. Al, honey, you'll knock 'em dead again. I really believe that. But right now let the Rudy Vallees and the Bing Crosbys do their share. You've done yours.

3

Ruby had prodded Epstein into finding an engagement for Al as a means of bolstering her husband's morale.

A vaudeville spot would be great, could give him that one lift he needs, said Ruby.

I'll do my best, Epstein promised.

He did succeed in landing two engagements for Al—one at the famed Palace in New York, the other in New Orleans where they were most anxious to hear the sponsor of their native music.

At the Palace Al sang to a packed house for one solid week. In addition to his salary of $15,000, he had been promised a percentage of the gross if it exceeded $100,000 per week. Though he didn't go over this figure, this might have been due to some of the patrons remaining in order to hear the new songs that Jolson usually introduced in his second performance.

In New Orleans the attendance exceeded all expectations and many were turned away. Jolson was at his top form. Once again his personality held sway, his voice thrilled them with "My Mammy," "Swanee," "Rock-a-Bye Your Baby with a Dixie Melody," and a score of others.

They kept calling "More! More!".

Once again Al Jolson was in his glory.

It seemed that the roar of an approving audience was a life-giving serum to him and he became his old confident self, laughed, quipped, lived life with zest.

Ruby, of course, was happy for his sake.

But when Al asked the Shuberts for another musical on Broadway he met with an emphatic No.

Lee Shubert shook his head. Al, in short individual spots you'll do all right. People will come to see you for old time's sake. And once seeing you, they'll be satisfied. That's why a regular show wouldn't jell. Why take a chance on a possible flop? Could be disastrous to your own reputation. Why kill yourself? You don't need it. Why don't you go on like this—with vaude spots?

I get you, said Al. A show is out. All right, I can finance my own show.

Al, you're asking for trouble. You did all right in Hollywood. Why not continue in pictures?

So Al walked out of the Shubert offices, his mood downcast. It was disheartening. After so many years in show business, to be turned out to pasture.

Despondency came over him once more. From now on he would feel irritated at the slightest provocation. He would be difficult to associate with. Ruby would have her hands full.

4

Al made up his mind to leave New York and Broadway perhaps for good. He felt the Great White Way had finally rejected him, and decided to go back to his beloved California. The Jolsons arrived in Hollywood one morning in the spring of 1932, and this time Epstein made his greatest sales pitch and succeeded in landing a radio program for Al. Radio had become a tremendous medium with a nationwide audience measured in the millions.

He had a weekly show, broadcast from Hollywood on the Columbia network, with Parkyakarkas and Martha Raye supplying the comedy relief. It was a forty-week contract, salary $5,000 per week.

Al had his chance to sing his trademark songs to his heart's content, along with some new numbers he made popular. He was fairly sure that California would be his state from now on, since he had fulfilled the words of the famous song, "California, Here I Come."

With Ruby he looked about for a permanent home with plenty of open space. He was positive now that, in this locale of sunshine and roses, he would at last find himself and settle down to a mode of life at once tranquil and satisfying. With Ruby at his side he knew he would be as happy as any man could ever hope to be. After all, life had been good to him. It had given him success, fame, financial independence—and Ruby. What else could there be?

His one regret was that he was far from his parents, but he promised himself he would visit them as often as possible. He knew that his father was ill, and that worried him.

There was a ranch on the edge of Encino near the Ventura Boulevard, about twelve miles west of Hollywood, that immediately appealed to Jolson and Ruby, so Al lost no time in purchasing it. Soon they were settled on it, and Epstein commented, Now I can breathe easy. You two have finally come to roost. The next thing on the agenda is a family.

Ruby's eyes glowed. Of course, Lou, a family. I've always wanted lots of children. She glanced at Al. Now it's up to the boss man.

Al nodded, grinned. Ruby, this ranch is for raising oranges, melons, sweet potatoes, and kids. Yes sir-ee. Ol' Jolie's goin' to be a real cracker-barrel farmer, you can tell the world.

And so the Jolsons became entrenched in California, not far from the scene of their career activities, but far enough to make it easy to forget about show business.

5

A visitor came to the ranch from the Hollywood studios of Warner Brothers. This time it was not Al Jolson that the studio representative had come to interview but Ruby Keeler, the actress. Our studio is starting a musical and there's a part in it calling for a good tap dancer with a nice singing voice. Must be young and pretty. The brass have decided on you, Miss Keeler.

I'm sorry but—

The agent interrupted. Before you say anything, Miss Keeler, why not consult Mr. Jolson? If he nixes the idea, then we forget the whole thing. If he votes "yes," then it's your ball.

I promised Al no career.

Think what it means, Miss Keeler. The studio chiefs are banking that you'll break big. America's new sweetheart—the Mary Pickford of the talkies.

The agent left with the comment that he'd phone her the next day.

Ruby thought about her vow to Al that her place was in the home.

But when she broached the subject to Al, his answer came without hesitation. It sounds great, baby. We can't let it go by.

You can't keep your talent bottled up. I know how it is, believe me, sweetheart.

Al, but I promised you—

I promised you many things too, kiddo, but along comes destiny and we have to make a change. That's another thing I've found out.

Inwardly, Al was wondering, if she becomes a movie star how much of Ruby will be taken from me?

25

1

Though Ruby had been loath to leave her post as a housewife, now that she had the approval of her husband, and with the urging of the studio heads, she signed a contract which instantly placed her in the category of star, bypassing the stints of extra, bit player, and supporting actress. She played opposite Dick Powell, the singing sensation, and even while her first picture was being shot, the director, his assistants, the supporting cast, even the stagehands immediately recognized in her performance the makings of a great star.

As for Al, in the year 1932 he took part in the election campaign, stumping for Franklin D. Roosevelt. Al sang at political rallies, and the crowds gathered eagerly to listen to Jolson rather than to the boring vote-begging harangues of the politicians.

The people were looking to FDR as the next president—a president who would soon plug up the broken dikes of the national economy with startling new measures, beginning with bank holidays and the repeal of prohibition.

Jolson was fairly happy on his Encino ranch during the term of his radio broadcast contract. The money was good and the job gave him a sense of fulfillment and belonging. He felt like someone who had been snatched out of the depths of oblivion to live and breathe again.

And feeling happy, he made others feel that way too. With Jolson it was always a matter of achieving, of doing to the utmost what he was best equipped to do. Of course, he missed the applause of great audiences in theaters where he could look at the people he was entertaining, but he contented himself with radio where he sang and performed for an audience thousands of times bigger, though unseen and unheard. To him it was like groping in the dark, feeling his way along, not knowing whether he was going in the right direction or not.

2

Al had slowed his car on Sunset Boulevard in Hollywood and stopped at the curb. He honked his horn to attract the attention of his brother Harry, whom he had detected walking on the sidewalk.

Harry, surprised, turned and approached Al's car.

Harry, please get in. I wanna talk to you.

Harry hesitated, his fingers clenching and unclenching nervously. Finally, he made his decision and got into the front seat beside his brother.

Harry, I admit I pulled a dirty trick on you, but I already explained my reasons. I'm supposed to be a big star, you know, and a big star needs a well-known agent to take care of his interests. Harry, I would like to do something for you.

Al, the matter's been closed and almost forgotten and you're not obligated to me in any way.

Don't be so sure about that, Harry. Is it fair to Lillian for you not to have a car? Maybe she would enjoy some nice drives. Harry, I'll phone the best auto dealer in town. You can pick out any car you want. No limit, no strings.

Harry was somewhat stunned at this and did not know what his answer should be. Al looked at him closely. Still sore at me? I did offer you a position but you turned it down.

Al, I'm not sore. That's in the past. But about that car—I better talk to Lillian first.

Sure, do that. Then pick out a car.

When Harry mentioned this to Lillian, he received her nod of assent with the comment that after the way Al had mistreated him with that agency routine, the car was justifiable compensation. Besides, to a wealthy man like Al the price of an automobile meant nothing.

That evening Al informed Harry by phone of the dealer's name and location. Harry made his selection, and his resentment against his brother took a nose dive.

Al wasn't such a bad guy, after all—but he was truly unpredictable.

During this time of comparative contentment, Al and Ruby literally had a "ball." Soon she was working in the production of *Forty-Second Street.*

In their spare moments when not occupied with their careers, they attended parties and friendly gatherings of the Hollywood set. They had grown quite chummy with the Cantors, Eddie and Ida, who lived in Beverly Hills.

Al was a great practical joker when a good subject came along—in this case, Mrs. Cantor. He was delighted with Ida's credulous nature. He could tell her almost anything and she would be ready to believe it, without question, for she was a thoroughly trusting soul. She was surprisingly unassuming and the antithesis of what was pictured as a Hollywood wife.

Ida, as Mrs. Eddie Cantor, was more like the wife of a typical American business or professional man, attending to her wifely duties with the utmost sincerity. To her, Eddie's welfare came first, and the children, of course. She was patient with Jolson, who had drifted into the habit of kidding her quite a bit. She reminded him so much of his own mother—they even had the same first names.

There were several occasions when Jolson played practical jokes on Mrs. Cantor, at which Eddie smiled tolerantly, but with some misgiving for he was always afraid that Ida might be hurt. But she never was. Eddie was to find that she "could take it," though she never thought of "dishing it out."

On one such occasion Jolson called Mrs. Cantor on the phone from his ranch home, while Ruby sat alongside him, listening and bubbling over with high glee. That Al of hers! He was liable to do anything.

Am I speaking to Mrs. Cantor? said Jolson in a disguised, authoritative voice—the voice of a bill collector, no less.

Yes, this is Mrs. Cantor, came a rather diffident housewifely voice.

Al continued, Mrs. Cantor, this is the Beverly Hills Electric Company. It has come to our attention that you are somewhat behind in the payment of your electric bills. Consequently, Mrs. Cantor, we are sending our man to shut off your supply of electricity.

A brief intense silence on the other end. Then Mrs. Cantor's anxious voice, Please, sir, don't shut off our electricity. There must be some mistake. I definitely remember paying our bill. I'll look for the cancelled check. But if we owe anything, sir, we will pay it, whatever it is. But please don't shut off our electricity.

Well, we'll check further. If your bill is paid, then we won't bother you.

Please, Mister, make sure not to shut us off.

Good day, Madam.

Al hung up, and burst into laughter. Ruby laughed too, but she soon stopped. Al, maybe you better call her back. The poor woman will be frantic. And when she tells Eddie—well, he's liable to blow his top.

Al shook his head. Ruby, doll, telling her now would spoil the whole joke. Let it ride for a while. I'm sure Eddie will have a good laugh himself when he finds out.

There were other little jokes he played on Mrs. Cantor. Once he phoned and told her Eddie had left suddenly for the East Coast on important show-business matters in New York and that he would be home in a month. Eddie came home as usual that same evening. Another time Jolson called Mrs. Cantor and told her that the home-cooked meal he had eaten at her house the night before had landed him in the hospital and that a stomach pump had to be used to get the food out of his system.

There was one more occasion, after a suitable lapse of time, when Al, in his most authoritative voice, phoned Mrs. Cantor. Mrs. Cantor, this is the Beverly Hills Water Company. We have an emergency on hand due to a breakdown in our plant. We're going to shut off the water supply for forty-eight hours. We therefore suggest that you fill up all available containers with water to last you over a period until the water is turned on again. We regret this inconvenience to our customers but there is nothing we can do to prevent this. Please accept our apologies.

Not wasting a moment, Mrs. Cantor gathered together all the pots and pans in her kitchen as directed by the "kind man" at the water company, and filled them brimful with the precious liquid. Eddie, coming into the house, listened to Ida's explanation and nodded. Nice of them to warn us, said Eddie.

The following day Al and Ruby dropped in to visit. Ruby, of course, was aware of the joke, and though she had pleaded with Al to phone Mrs. Cantor and ease her anxiety, he had insisted again it would spoil the whole idea.

To Mrs. Cantor, Al said, Can I trouble you for a glass of water?

We have plenty, she said. I got all my pots and pans filled.

Eddie had a proud grin. Folks, there's no one like my Ida.

Al nodded. You're right, Eddie. And she can take a joke, too. For your information the water company was me.

Ida and Eddie looked at each other. Jolie, you *are* a dog, said Eddie. I ought to—here, have another glass of water.

Ida's face was a mixture of relief, perplexity, and resignation.

Mr. Jolson, she pleaded, please—no more jokes—

Al raised his right hand. My word of honor, Ida, this is positively the last one.

3

But underneath all this, Jolson had a genuine admiration for Mrs. Cantor. He told Eddie that the latter was a lucky guy for having such a jewel of a wife.

Eddie, my boy, I'm goin' to train Ruby to be like Ida.

Jolie, you're kidding no one. You know you like Ruby just as she is. Any time you get tired of her send her to us. We can always make room for another daughter.

On an auto jaunt into Mexico toward the end of the summer, Jolson received another good laugh. Eddie and Ida had come along and the quartet had driven across the border with high spirits and much singing. The weather was ideal and they were glad to get away from the hurly-burly for awhile.

In Mexico City, Eddie urged Jolson to stop in front of an inviting store. He purchased an expensive bottle of perfume for Ida, price fifty dollars.

Ida, ain't you goin' to give him a kiss? asked Al.

Ida nodded, put her arm about her husband and kissed him. Eddie rolled his eyes.

Jolson chuckled. Eddie, my boy, a fifty-dollar bargain.

All right, Mistah Bones. I'm going to win back that fifty in the Casa Loma Casino.

They visited the Casa Loma. Eddie stationed himself at the craps table. There were also roulette and blackjack games in the room but the dice charmed Eddie.

Al, Ruby, and Ida watched Eddie throw the dice. The other players at the table covered his bets. A crowd of onlookers gathered. Eddie's eyes gleamed.

Eddie, I think you'd do better betting on the nags, said Al.

Maybe you shouldn't play, said Ida. Gambling is always losing.

Eddie said, Ida, this is my lucky day. He spat on the dice, shook them in his hand, listened to their rattle, then threw them across the table, and lost. The game went on. Ida was concerned. Eddie had never been so reckless. He became immersed in the game, and his losses snowballed. When it was over, the bottle of perfume had cost $11,050.

Jolson took one look at Cantor's face and burst into a laugh. Ruby pleaded, Please, Al, Eddie lost a lot of money.

Al turned to Eddie. My crap-shooting friend, just in case you need some ready cash to tide you over—to pay your electric bills, for instance—

Eddie pointed an accusing finger at Al. Jolie, you can stop gloating. From what I hear, you haven't been too lucky, either in your pinochle games or at the track.

Jolson shrugged. Right now I feel mighty lucky.

They drove out of Mexico City, southward into the heart of Mexico. Ruby smiled at Ida. Ida, don't waste a drop of that perfume. It cost a fortune.

Jolson laughed again and said, For that money, Cantor, you could have bought yourself a Rolls-Royce. When we get back I'll take you to the track and show you some real winning.

After they returned from the trip they did go to the track, and Al showed Eddie how to bet on the ponies.

When they left the track, Jolson had dropped fifteen grand.

4

When *Forty-Second Street* was released in 1933, followed by *Gold-Diggers of 1933*, the public acclaimed Ruby Keeler at once, and she did become America's new sweetheart.

The freshness of the personality that had won Al Jolson now won the admiration and love of millions of moviegoers. Her career had become a fact and it filled her life.

Al had to stand aside. Almost all her time was consumed by her work at the studio, by personal appearances, conferences, invitations to receptions and parties. Al felt himself dragged along like some kind of bodyguard instead of a husband. He had to take a back seat while executives and fellow actors gathered about Ruby, like bees around honey, conferring with her, engaging her in small talk, a language he did not comprehend.

Al himself had the title role in a film, *Hallelujah, I'm a Bum,* produced by Joseph Schenck for United Artists, rather a backward step from his previous movie work. The picture hardly earned the cost of production. It was more or less of a fill-in feature which the public passed by with a cursory glance, wondering what had happened to a great performer named Al Jolson.

Meanwhile the name of Ruby Keeler became a common sight in electric lights over the breadth of the nation. Her earnings, consequently, increased and she became financially independent. And with fame and fortune, inevitably, that "little girl" innocence that had so charmed Al Jolson, was outshone by the glamor of her success. Her personality had gradually taken on a coating of sophistication, although the little things of life that had fascinated her before still held her attention. It would have been difficult, if not impossible, for a young girl to remain naïve in the face of such popular adulation. As that agent had originally prophesied, she did in fact become the Mary Pickford of the early talkies.

Underneath all this excitement, which would have shaken the strongest individual, she was basically the same girl—the Ruby Keeler Al had married. He would just have to be patient until the turbulence about her died down.

But Al was in no shape to understand this. He saw her now as a great celebrity, with himself the lesser in importance. He was chagrined. The world had politely but definitely urged him to the sidelines. Even Warner Brothers had relegated him to supporting roles, and Al wondered sometimes whether they didn't give him work for old times' sake and because they felt they had a moral obligation because he had rescued them from bankruptcy.

He tried to busy himself on the ranch. He planted orange trees and tended them. He planted sweet potatoes and cantaloupes and, with the expert help of his dependable farm manager, succeeded in bringing forth a crop. He planted plots of roses and tulips, but his heart was not in it.

5

In 1933 a refinement of jazz came in the form of a rhythm called "swing." It served to eliminate the "choppiness" and discordancy of ragtime. Among the first sponsors and interpreters of this new music were Glen Gray's elegant group, Stuff Smith's individualistic musicmakers, Bunny Berigan's peppery jam boys, Paul Whiteman's aristocratic band, Louis Armstrong's Dixieland hot trumpet. There were also Artie Shaw's magic clarinet and Mildred Bailey's sending voice.

At Carnegie Hall Benny Goodman tried to educate music lovers with his own unique impression of "swing," to which the youth of the land were already responding in "jitterbug" jam sessions. But it was Paul Whiteman who was able to "send" the sophisticates and win them over to his "sweet" edition of this new strain.

Jolson, in the midst of this bewildering evolution, found himself in an eclipse that was virtually total.

Each day he drove to the studio and brought Ruby home, as from a different world. She was busy, always had commitments for more pictures, and the studio had come to regard her as a most valued asset. She dressed like a princess, and Al, in his work clothes and turtleneck sweater, sometimes felt entirely out of place, escorting her to the studio in the mornings and back to the ranch in the evenings.

He found it more and more difficult to kid around with her as he used to do. He had the feeling that she did not belong to him alone that her beauty and charm were now shared by millions of others. Perhaps, he told himself, he had made the wrong decision in assenting to her career. He could have prevented this at the start, for she had left it up to him entirely.

25

1

It was a quiet breakfast at the Jolson Encino ranch home—Al was reading the morning newspaper, and Ruby, as was her custom, was reading the gossip columns and sipping her coffee.

Suddenly there was a sob from Ruby.

Doll face, you cryin'?

Oh, Al, what am I going to do? Here's an item that says Winchell has written a story linking me to gang life.

Al looked at her with an unbelieving stare.

There must be some mistake, kiddo.

No mistake. Read for yourself. Oh, Al, that isn't fair. You know I've had nothing to do with that sort of people.

Of course not, Ruby. I'm surprised at Winchell. Why should he do that? Nobody—not even Winchell—is going to taint your name.

Al was wondering what to do about it. Well, he'd see his lawyer. The matter would be settled at once, and legally.

Now, look, Ruby, don't you worry about it and spoil your day. I'll have my lawyer nip this in the bud, pronto.

Al, honey, I hope we will be able to stop him.

Sure we will, Honey Chile. Just leave it to your ol' Jolie.

Ruby was mollified for the time being. She felt confident the matter would go no further and tried to put it from her mind. In time the wound eased. She went out to parties and shows with Al. Life resumed its normal stride.

On a July evening in that year of 1933 they attended boxing matches, as was their custom, at the Hollywood Bowl. They had just made themselves comfortable during a preliminary bout, when Jolson spied Winchell sitting not too far away.

Something snapped within Al. He sprang up and, without even excusing himself, made a beeline for Winchell. Quickly he stood directly over the columnist. Winchell looked up, smiled when he saw his old friend.

Winchell, you go any further with that story about my wife having any connection with gangsters and I'll sue you for all you've got.

Al, you don't understand—

Al's temper boiled over, exploded, and before he himself knew what had happened, he had socked Winchell with a hard right to the jaw. Winchell, shaken and swept off his feet by surprise, rose in an effort to defend himself. Jolson's right shot out again, striking Winchell another blow on the cheek and this time the columnist went down.

The boxing fans were all watching the impromptu bout in their midst instead of the professional match in the ring. The police restored order. Winchell received medical attention and Al went back to a frantic Ruby.

Al, for heaven's sake, you didn't have to do that. I thought you said you were going to have your lawyer handle this.

Ruby, I'm sorry. I saw red. I lost my temper.

I'm sorry, too, said Ruby. And believe me, this isn't the end of it. Maybe you made it worse.

Now, baby, he had it coming.

Yes, but through the law. You didn't have to wallop him. You could have crippled the poor man.

Poor man? Whose side you on?

Don't act like a child, Mr. Jolson.

Sometimes I can't understand you, Ruby. I did this because of you.

You didn't have to act like a—a thug.

Honey Chile!

Oh, I'm sorry, Al. I'm to blame anyway. Please take me home.

They left the arena, and for the rest of the evening there was a strained silence between them. Al made several attempts at reconciliation but Ruby was not too cooperative.

Her fears of trouble were not unfounded.

Next morning the papers were full of the incident. Then the evening papers followed suit and so the whole country was informed of the impromptu bout. Al Jolson became, unexpectedly, a fisticuff champion without portfolio.

There were, of course, repercussions in the form of reports that Winchell was formulating a suit against Al for $500,000. At the same time this was the starting point of a well-publicized feud between the two.

These developments provoked Ruby, and the tranquility of the Jolson household was disturbed.

Al had remarked to reporters who were describing him as the Hollywood Carnera (after the massive Italian heavyweight contender), "A man can sing 'Mammy' songs until his knee is worn tissue-paper thin, and the public pretty soon pushes him into the sidelines, but let him sock a columnist and, man, he becomes suddenly world famous again."

But despite all the publicized animosity between the two men, before long Jolson simmered down and realized the brashness and recklessness of his action.

He heard from a mutual friend that Winchell was suffering from some sort of nervous itch. At once Jolson sent the columnist a jar of his private "sure-cure" salve. This marked the official end of the feud and thereafter they were, as before, on a friendly basis, and the whole subject of the offending story was dropped and forgotten.

Jolson himself, at this time, had a regular stock of remedial medicines, pills, and salves for various ailments, real or imaginary. He was always trying one elixir or another for his throat, his stomach, his wind, and his so-called rheumatic pains; he experimented secretly with vitality pills.

During this period, while Ruby was busy with the starring roles in such pictures as *Forty-Second Street, Gold-Diggers of 1933,* and *Flirtation Walk* with co-star Dick Powell, Al received bit parts from Warners which gave him a little something to do after his radio contract had expired. Epstein did his best to snare a renewal of the contract or a program on another network, but all he could garner were spasmodic guest spots. Into the radio field, as into other areas of entertainment, had come a tidal wave of new and powerful personalities who had brought with them new styles, novel formats that captured the fancy of the fickle public.

Red Skelton, an amazing new comedian; Rudy Vallee, with his "Hi-ho Everybody"; Edgar Bergen and his ageless Charlie McCarthy; George Burns and Gracie Allen, with Gracie's "You say that to all the girls, George"; Eddie Cantor, with his "potatoes are cheaper"; Joe Penner, with his "Wanna buy a duck?"; Kate Smith, with her "When the Moon Comes Over the Mountain"; Jack Benny, with his "Jello Again"; Jack Pearl, with his "Vas You Dere, Sharlie?"; Paul Whiteman, with his Gershwin's *Rhapsody in Blue*; Phil Baker, with his "Bottle" and "Beetle" foils; Bing Crosby, with his "When the Blue of the Night Meets the Gold of the Day"; Ben Bernie, with his "Yowsa, Yowsa"; Amos 'n' Andy, with Andy's "I'se regusted"; and scores of others.

2

Something was missing in the Jolson marriage and it was Ruby herself who brought that up one evening as they were sitting on the veranda.

Al, it just struck me, we're married five years, and no children.

Al caught his breath. He felt that same familiar guilt. I know, Ruby.

I'm sorry about that, she said. I've always wanted children but I suppose we can't help that.

Al nodded. He was silent, staring off into the early darkness, watching the stars twinkling above the pine trees at the edge of his land. The sounds of innumerable insects came to his ears. It was too quiet, too peaceful here for him. Strange that he should feel a longing for the sights and sounds of a Broadway he had vowed to forget.

Al, honey—

Yes, Ruby.

I still want children.

Sure, baby. We'll have them—yet.

Al, you're broadminded, I know. Once you told me you'd be willing to adopt a child if we didn't have our own.

Any time, Ruby.

As soon as I'm through with the picture I'm doing we'll go through with that. Okay, Al?

Anything you say, Ruby.

He was thinking of another day, another Mrs. Jolson, when this subject had come up. There would always be the question of children. It was something Ruby had dreamed about since her first doll.

He rose and paced the floor of the veranda. He had to do something to break this monotony. It was getting him down, but good. He felt himself being wasted—disintegrating by degrees. He had to do something for excitement. Ruby had her career; her life was full, but his was incomplete. Tomorrow he would go to the track. Excitement. To him there was nothing more satisfying than the track. In the evenings he'd have his card games. He had become an habitué of the racetrack.

He bet heavily. Usually he lost. There were days when he dropped five or six grand, sometimes as much as ten grand.

He buried himself in card games, losing continually in these, but it compensated for hurt feelings about Ruby's career. Once they had been very close; they had confided in each other their hopes, their dreams. Now she had her own world of a movie queen from which he felt excluded. Despite his desire to be nonchalant about it, the embers of resentment glowed ever brighter within him.

In the summer of 1935 Ruby took a vacation from her film work. They visited an adoption agency. Al was happy about this; it might break down that barrier between them, a wall that thickened with the advancement of her career.

The adoption board, on making its investigation, noted the comfortable, adequate ranch home, the favorable surroundings. There was also the assurance that Mrs. Jolson would end her career abruptly as soon as a child entered their home. Under these conditions, which were certified in the report of the investigator, the Jolsons were notified in surprisingly quick time that they would receive a seven-week-old son into their home.

We'll name him Al, Jr., said Ruby.

3

It was difficult for Al Jolson to believe it was happening to him, but for the first time he found himself without engagements, nor the prospects of any. Epstein told him one morning: Al, there's something happening which maybe we didn't see too close. But it's happening. There's a new trend in singing, and the people go for it. It's what they call crooning, like Rudy Vallee, Bing Crosby, Dick Powell—all making tremendous hits. Reminds me of the old days when you were in their place.

But, Eppy, this crooning—there's no voice in it.

The people don't seem to mind. Maybe they got tired of listening to big voices. Now they want peace and quiet, and so they're getting it.

Does that mean I've gotta croon?

Not you, Al. You're not the type. You're strictly for full voice delivery, but the public—well—they have put thumbs down on your kind, but definitely. They all know you and what you can do. That puts the stamp on you—obsolete. Like a piece of machinery.

Al paced the floor of his living room. He stopped at the window and looked out at the California landscape. Then he turned again to Epstein.

Eppy, the way they used to listen to me—I had them hypnotized. You know that, Eppy!

Sure I do, Al. But what was new then is old today. Admit it. There's a new generation. They like their own type of music and it's not the type of the twenties. Maybe it's better. Anyway there's more to it. You were the one that first pushed this jazz singing and they've taken it and refined it and added to it. So it's not the same any more.

Al stared at Epstein. The meaning of Lou's words engraved itself in his mind. It was a new public that had no use for him. Yes, Epstein was right, as usual. Jolson was obsolete.

Al envisioned the days stretching ahead of him in an endless procession. A fear took hold of him. What could he turn to?

Eppy, what am I supposed to do?

If I know you, Al, you'll find something.

4

After Lou had gone, Al sat in the living room alone. Ruby was out with Al, Jr., visiting some of her neighbors. On an impulse he placed one of his hit records on the phonograph, "Swanee" on one side and "My Mammy" on the other. He sat down on the sofa and listened. Memories came back to him of another, a gayer time, when he had been king of Broadway. He listened to the recording of his voice and he still couldn't understand why the present generation had chosen to push aside a Jolson for a Vallee or a Crosby.

Al was worried, too, about Ruby. She would get tired, sooner or later, or having a man about the house who did nothing—a "has been" who had lost his place in the world.

He remained on the sofa as the twilight shadows gathered close about him. He didn't move even when Ruby with Al, Jr., came into the house.

Jolson took the boy into his arms. Ruby laid her hand on her husband's shoulder.

Al, what's wrong? You look ill.

I'm getting sick and tired of hanging around the house doing nothing. I tell you, I've got to find something—I'd even go back to burlesque.

Al, don't you think you've had enough of the stage for a while? There's plenty of work right here on this ranch.

Ruby, I'm no farmer. Besides, farming gives me the blues. If I could get some spot, maybe in a night club. I can still wow them. I tell you, I'm the same old Al Jolson.

Ruby's face flushed. All these years she had always babied him, acceded to his demands. Why didn't he grow up? But now something seemed to click inside her. He deserved a scolding.

Al, when will you settle down? We have a nice home, we have Al, Jr. We're a family. But all you think about is a career on the stage—as though you were just starting out. You're always talking about making a comeback, and going through the whole routine again. Al, you've done your share. Let the new ones do theirs. Don't you see?

Jolson stared at his wife. She was young enough to be of that new generation that had rejected him.

Baby, you don't like the way I sing.

Al, honey, anyone who doesn't like the way you sing is a fool.

Jolson's eyes smarted.

Ruby, I flew off the handle again—

Al, we're beginning to snap at each other. That frightens me. Shall we go to dinner?

His temper subsided. He looked at her in hang-dog fashion.

Baby, I'm sorry. I've been a dog—and a mean one.

He put one arm about her, while the other held Al, Jr. Son, I'm goin' to buy you the biggest set of trains in Los Angeles, and we'll put them up together. Okay, boy?

Al, Jr., gurgled up at Al, Sr.

27

1

In the middle thirties, to fill the crying need of the talkies for romantic leading men who were also articulate, came the invasion from Broadway of stars like Rudy Vallee, Tony Martin, and Don Ameche, good-looking and top-flight singers; Jack Haley and Georgie Jessel, besides singing, with a flair for comedy; Charles Laughton and Leslie Howard, British dramatic imports; Nelson Eddy, musical comedy star; Paul Muni, master of characterization. Hollywood's own contribution to the talking male personnel included such luminaries as Gary Cooper, Clark Gable, Warner Baxter, William Powell, Robert Taylor, and Spencer Tracy. With this array serving the public's every taste for personality and talent on the screen, Al Jolson found himself gradually but surely being pushed into the background, out of focus of the camera's eye, being thrown a bone now and then by Warner Brothers.

Another batallion of masculine screen giants almost completed the blackout for Al Jolson—Eddie Cantor, Robert Montgomery, James Cagney, George Arliss, Lionel Barrymore, Ronald Coleman, Fred Astaire, and the new King of Hollywood, John Barrymore.

Suddenly Al Jolson's own light dimmed in this dazzling galaxy. He was glad enough to get roles in the film productions of *Wonderbar* and *Go Into Your Dance* in 1935, though they were almost ignored by the public.

Al and Ruby, to the outside world, seemed a well-adjusted couple, and with their adopted son, Al, Jr., there appeared to be now a completeness in the Jolson abode.

Al tried to interest himself in the work on the ranch, tending the orange grove, the vegetable crops, the horses. Al, Jr., romped about the place and found his father a great pal, but Al, as he had often asserted, did not find full satisfaction in farm work. The old call of Broadway was still audible and he fought a losing battle against it.

His future appeared drab. This inactivity and hermit-like existence was not for him. He grew restless; he returned to the racetrack and resumed his gambling. Epstein, in answer to Ruby's plea, worked hard to get Al suitable engagements, and did secure periodic radio guest appearances or benefit spots. But it seemed that there was no eager audience for Al's type of singing.

This state of affairs played havoc with Al's morale. He became curt with Ruby, bridled at her comments on his gambling excesses or his brooding, unpredictable conduct. She found living with him increasingly difficult. They would sit in the same room for hours, their conversation limited to a few brief comments about the weather or the neighbors.

For him at this time it was a period of involuntary exile. He walked about the precincts of his ranch, trying to accustom himself to this new mode of existence. Jolson was, primarily, a man of action. He could not remain static and enjoy the overflowing charm and beauty of the countryside about him— the forests, the undulating hills, the mountains in the background. Every now and then the craving to face an audience seized him and he would suffer frustration.

His temper was sharp these days. He increased his visits to the racetracks. He played cards almost nightly. He did not laugh so much as in the old days. The clowning had almost gone out of him. He spent less and less time with his son. He would start a game with the boy and then stop suddenly in the middle of it, get

into his car and drive off to the track, or join the boys in Encino in the eternal card game.

He woke in the mornings, confused, hesitant. Life for him seemed to have no purpose. The great well of energy within him boiled and seethed like a volcano, with no outlet.

And yet, he knew that he still had his talent, his voice. He could sing as well as ever—if only they would permit him. But there were no offers, and Epstein, despite his efforts, could land nothing suitable. Of course, there were always the cheap bistros, the honky-tonks, and, as a last resort, burlesque. But Epstein would never permit Al to disgrace himself. Al, you don't need the money. If you can't sing in a fit place, then you won't sing at all.

Al shrugged. Warners hand me a crumb once in a while, but I tell you I'm a forgotten man. I never thought this would happen to me. Me—the great Al Jolson—the guy who used to pack them in like sardines.

Epstein told him to calm down. Look around you, Al. Exit blackface. Enter the handsome romantics. These boys croon lullabyes to the female of the species. The music is called "swing."

And a new dance is born—the "jitterbug." To the jitterbuggers you are ancient history. Their word for it is "corn." The world changes. Sometimes we can't change with it because we are what we are. Besides, youth always has the advantage.

I think I understand, Eppy. But I still say Jolie ain't finished. I can still tell them, "Folks, you ain't heard nothin' yet."

Sure you can, Al, but there's one thing they can't take away from us—a good game of pinochle.

So they played cards—the avenue of escape.

3

Ruby had just finished giving Al, Jr., his evening bath. She watched her husband at the table in a card duel with Epstein. Of late Al had grown resentful of her own calm, secure hold on life. At times he accused her of pitying him, and he wanted no pity. She was remembering that a day earlier, Al had told her, Look, baby, Jolie's comin' back, understand? You think I'm through. You think I'm an old "has-been." Maybe you're sorry you married me.

Al, why do you talk to me like that?

It's the truth, ain't it?

It's not the truth. I am not sorry I married you.

Ruby, you were too young to see your mistake.

Al, please—

The way you look at me sometimes—I know you're pitying me.

Al, for heaven's sake, you don't know what you're saying.

He looked at her for a tense moment. Then he slumped down on the sofa. Honey Chile, I'm all kinds of a fool.

Ruby sat down beside him. She took his hand. Al, I know how you feel. Nobody has forgotten you. All those great performances—

Al glanced at her, his eyes moist. You're an angel.

She stroked his forehead with gentle fingers.

Al said, Ruby, I'm sorry. Another one of my tantrums. I wonder if you can forgive your ol' Jolie?

Of course.

Ruby, doll, you're my whole life now. You and Al, Jr.

You have lots of friends, Al. Don't you know that?

4

As time went on, uneasiness developed between Al and Ruby when they had to spend hours in each other's company.

One solution of this was for Al to escape to his card games and his group of friends in Encino or Hollywood.

When Ruby would mention that Al's gambling might influence their son, Jolson would lose control of his volatile temper. He

always had the feeling that Ruby, being so much younger than he, had no right to tell him what to do, though in the beginning he had not minded it and had considered it rather cute.

But now advice from her only irritated him, brought to his attention this other growing impotence on his part—the matter of his career. The World's Most Unwanted Entertainer.

Ruby found her own life dull, unsatisfactory, even lonely. Al's old buoyancy, his bouncing good humor which she had admired and loved so much, was now replaced by an unbecoming taciturnity.

Al, what's happened to you? You used to be so jolly.

I used to be King of Broadway too.

Al, why don't you stop living in the past?

You think I'm finished. Remember, I told you Jolie never quits.

Al, every time I say something you take it as an insult.

Now wait a minute, baby—

Oh, leave me alone.

Al hurried out of the house, got into his car and drove off. Any place would be better than to continue this nerve-racking tussle.

5

During the latter thirties Jolson continued to receive supporting and bit assignments in Warner Brothers productions.
Apparently Warners were paying him in full for the lift he had
given them with *The Jazz Singer*.

He had his last main role in *The Singing Kid,* followed by a
period of virtual inactivity, alleviated somewhat by the tidbits
thrown his way by the sympathetic Warners and by people who
had known him "when." He was also favored with intermittent
radio guest spots. In 1939 he had a small part in *Rose of
Washington Square,* in which Alice Faye and Tyrone Power were
co-starred. In this picture Jolson repeated his hit songs, "My
Mammy," "Toot-Toot-Tootsie," and "California, Here I Come,"
but his performance was overshadowed by the fine acting of
Power and Miss Faye.

Meanwhile, his homelife was becoming more and more a
strained affair. Ruby, so much younger than Al, and of a volatile,
impressionable nature herself, might have been happier with a

man who was of steadier temperament, or else with one youthful enough to be a partner with her in life's little experiences, the small everyday things which the young find so delightful. She needed someone who would have been patient enough to work at making and keeping her happy; someone on the same level with her, who could laugh at the same things, dream the same dreams of a future, and, for the present, live in the same world; someone, in fact, with whom she could have had the children she had always wanted—her own.

But with Al Jolson, it was a different situation. He lived in a world of his own making, filled with his own ambitions. He did not have the patience or the fresh viewpoint of youth. With him it was the subconscious feeling of his shortage of time. Of this time allotment he had to make thorough use. No waste. No stopping too long to laugh, to play. He truly believed he had a predestined mission to sing to audiences and he had to find the audiences. Otherwise, his golden nuggets of time would be squandered—and that would be failure.

This obsession to keep his career alive raised a curtain between Ruby and himself. Before long the curtain was so thick she could not reach him. At times she felt more like an interloper than a wife.

But all things, good or bad, must eventually come to some sort of ending—or solution.

Al came home one night, and found the house unusually quiet. It was past midnight and no one was home. He assured himself that Ruby, with Al, Jr., might be staying overnight with one of her friends. But the next day he waited in vain; there was no sign of Ruby or the child. Now, Jolie, don't panic, he told himself. He went to the telephone. He phoned her friends, also the neighbors. No, they had not seen her and the boy.

Minutes later the phone rang. It was Ruby.

I'm sorry, Al, but it's better that we live apart for now. Things were getting awkward between us. Maybe matters will adjust themselves. Junior is fine. You can stop in and see him any time. Please take care of yourself.

That was it. Al had to make his plea, Ruby, listen to your ol' man Jolie. I'm tellin' you, baby, come back and I promise you absolutely I'll be a changed man. Look, I know I've been a bum— a one hundred percent no-goodnik. I admit it. But from now on you're goin' to have a new Jolson. I'm waitin' for you, honey. This shack don't mean a thing without you—and Junior. Please.

Don't beg, Al. I know you mean what you say but I really believe this is better for both of us. Being separated will give us a chance to think over what we're going to do. Good-bye, Al.

Now, baby doll, wait a minute—

The phone clicked. It was over.

6

Once again he was alone—right back where he had been in the beginning. At once he realized that he himself had been at fault. Once again he had permitted his preoccupation with his own career and his own follies to steal his happiness. He felt lost. Yesterday he had a family and a home. Now he had nothing. He walked about the ranch aimlessly.

But he was Al Jolson and, as in critical situations before, hope began to build up within him. Ruby had not actually mentioned a

permanent separation. The way she had spoken could very well imply a temporary split-up. That meant a chance of winning her back.

Al lost no time in paying his first visit to see Ruby and his son, Al, Jr.

When he entered his wife's apartment, he found Ruby showing the child a picture book. Al, Jr., now all of four years, was a cute wide-eyed tot. When he saw his father he held out his hands—Daddy! Daddy!

Al swept the boy up into his arms and lifted him high overhead. How y' doin', Mr. Jolson, Jr.? Is that pretty lady over there treatin' you right? If she ain't, then I'll put her across my knee and give her the spanking of her life!

Ruby laughed. I dare you. The same old Jolie.

The same? No. I won't beat around the bush. How about coming home with me? It will be different now.

Al, I wish I could say Yes. But I can't. There's such a thing as two people not being suited to each other. That might be our problem. Anyway let's try being apart for a while.

Sure, baby. Take your time and think it over. I'll wait. But I'll count every minute. One thing I promise you, sweetheart. You

come back and you'll find me a changed man. My one ambition will be to take care of my family and be the new Jolson I promised.

Al, I believe you, but I don't want to be a drag on you, to interfere with your work. So we'll see. Okay, Al?

Ruby, I'll take the kid for a walk. All right with you?

Of course, Al. He's your son.

Al made more visits to Ruby's apartment. He did not press her too forcefully. He spoke with tact about getting together again. He made his plea each time, as calmly and as gently as he knew how. He tried to put her at ease, so that the way would be open for him to be with her, to talk to her, to spend time with his boy.

But the realization slowly but gradually dawned on him that Ruby might not intend to come back. Her answer was always a negative one, though she always greeted him with that dimpled smile of hers, that twinkle in her eye. On these occasions she seemed to be the very same Ruby he had first met a dozen years ago.

Epstein called at the Jolson ranch often, for he hated to see Al left by himself, living like an exile.

Al, why don't you wise up? If I were in your position—financially—I'd take a boat to South America, Europe, or the

South Sea Islands. I'd travel. I'd have myself a ball. I'd live like a king. Why don't you give yourself a treat? Don't be a *yold*. You had trouble enough in your life. Now enjoy yourself. What will it get you mooning over a lost cause. When a woman says Good-bye, Charlie, she usually doesn't mean Hello.

So you think I've lost Ruby. Eh, Eppy?

You want the truth? Cross Ruby off your list. For you she is already a memory. She belongs to your past. So who wants to live in the past?

She said that to me once—about living in the past. Eppy, what's wrong with me? A man loses his first wife. It may be unavoidable. A man loses his second wife. Well, maybe there was another good reason. But when that same man loses his third one—after twelve years—I tell you that jerk is a no-good guy.

Al, it's the breaks. Like those prize bags we used to sell in the burlesque house I managed in Scranton, back in 1912. You remember. A man bought one, opened it, expecting to find something wonderful. So what did he find? A five-cent ring or maybe the picture of a naked lady stepping into a bath tub. Or maybe an extra piece of milk chocolate. You have some years left. Stop worrying about what you can't get and grab what's easy for you to take.

But, Eppy, I miss her awful. You don't know what her going away did to me. If she'd come back I'd get down on my knees and kiss the ground she walks on. Now you know.

Al, I know one thing. My advice you're not taking.

Eppy, listen to me. Maybe if you talk to her. Tell her how much I need her. That I'm miserable without her and the boy.

All right, so I'll talk to her. I'll be your *shadchen*.

Thanks, Eppy.

Epstein did talk to Ruby. He tried to convince her to return to a heartsick Jolson, but Ruby's answer was brief and final. Lou, I might as well tell you. I don't believe I'll ever go back to him. Tell him that in time he'll find someone much better for him than Ruby Keeler.

Epstein broke this news gently to his friend. Al did not accept the finality of it.

You got the message wrong, Eppy. She's taking time to let things settle a bit. I tell you she'll be back.

28

1

In time he received a formal notification from Ruby's attorney that she had filed for divorce.

Al made no contest. In due time, Ruby was granted the divorce and the custody of Al, Jr., by decree of the court.

Finished. The end of another ecstasy.

For some days he kept to his Encino ranch home, seeing no one, avoiding the press and the curiosity seekers.

Only Epstein was permitted to come and go, and it was he who did his best to bolster Al's ego.

Eppy, I sure was nuts about that gal, and still am. But I guess I never realized how much.

Al, my friend, it's all over.

No. It's not over. I'm goin' to put up a fight to win her back. It's been done before. What the hell's the good of bein' a millionaire if you can't have the wife and kid you love?

Epstein spread his hands and shrugged his shoulders. What could he say to that?

Al, if there's anything I can do—

Eppy, first let me say it's all my fault. Ruby took a beating from me. In my book she's still the prettiest, sweetest, most understanding kid in the world and I probably don't deserve her. But until I win her back, Eppy, you're goin' to have a mighty unhappy mammy singer on your hands.

Epstein shook his head. Look, Al, let's be sensible and grown-up men. What do you want me to do? Name it and I'll do it. And if I can't do it, so I'll jump off a cliff. Okay? Eppy, I've got a plan. It hit me like that. Maybe it's gonna work. I've got to take a chance on it. You with me?

I told you—otherwise the cliff.

Eppy, I want you to get busy on a new show for me. I'm goin' to surprise the show-biz world and the public. I'm headin' back to old Broadway in the biggest, most dazzling show the street's ever seen. Anyway it's been in my mind a long time—to get back before a real audience. I'll show them ol' Jolie is far from through. How does that sound, Eppy, ol' boy?

Sounds okay. But what's that got to do with getting Ruby back?

Tell you in a minute. I don't care how much of my money you spend. Go the limit. I've got a few million. Exactly how much I'll never know. Money I can afford to lose. But I can't afford to lose Ruby.

I still don't see how this is going to help you get her back.

I'll draw you a picture, Eppy. I'm goin' to have Ruby play a role in the show. How about that?

Sounds clever. If she agrees you'd have her on tap all the time, so that you can take up with her where you left off. Nice maneuver. When do I start with the finagling?

Right this minute.

Any ideas about the show? Who, what, where? Enlighten me, Mr. Jolson.

Eppy, listen good. Here's what we'll do. . . .

Epstein was witnessing a miracle. He was listening to a man who had suddenly become alive, tingling, eager. Surely, this was the Al Jolson of the smash hits, the Jolson sweeping his way to the legendary heights, the real Al Jolson.

2

The new show, which was to have the usual Jolson routines, went into rehearsal in the early summer of 1940.

Epstein was fearful of the fact that Jolson was not going to perform in his traditional blackface. At the same time he realized there was a new state of affairs. Minstrels were out of style, and there was pressure against the delineation of characters in burnt cork. Epstein had his doubts about the outcome of Jolson going on in the "natural," doing outmoded routines in the face of the competition of new and modern trends in entertainment. But Al was determined to go through with it, and the sky was the limit. The show, *Hold On to Your Hats,* opened at the Shubert in Philadelphia on September 14.

Jolson, with Epstein as emissary, had convinced Ruby to accept a role in the show, joining the cast when it reached Chicago. This was good enough for Al, who felt that his plans were working out. He soon would have Ruby with him, and that meant he could speak to her whenever opportunity presented itself. Also, he would have his son again. Things were shaping up. It seemed the clouds on his horizon were drifting by.

Hold On to Your Hats was an all-out effort. The book was composed by Guy Bolton, Matt Brooks, and Eddie Davis. Lyrics were written by E. Y. Harburg. Co-producer of the extravaganza was George Hale, with Jolson taking on almost the entire financial burden. The show was staged by Edgar MacGregor and directed by George Hale. Al had secured the services of Catherine Littlefield to create and direct the choreography, and he had spared no expense in collecting a capable cast which included such luminaries as Martha Raye, the wide-mouthed comedienne, Eunice Healey, Jack Whiting, Gil Lamb, Russ Brown, Jinx Falkenburg, Joanne Dru, and a chorus line of delectable cuties.

After a ten-year absence from the theater Al Jolson had come back, but to a strange new world of show biz. It was not, he soon found out, the world he had known.

The attendance was fair, but below expectations, nor was the show to be considered a smash hit in line with the old Winter Garden spectaculars. There were many old timers in the audience who had come to see Al Jolson perform again, and there were the curious who had come to see what all the shouting was about. But though there were such new song numbers as

"Walkin' Along Mindin' My Business," "World Is in My Arms,"
"Don't Let It Get You Down," "There's a Great Day Coming,"
"Would You Be So Kindly," and "Down the Dude Ranch," these
made no special impression on the audience, and Jolson had to
resort to his old standard proven hits. He sang them again in the
Jolsonesque style, his faithful standbys: "My Mammy," "Rock-a-
Bye Your Baby with a Dixie Melody," "Swanee," "Sonny Boy,"
"Toot-toot-tootsie," "You Made Me Love You," "California, Here
I Come," and "April Showers."

When the show had opened there had been a good house, but
as the run continued the box office lagged. The show barely met
its cost of operation. Jolson threw himself wholeheartedly into
his performance, but perhaps there was too much straining on
his part to hold an audience that was now accustomed to
smoother efforts on the part of performers. It was, for the greater
part, a new brand of listeners who already had their relaxed,
sophisticated, streamlined ideals, and in Al Jolson they saw an
oldster, a once-famous star trying desperately to make a
comeback. Though they were sympathetic, they regarded the
strutting figure on the stage as a "dated" ham. And their word for
it, of course, was "corn."

The public was loath to go back; only forward, with new faces,
new modes of singing. It was human nature, and so there were
vacant seats in the theater, more and more with each succeeding
performance.

Jolson was relieved to have the show open in Chicago.

3

Ruby had come east from California to join the show, and
Jolson had arranged for her to stay at a hotel.

Once she was settled, he paid her a visit one early afternoon.
He picked Al, Jr., up and swung him onto his shoulder. How's my
boy, eh? Beautiful mommy treatin' you nice? You be a good kid
and I'll take you to the zoo. See the monkeys.

Wanna see monkeys, daddy.

Pretty soon. Now here's something for you to play with while I speak to your mommy. Al gave his son a tiny Jack-in-the-box he had picked up from a street hawker. Then he seated himself on the divan and looked at Ruby. Baby, I've missed you. Thanks for helping me out with the show.

Al, I thought it would be nice to get back on the stage.

Almost without being aware, he came out with what was in his mind. Ruby, I know you're free now, with the divorce. But you can't stop a guy from making a second try.

Al, we can be good friends.

Ruby, we can be more than that. I want you to know I'm still crazy about you. I blame myself for what's happened. I was a dope.

Don't scold yourself, Al. It was something we couldn't help. If I had had enough will power maybe I would have hung on. But, Al, that would be no good. You don't want a wife that hangs on.

Ruby, remember how it was in the beginning? I mean, it could be that way again. One more chance, baby.

Please, Al. I came here to work in your show.

Okay, sweetheart. Okay. I'll stop pestering you. Good luck in the show.

Now Al knew where he stood thus far. It was apparent that Ruby had not come hoping, as he did, for a reconciliation and a possible remarriage.

With Ruby Keeler now added to the cast, *Hold On to Your Hats* made a better impression, even though Jolson could not make it a hit on his own.

The critics praised various members of the show and commented favorably on the individual supporting performances, but their opinion of Al's own part was only too apparent—a "nostalgic flashback," a "legend on a visit from a horse and buggy era," and a "fond memory come alive, but still a memory."

As the show ran on Ruby remained indifferent to Al's careful advances and suggestions. He was skating on thin ice, for he was in constant dread that he would frighten her off and lose his final chance.

Soon there were items in the newspapers suggesting in no uncertain terms that Al had produced the show with the main objective of bringing Ruby within his reach. Eventually these reached the attention of Ruby herself, and her eyes glowed with a burning resentment against the gossip-mongers.

It seemed one could not remain on a friendly basis with one's divorced husband—there would always be allegations.

On the day before the show closed in Chicago to move to Broadway, Al decided to speak to Ruby and lay his cards on the table. He could not go on like this, hanging by a thread. The matter had to be settled.

He greeted Al, Jr., engaged the tot in an imaginary boxing bout. Then he sang a verse of the boy's favorite—"Camptown Races"—in which the tot seemed to find great delight. Al finished the verse. Daddy, sing again. So Al sang another verse. When he finished, he turned to a smiling Ruby. She seemed more attractive than ever. To Al she was a flower in full bloom. What a *schlemiel* he had been to let her get away from him.

Ruby, you're great in the show. In New York you'll wow them.

Al, I'm not going on with the show.

Now, baby, don't talk like that.

I'm sorry, Al.

The show needs you. As a favor to your ol' Uncle Jolie, don't leave us.

Ruby rose and moved toward him. Al, I thought it would work out but—well—I don't think so now. There are certain rumors cropping up about us being together.

Now, look, baby doll, you're not goin' to let a bunch of busy-bodies interfere with your life?

I'm sorry, Al, but I have no choice. There's Al, Jr., and we're divorced.

Al stood up. He realized that the moment of decision had come. He had to make his plea now. It was his last chance. He had to convince her. He had to make her agree to a reconciliation.

Ruby, I have something to say and I want you to listen.

I'm listening, Al.

You'll admit that we were happy together for quite a time. I know we can make a go of it again, if you come back. We've got a nice place in Encino and the kid can have the time of his life there.

Ruby, I don't know when I will see you again. I know this is my last
chance with you. Come on, baby, make ol' Jolie the happiest guy
in the world. Just one little word Yes. Do I hear it? Will you say it?

She took his hand. Al, don't you realize I've thought about it,
too? I've considered it and reconsidered it. But I always get the
same answer. I am not the one for you. Sooner or later we'd
reach the same point again and it might be worse then.

There was a sinking sensation within him. He saw his hope for
winning back his happiness receding fast.

Ruby, won't I see you again?

Good-bye, Al. And thanks.

He started toward her, as if to kiss her, and she drew back.
Don't kiss me, Al.

He stood there motionless, for one brief moment. Then he
turned to Al, Jr., picked him up and kissed him on the cheek.
Now, looka here, Buster, you be a good boy and do what
Mommy tells you. He put the boy down. He started for the door,
opened it. He heard Ruby say, Al, I want you to come and see
Junior whenever you feel like it.

Sure, Ruby.

He was out of her apartment, and out of her life.

4

He walked back to his hotel, trying to adjust to the new
situation.

If only there were some way he could stop thinking about her;
if only he could stop that ache for her.

He knew he was in for it. He would suffer being away from her
and now she would not come back to him.

If he were a drinking man he could perhaps have drowned his
grief. As it was, he had to go on living and working. There was a
show that had to go on.

From that moment on his heart was not in his performance.

He went through the motions, sang his songs. *Hold On to Your
Hats* began to waver. He himself was surprised it held up as well

as it did. There were people who truly wanted to see Al Jolson, at least once in their lifetime, and so the show limped along to an inevitable demise.

It was with almost a sigh of relief that *Hold On to Your Hats* finally folded in November of 1941, after a total of 158 performances. Once again the Greatest Entertainer in the World found himself cut off from the scene of his former glories.

After the close of the show he become an involuntary member of the unemployed. He was like a man for whom everything has completely stopped. He might have been an exile, banished to spend the remainder of his days in total exclusion from a world he had loved, worked in, been a part of.

It seemed as if that great public, which had once placed wreaths of victory about his head, had suddenly turned its thumbs down, telling him: Jolson, we don't want you any more. You've been replaced. You're through.

He was like a baseball player stepping up to bat and striking out—with Ruby, with Hollywood, with Broadway.

The long, gray days stretched ahead of him, leading into nowhere. He had two hands and could do nothing useful with them. He had no hobby, no other interest in life with which to occupy himself, and make his life meaningful.

He walked the streets of Manhattan and he envied the newsboy on the corner or the bootblack who shined his shoes— they were competent citizens, with a mission to perform.

There were moments when he thought of his family in Washington and that they would be justified in being ashamed of him. Could it be then that after all the triumphant events of his past life, he had reached the end of the road?

He had had his chance to face audiences once more in *Hold On to Your Hats* but he had bungled the opportunity. Now there might be no more chances. Was he finished? He himself would never admit it.

Epstein stood by his friend. Al, do me a favor and enjoy your life. Retire.

Eppy, you're speakin' to Jolie. He never retires. But I did make a mess of things. Eppy, I don't know why you hang around. The general opinion is that I'm done. Maybe that's your opinion too.

Epstein grinned. He was a patient man, but a tenacious one. Al, my opinion is you'll never be done, and anybody who thinks so is crazy. Even if the public today doesn't want any part of you, Al Jolson won't be forgotten. But right now I have an idea. Let's pack ourselves off to Florida for the winter. You can spend your time at the racetrack and sunbathe on the beach. You always forget your troubles when you're betting on the nags.

Maybe that's all I'm good for now.

So what's wrong with that? Everybody should be an expert at something. You can be an expert horse better. Maybe you'll teach me to be one too.

Eppy, you're a pal. What's for tonight? Let's have ourselves some pinochle.

But no matter what Al did, visiting the track, playing cards, taking in the Broadway shows, the feeling of being a "has-been" grew upon him.

He watched other, younger performers reach toward the heights that he had once trod, and he marveled at their amazing new skills. And then he would experience once again that urge to face an audience himself, to watch their faces as he sang to them, to inspire them and be himself inspired.

The image of Ruby would come back to him in the nights when he was alone, and the sense of lost happiness saddened him.

If she were here beside him, he wouldn't have cared about anything else. He would have basked in the warmth of her charms and lived for the purpose of making her and Al, Jr., happy. He would have gone back to Encino and finally settled down.

5

This was a period in Jolson's life when he found himself a lonely unwed man, out-dazzled by the tremendous legit and musical shows on the Broadway that had turned its face from him— shows that brought a new artistry and sophistication to the theater that made Al's former Winter Garden hits pale by comparison. Jolson himself witnessed many of these spectacles, which only added to his despondency by emphasizing his own ineffectiveness.

Among the legit hits were *Victoria Regina*, with the twinkling Helen Hayes; *The Philadelphia Story*, with the debutante charmer Katherine Hepburn; *The Little Foxes*, with the amazing husky-voiced Tallulah Bankhead; *There Shall Be No Night*, with the engaging footlight sophisticates, Lynn Fontanne and Alfred Lunt; *Tobacco Road,* a revealing and astonishing cross-section of the Southland's "white trash" that broke records in a seven and a half year run on Broadway.

Jolson shook his head at his own eclipse in the blinding glare of such musical comedy spectaculars as *Oklahoma,* the Rogers and Hammerstein masterpiece in which Celeste Holm and Alfred Drake took first honors; *Winged Victory,* an Air Force extravaganza in which Lee J. Cobb, Peter Lind Hayes, and Edmund O'Brien starred; and *Something for the Boys,* produced by the energetic Mike Todd, written by Cole Porter and featuring the devastating Ethel Merman, scored with Allen Jenkins and wide-eyed Betty Garret. Then there was the fabulous Ziegfeld Follies, 1943, featuring the young Milton Berle, the lithesome Ilona Massey, and that impeccable gentleman's gentleman, Arthur Treacher.

Jolson, almost convinced now that his place in the American theater was a matter of past record, would slink out of his hotel, get into his automobile, and order Jimmie, his chauffeur, to drive out of New York and keep on driving. Sometimes, these drives with the perplexed chauffeur continued for days, westward across the states until they ended up, at last, in San Francisco or Los Angeles, with a final stayover at Al's Encino ranch—all this against the argument of Epstein for Al to rest on his laurels, to announce his retirement.

It seemed that Jolson had to run away from his own sense of inadequacy, for as soon as they had arrived on the West Coast, he wanted Jimmie to drive back again, across the country, to the East Coast, and Manhattan. There was one occasion on which he ordered his chauffeur to drive from New York to Encino, while Jolson himself took passage on a steamer that sailed southward on the Atlantic into the Caribbean, through the Panama Canal, and out into the Pacific, finally docking at San Francisco. Here Al boarded a train for Encino.

It was a lonely life—but eventually he began to understand there was no escape. He had to accept the inevitable—that he was finished.

But he still felt that longing to entertain seething within him, seeking an outlet, like a welling current that couldn't be dammed. He was ever watchful, looking out for some stray opportunity that might place him before an audience again. He ignored Epstein's continuing plea, Al, why do you aggravate yourself? You've already accomplished more than any dozen of these newcomers. Take it easy, and enjoy life.

But being alone with no one to look after, he had no positive incentive. Again and again he felt sorry he couldn't drink to forget.

On December 7, 1941, he had received a jolt that knocked him out of his impasse. Over the radio came the announcement: "Japanese planes have just bombed Pearl Harbor." At once he put everything else from his mind except the desire to help.

There must be something he would be able to do. He was too old to carry a gun, but surely there was a task for him in which he could best serve.

Lou Epstein, after several months, came to him with a bit of information that thrilled Al, and lifted him out of his doldrums.

BOOK FIVE

War Years
1942–1950

Troup Entertainer in World War II and Korean War

1

Al, there's an organization forming to entertain the American troops. They call themselves the USO.

Jolson shrugged. Eppy, another alphabet group. They've got a million of them.

Al, this is something you can fit into. The USO recruits entertainers and ships them overseas or into the camps in the states to perform for the soldier kids. Great for their morale. How does that sound to you?

Eppy, you've saved my life. Where do I go? What do I do?

I'll take you tomorrow. Before you'll know it, you'll be having yourself some of the biggest audiences in the world—real young audiences. GI Joes, they call 'em. And you're the guy to cheer them up, if anyone can.

Eppy, do you think they'll know me?

Know you? Look, my friend, their mothers probably told them all about you when they talked about their girl days.

Eppy, you're a dog.

2

In a private's uniform during World War II, Jolson, the first show-biz notable to volunteer his talent, toured the front lines of the American and Allied forces. The boys looked upon a

bareheaded, balding, graying man, swinging his arms in that
Jolsonesque manner and bringing to them the repertoire of his
famous songs, including their favorite—which he was called upon
to sing over and over again—"Sonny Boy." Perhaps, it reminded
them of Junior back home, toddling about the house and waiting
for his soldier daddy to return from the wars.

Now it came back to him—the birth of that song. He enjoyed
going over the incident in his mind. Back in 1929, while filming
The Singing Fool, he had thought a song would come in handy in
which he talked to his three-year-old son. But he had had none
ready and no one at the studio had been able to think of anything
appropriate. At once Jolson had thought of his friend, Buddy De
Sylva, who was vacationing at that time in Atlantic City. Al had
wasted no time. He had phoned De Sylva who had listened to his
problem.

How old is the boy? De Sylva had asked.

About three, Al had answered. And he's standin' right at my knee and lookin' up at me.

Good, De Sylva had declared. Two lines I've got already:

Climb upon my knee, Sonny Boy—
Although you're only three, Sonny Boy—

Jolson had been delighted. Great! Great! But what about the rest of it?

You're going to finish it yourself. You know you can do it.

And Al had done it, and that song had scored an emotional triumph in the picture; thereafter it had been brought to the public in the form of sheet music and records to garner another fortune into the Jolson treasury. But that was ancient history.

Now, after thirteen years, "Sonny Boy" was the favorite song of his GI audiences on the battlefronts.

3

Jolson, standing on a hastily built platform stage somewhere in the Aleutians, performed in his army issue blouse—bareheaded, though the thermometer registered far below freezing.

Harry Akst, his accompanist at the piano, begged him to wear a hat, lest he catch cold, but Al always laughed about this and ignored Akst's concern. After that, Jolson singing at the front lines in an Italian mountain glade against the thunder of field artillery, singing in a freezing rain or a cascade of heavy snowflakes in northern France, singing with enemy planes zooming by overhead and dropping their deadly payloads on the sand-dune beaches of North Africa, singing in the vineyards turned into battlefields in Sicily, singing in the jungles of the South Pacific, singing until his amazing voice hoarsened and his heart protested and his lungs almost burst, until the fangs of malaria licked at him and he was carefully hauled to a hospital and tucked into bed, his body and mind tortured by the white-hot breath of the fever.

An iron man, a human dynamo—so often was he called that—
but there was a limit, and if Jolson himself did not observe that
limit, then nature stepped in and forced the issue.

As soon as he was well enough, he returned to his USO battlefront bookings. The authorities suggested a rest. And Jolson's
answer? Rest? The hell with that.

4

In 1943 Jolson returned to the States and was stricken with a
serious attack of recurrent malaria, complicated by a rundown
physical condition. For days he lay helpless in a hospital. His
recovery was slow.

Epstein had been a daily visitor, bringing him the news of the
war and how the tide of battle was beginning to turn. Al writhed in
his inactivity, and his restlessness grew hour by hour. Epstein
shook his head, thinking that here was a man who could not
remain still, who had to be moving and doing.

Al, my friend, maybe you'll take it easy now.

Sure I will, Eppy. As soon as I feel strong enough I'll be off to see
the boys again.

You mean you're going back with the USO?

The war ain't over yet, Eppy.

Al, you're not a well man. You've been a serious hospital
case—you're subject to malaria attacks. You were almost a
gonner—and you're going back?

But Epstein knew it was useless to argue with Al Jolson. Once
Al's mind was set on a plan, that was it, come hell or high water.

And Al did fly back, this time via South America.

In a narrative letter to *Variety* Al wrote in that year 1943:

"I never knew such hell-holes existed. On this trip Akst and I,
on our first stop out of New York, landed at Georgetown, British
Guiana. We arrived at 4 P. M., did two shows and left by plane for
Belem, Brazil. We had some powdered eggs and powdered milk
for breakfast, then clowned around and did a few songs for the
boys till show time. At our regular show, we performed before

3,000 G. I.'s. Right after that, we did another show for the Navy and a third for the local population. The mosquitos gave us a rough time all night but we had to get up at 5 A. M. in order to make the plane to Recife. After our show there we flew back to Natal, did a number of hospital shows and got up at four the next morning to fly the South Atlantic. It was raining cats and dogs at four, so we waited around till the weather cleared up and, in the meantime, did another hospital show.

"We finally made the nine-hour flight across the ocean. Arrived at Dakar at 9 P. M. What a hole this is! We had a dinner of spam and atabrine tablets, then raced by jeep over dusty roads for twenty miles to a G. I. camp. We had to do a big outdoor show in darkness because the lights went blooey, but luckily there was an army truck that put the spotlight on me so the boys could see me. Would you believe it, it began to rain just as I sang 'April Showers!' On the way back to Dakar the jeep overturned in the mud, but some engineers helped us out. We did a number of shows the next few days for the Air Corps, Signal Corps, and Engineers. Then we took a bumpy plane ride over the Atlas Mountains, arrived in French Morocco, and got our first good night's sleep in weeks. We did a few shows there and flew here to Marakesh. We're eating spam today and we've got three shows to do tonight and then we'll be off again, but after all, who are we to complain?"

It was the same story repeated. He joked with the GI's, he sang to them the Jolson songs: "Swanee," "You Made Me Love You," "My Mammy," "Waitin' for the Robert E. Lee," "Toot-Toot-Tootsie," "California, Here I Come," "April Showers," "Rainbow 'Round My Shoulder," "Blue Skies," and, of course, the most requested, "Sonny Boy." He was received by the boys with great affection. Wherever he went they listened to him almost with reverence. Here was a man, not in good health, who did not have to do this, who could have lived in the lap of luxury, away from all this hardship and danger. Yet here he was, trying to make them feel better, singing to them, talking to them, as though they were all his own sons.

And out of these experiences a lasting friendship grew between this aging performer and his youthful uniformed listeners. They would carry the memory of him through the years, when they'd resume their civilian pursuits.

And wherever Al traveled and performed, he felt that he was merely trying to pay back a part of the debt he owed to America for all it had given to him. At the same time he was happy to stand in front of an audience again, to be appreciated, applauded, and beseeched for encores. There were times when he thought he was back in the old Winter Garden, putting over his best performances, listening again to the approving roar of the crowd as he finished each smash number.

That was his recompense.

Once more he was recognized, he was important, he was part of what was going on.

It was a fulfillment that erased his previous sense of inadequacy. There was a sparkle in his eye, a spring to his step.

5

Back in the States in the summer of 1944 he entertained the troops in their camps and in the military hospitals. Epstein tagged along, watching over him like a mother hen. It was while singing to and quipping with the boys at a hospital at Hot Springs, Arkansas, that Jolson noticed a dark-eyed, dark-haired willowy beauty in nurse's uniform sitting with a few of the other nurses in the front row and watching him steadily.

On the following morning, with Epstein and Harry Akst waiting in the car, Al was getting his gas ration ticket for the trip to his next stop, which was San Antonio, Texas. He saw the dark-eyed beauty approaching with an autograph book in her hand.

Mr. Jolson, sir, may I have your autograph?

She spoke with a marked Southern accent.

Sure thing, honey chile.

He signed his name. Then he looked at her closer. You were the one sitting in the front row last night at the performance. Like the show?

Mr. Jolson, I simply adore your singing. I have some of your records at home.

Honey, you're wonderful. Well, next stop, San Antonio, Texas. See you.

She stood there without moving, watched him get into his car, watched him drive off. He waved at her. Epstein shook his head in resignation. When they arrived at their destination, another military hospital, Al could not forget that enchanting girl, her understanding eyes, her smile, her cute Southern accent, her graceful movements. He remembered the way she had looked at him, as though she had been sorry to see him leave. The fact that she was so much younger than he did not seem to bother him in the least. He knew only that he would have liked to learn more about her. He didn't even know her name.

He felt the urgency of keeping her in his life. A girl like that came along only once in a lifetime. She spoke to me, Eppy. None of the other babes did that. Jolie, you old lover boy, looks like something is in the wind, he addressed himself. Eppy frowned. Not again, Al. Not again.

Al made his way to a phone and called back to the hospital at Hot Springs and asked for the commanding officer. Sir, this is Al Jolson—

Yes, Al. Something we can do?

Yep. Name of that dark-eyed young nurse with the Southern accent so thick you can cut it with your pen-knife.

Got you, Al. Her name is Erle Chennault Galbraith, age 21. X-ray technician. Niece of General Chennault. You know, of the "Flying Tigers." Her father is a Southern colonel of the old school. Still excited about the Civil War. Her mother, old South social register. Enough?

Commander, you're a pal.

Anything else, Al?

If you get an inside tip on a good horse, let me know.

So her name was Erle. Unusual but nice.

When Al returned to the waiting car, Eppy seemed to read Al's thoughts. You called back about that black-eyed *shiksa*.

Al said, Now look, Eppy, no law against a guy getting a line on a gal.

Epstein and Akst exchanged wise glances. Akst was diplomatically silent. Eppy couldn't hold back the words. Al, right now you're a fairly happy man. You're working. Everywhere you go the kids like you. So why make complications? Believe me, my friend, you're playing with dynamite. That kid's a child alongside of you. Al, why don't you wise up?

Al patted Epstein on the shoulder. Eppy, old boy, you're way ahead of me. All I did was find out about a girl's name. Maybe I could get her a spot in Hollywood. She's pretty, real class, and smart as a whip.

Epstein shrugged. So now you're dishing out movie careers to good-looking chickens. Such a hobby I would like myself. But the complications I don't like.

Harry Akst grinned. Come on, Eppy, let Al alone. He's free and over twenty-one.

Free he is now, said Epstein. When the complications come, freedom is *kaput.*

Al continued entertaining the G.I.'s wherever the USO sent him, and often paid his own expenses in order to bring his show into hospitals and camps not pinpointed by the organization.

And then, suddenly, two explosions in Japan of what they called "atom bombs," one over Hiroshima and the other over Nagasaki, and the Japanese military forces surrendered, and the war was over. With the cessation of all hostilities, the world went wild with relief and indulged in a joyous celebration, but for Al it marked the end of his newly found audiences. Once again he was on the sidelines, as unwanted as before.

Harry Cohen of Columbia pictures gave Jolson a job as producer, and within a brief time he found himself sitting in a comfortable, spacious office, elegantly furnished and decorated. He sat in a deeply upholstered chair in front of a wide glass-topped mahogany desk and waited for something to happen. Cohen had promised him a script as soon as he found one suitable to Al's experience. Meanwhile it was a matter of sitting through an inactivity that almost drove him frantic.

This was not to Al's liking at all. He made use of his time by writing letters to Miss Galbraith, asking her to come to Hollywood and join the Columbia Studio starlet training group at $75 a week. In his letters Al assured Erle that she had the beauty, the intelligence to be successful. Besides, he would be there to help her, "so why not take a chance?"

But Miss Galbraith indicated that she really had no particular inclination to be an actress and wouldn't it be a waste of time and money on the part of the studio?

Al read her letters and fell to dreaming over them, envisioning the lovely Southern beauty standing before him, smiling at him.

How would it be to take her out, to dine, to dance, to show her a real time?

Then he reminded himself that his motive was to build a career for her, to make her a star. It was purely a matter of business. Impersonal. He must not forget Eppy's warning about "complications." But he wrote to her again, and when he received her letter advising him that she was coming to Hollywood, his heart leaped, and he wanted to sing a song right there in his impressive office. Harry Cohen, passing by and noticing Al's sudden elation, shook his head and decided that Jolson had finally won the daily double at the Santa Anita track.

30

1

When Erle walked into Jolson's office, it was a high moment in the singer's life. As he had dreamed, there she was—standing in front of him, in all her gracious, refined beauty.

Well, here I am, Mr. Jolson. Hope I don't disappoint you too much.

Honey, you can never disappoint anybody. First thing, you deserve a welcoming ceremony. You're going to lunch with me, and I'll introduce you to people.

From that moment on the current of Erle Galbraith's life quickened considerably, as Al escorted her about the studio, introducing her to the executives, the stars, and the hopeful newcomers like herself.

Erle began her training in the Columbia Studio beginners class. The coach of elocution and vocal control had a word with Al.

That Southern belle—I'm afraid we have a problem.

How come? asked Jolson.

Her accent. We'll never iron that out. It's too much a part of her. Generations behind it.

You mean, she won't make it?

Frankly, no.

When the coach had left, Al rose and paced the floor of his office. He realized he had pulled a boner. He should have known about her accent. He would have to break the news to her— somehow—but later.

He was attentive to her every desire. He took her out on the town and they became a familiar twosome in the Hollywood night clubs—dining, dancing.

At the same time Jolson was disappointed with his role as producer. It seemed that the studio heads were not anxious to trust him with the actual production of a picture. He just sat at his big desk, day after day, and he was nearing the breaking point. He had to correct the situation, and fast—before I go completely nuts, he said.

Epstein tried to convince him to stay on. Al, I'm talking to you like a father. You've got yourself a nice little office here, comfortable, nobody to bother you. Little by little you'll get into the producing game, and you'll make it, I tell you. Walk out of here and you have nothing. You know how you stand with the public. They're not going to take you back, Al. You've had proof enough of that. Don't be a *chiam yonkel.*

Eppy, once, when I was a kid in a boy's home, they put me in solitary confinement and I screamed and kicked, trying to break out. This office reminds me too much of that place. Eppy, all I do is sit here and kill time, and, pal, that's one thing I can't afford to kill. I wanna sing. Maybe you can get me a few bookings. Anything—entertainments, benefits, society functions—so long as I can face an audience again. What d'you say?

Epstein sighed in resignation. Al, you're stepping out of a nice berth into a jungle. You're asking for trouble, but I can't stop you.

I gotta sing, Eppy. You know that. So try to get me something.

Al quit his job—walked out of his producer's office—and once again tried to break through the barricade for a comeback.

But Epstein had no good news for him.

Al, there just isn't any demand for your type. There's an old man character bit in a movie I ran across today.

Eppy, Al Jolson's not ready for that yet. Keep looking. Maybe a benefit show.

Beset with his own problem, he had put out of his mind the problem of his protégée, Erle Galbraith. She was still with the Columbia Studio, being groomed for bit parts where her personality might fit in. She was trying very hard to smooth out her Southern accent.

2

In the winter of 1945 Al had a severe attack of grippe that developed into pneumonia. He was confined to a hospital and for several days he suffered from a grave fever that ravaged his body. Two ribs and part of his left lung were cut away. With a tube in his back, he lay in critical condition. Epstein visited him daily, learned from the doctors that Al's recovery hinged on his will to live. Right now there seemed to be no incentive in him to keep on. He was like a man who had lost his enthusiasm and for whom there was no place.

All Epstein's efforts to cheer up the failing Jolson were in vain. On the bed lay the washed-out remainder of a man, staring almost blankly up at the ceiling with lackluster eyes.

He looked at Epstein who was sitting by the bed, trying to cheer him with recountings of old times. Al shook his head weakly. Eppy, he said in low, almost inaudible voice, I guess you were right. Maybe I *am* finished. Look, why do you waste your time with me? I can't do you any good.

Al, are you trying to fire me? Because if you are, I'll just hang around and picket you.

There was a slight upturning at the corners of Al's mouth. Eppy, tell me the truth. Am I through?

Who said you're through? Did I say it? I didn't hear anybody else say it. So now you get well. Don't keep those audiences waiting.

The following afternoon Al had a visitor who made his eyes shine for the first time in days.

Hello, Al.

Erle Galbraith.

Your big movie star. Al, I want you to get better. I do declare, you've been neglecting me. What happened to the gay times, the night clubs and shows? I know you've been avoiding me.

Al looked at her gratefully. For the first time during this siege, he smiled. Honey, I was afraid you were mad at me. Know something? You make ol' Jolie feel better, just sittin' there an' lookin' at him.

Al, promise to get well quick. She kissed him lightly on the forehead.

Honey, I promise. They laughed at each other. Al's eyes were brimming. Honey Chile, you is powaful medicine, sho' nuff.

She said, I'll be here tomorrow.

And that was the magic that brought Al about and sent his fever down and his pulse up.

After that it was Erle who helped him out of the hospital.

They became inseparable.

He spoke of marriage to her, told her he would write to her father.

Painstakingly, he composed a letter to her father requesting the hand of his daughter. He thought this would be the proper thing, fitting in well with the customs of the Old South. Erle beamed. She leaned over him and caressed his forehead with fingers that felt like flower petals. Al was living once more in a world of ecstasy. What he had lost before, he now found in increased measure.

3

He awaited Mr. Galbraith's reply. Soon it came and it was disappointing. In the sweeping penmanship of a traditional Southern gentleman, the letter advised Al Jolson the marriage to Erle was out of the question, impossible. First of all, Jolson was old enough to be her father, with a good many years to spare. Second, he was not the sort of man Mr. Galbraith had in mind for his daughter. Third, there was the problem of different faiths. Anyway, what in blazes was the idea of luring his daughter to Hollywood? Was it really because Jolson had a career for her in the movies or was he trying to put over some shenanigans? The Colonel made it plain that if he found out that Jolson was fooling around with his daughter, "then, by heavens, sir, you'll answer to me."

Erle's dark eyes glowed when she read the letter, but her reaction was more amusement than anything else. Don't you fret, Al. Everything's going to be all right. I'll have a little chat with father. I can twirl him around my little finger. You wait and see.

And Erle did go home and speak to her father—not a very long conversation. At the end of it she had his consent. Her mother was still somewhat fearful that the whole thing was a publicity stunt. You know how those actor people are, my dear. Nevertheless, she wished her daughter the best. Erle returned to Hollywood and an anxious Al Jolson. On March 22, 1945, they were married at Quartzite, Arizona, by a justice of the peace.

From that time on, Al began to enjoy a happiness he had hardly dared to dream about. It was a marvel to him that this slim, dark-eyed slip of a girl could so fill his days with delight. Once again he could laugh, let himself go.

He brought his new wife back to his ranch home. There was a welcoming committee from Encino and once more the ranch, which had been deserted for so long a time, was filled with the sights and sounds of happy living.

Erle gave up her career at Columbia Pictures and told reporters, from now on my career is going to be to take care of my husband. And from what I hear, I reckon that could be a full time job. But as the days passed the old restlessness began to creep back into Jolson's system. At sixty years of age he had no intention of stopping. Before long he was straining against his bonds again and complaining to Epstein that idleness was strangling him.

Eppy, you've got to find me something. For heaven's sake, don't be so particular now.

Epstein contacted the various agencies in Hollywood, Los Angeles, Frisco, with no acceptable results.

Al knew he should be thankful for what he had: a new lease on life, a charming wife, and a comfortable home. What more could a man desire?

And yet, after that first excitement of the marriage and "settling down," the situation had begun to resume its former aspect. He grew impatient loafing about the house. He had to get back before an audience—this much he knew. It was a craving he could not dam up or ignore. It was there inside of him and it played havoc with his peace of mind.

4

Al was in the living room of his Encino home, taking it easy.
Epstein was sitting in his eternal Morris chair and enjoying a good
cigar. The buzzer sounded.
    Epstein rose and admitted Harry's wife, Lillian.
    She seemed to be quite perturbed.

Al, I'm sorry for barging in like this. I know I shouldn't. Believe me, if Harry finds out I've been here, he'll skin me alive. But I had to come.

Harry in trouble?

Al, Harry will have a nervous breakdown any minute now if things keep up like they are. Since you fired him as your agent, he's not the same. I tell you the poor man is going out of his mind, trying to make ends meet. He's too old to go back on the stage and he has no profession or trade he can turn to.

Exactly the boat I'm in. Both of us a pair—we can shake hands.

But with Harry it's not exactly the same. Harry doesn't have millions. He's fighting for existence. He's tried one business after another. Now he's trying to build up an insurance business, but his money is all gone.

Al shook his head. Lillian, listen to me. The guy's ashamed to ask me for help. He knows I'd give him a lift. He could work with Eppy. Any time he needs help, I'm here and he can find me—the way you did. Ain't that so, Eppy?

Epstein nodded. No problem when it comes to financial help. Al is always ready. Besides, I could use a good right-hand man.

Lil, I'll give you a check for five grand, Al told her. That ought to start him off. Tell him to accept it for past and future services. He knows he has a standing offer to pitch in with me, to take care of the detail work. Harry is meticulous, keeps good records.

Al, I think I've misjudged you. I thought you'd be too busy to bother with Harry's problems.

He's my brother, ain't he?

Epstein wrote the check. Al signed it.

Lillian accepted it with trembling fingers. Al, you're a doll.

I'm just a lucky dog. Tell Harry there's always a job for him with me. Tell him to forget his pride. There's nothing to fight about now. After all, he sued me for $75,000 and he knows I hold no grudge.

Yes, Al.

And Lil, you're neglecting yourself. You don't look so hot. Better take it easy and stop worrying. Money is one thing the Jolsons should never worry about.

Erle had come in from the lawn, having just finished weeding the flower beds.

She greeted Lillian warmly, asked her to stay a while. But Lillian had to hurry home and break the glad news to Harry.

When she was gone Epstein looked at Al. Then he said to Mrs. Jolson, Mr. Philanthropist himself, and lighted a fresh cigar. Erle, he just slipped Lillian a small fortune.

What would you have done? asked Erle.

The same damn thing, said Epstein, taking an initial puff on his cigar.

31

1

In the spring of 1946 a columnist and recently appointed assistant producer at Warner Brothers, Sidney Skolsky, called at the ranch.

Al, may I have a word with you?

Two words.

Al, I have an idea that might be a big thing—to sort of commemorate the twentieth anniversary of talking pictures, and your first film hit, *The Jazz Singer.*

Has Eppy talked to you?

No, this is on my own. I want your okay to go ahead with this idea. Maybe it's a gamble—I don't know—but I have a hunch that it's sure-fire.

I'm listenin', man. I'm just achin' all over for good ideas.

Well, this would be the story of your life.

Al shrugged. Suddenly, he seemed resigned.

Not again, Skolsky. It's old hat. Who the hell wants to go through my life again? There was *The Jazz Singer* and *The Singing Fool.* Those pretty well covered it. Besides, everybody knows I'm a "has-been." Who would want to know about me again?

Skolsky was a patient, cool-headed man, big for all his five-foot-two stature. Al, do I have your okay?

If anybody is fool enough to take a chance on it, I won't say "no."

There's one more thing you should know, said Skolsky. This is going to be a bit different from before. Actually, you yourself won't be in the picture.

I don't get it. You mean you're goin' to do my story with another actor?

Yes and no. Skolsky, seeing Al's puzzled expression, quickly explained. We'll have a young man act as you, but we'll use your voice singing the songs, soundtracked on the film.

Clever. Tell me, Sid, who's the young guy?

Al, the thing's just in the idea stage, a bug in my mind. I don't even know whether the Warners will go for it.

2

And so the matter rested. Jolson mentioned the idea to Epstein who nodded approval. Good. Good. Just what you need. Might amount to something. That Skolsky's nobody's fool, believe me, Al.

Skolsky broached the idea to Jack Warner, who listened respectfully, but in the end shook his head. Sid, Jolson is passé as far as films are concerned. He had two good pictures—the first in talkies—which were more of a novelty than anything else, so the public went for them. After that it was a problem to get the people to look at and listen to him. I'm sorry, Sid, but we can't see it. Another Jolson picture? Forget it.

I don't think I can forget it. The audiences will be looking at a fresh young face with Jolson's voice for the songs. It's twenty years since The Jazz Singer and Jolson's life has been an interesting one since then. Much has happened to him.

Jack Warner was not impressed.

Even with some young actor mouthing the Jolson songs, I'm afraid it would be a bad gamble. All his last ventures, stage or screen, proved that Jolson was finished. He should be remembered for what he was. Why subject the old guy to more misery?

But Skolsky, though he had listened carefully and without prejudice, was not satisfied with Warner's answer.

Somehow he had the feeling that the life story of the blackfaced singer should be done now with a young man acting the part and

Al's voice actually singing the well-known songs. Skolsky was sure that such a combination could not possibly miss.

He spoke to Harry Cohen of Columbia Pictures. Harry, skeptical at first, gradually but surely came to agree with Skolsky. Accordingly the stage was set. Epstein got into the arrangements of the financial setup, holding out for and receiving a fifty percent share of the profits for Al Jolson. Ruby Keeler was interviewed and agreed to cooperate but stipulated that her name not be used for the female lead in the picture. This was agreed upon and a sum of $25,000 was paid to her. Other minor legal matters were disposed of and the way cleared for the actual production of the film.

During these negotiations Al Jolson was like a new person. At last he was busy, doing something, if not actually acting in a picture, then singing for it anyway, and that to him was good enough.

He was his old self again. He kidded around with his co-workers, with Epstein, with Sid Skolsky, with the Columbia studio heads, and with his wife, the lovely princess holding sway in her ranch castle. To Erle he said, Honey gal, your old Uncle Jolie has gone and done it again. Columbia is doing my life—it's my comeback.

Al, darling, I'm happy for you.

I thought they had forgotten me.

Why should they forget you? You are the "World's Greatest Entertainer." Everybody knows that. I'm sure the picture will be a success.

Al shook his head in disbelief. Al Jolson up in lights again—even if it's not really me on the screen, it will be my voice and my story.

3

Al was soon notified that somebody had been selected to play his part in the film—a thirty-year-old actor named Larry Parks. Al hurried to the Columbia lot and was introduced to the young man.

I'll work with you, kid. You'll be fine.

Soon the training period began.

Now look, Larry, watch me. Hold out your arms like this. Then swing them forward, with your hands held as in prayer. Then down on your knee. I'm talkin' the words, like this—get it? Now try it.

Parks went through the routine, somewhat too stiffly. Al stopped him. No, no, Larry boy. You're too reserved. You're too reserved. You're holding yourself back. That's not the way. You must let yourself go, kid. Just get loose all over—like this. Now watch me, watch me, kiddo, and you'll catch it. Like this—see? Loose—loose—let yourself go, kid. All the way. Try it now. . . .

Larry went through the gestures and expressions once more. He tried hard. He tried to forget his own personality, to lose it entirely in the personality of Al Jolson. He must feel the emotions as Jolson felt them; he must forget he was an average young man named Larry Parks. That was the trick: he must remember he was now Al Jolson. He went through the routine again and again, mouthing the words of the lyrics in synchronization with the recording, waving his arms, rolling his eyes, grinning, getting down on one knee, extending his white-gloved hands to the audience, an expression of heartbreak upon his face one moment, of high glee the next—he did this over and over, Jolson coaching him, Jolson always at his side. Larry was sure he had it now—that feeling of being the blackfaced Mammy singer himself.

As Parks completed his act, Jolson gripped the younger man's hand. Larry, my boy, you were old Jolie himself. I swear you were. Keep it up. Don't lose it, boy. Hold on to it and I think we'll have it licked. We'll give the public a look at the Jolson I used to be—a long time ago, before you were born.

The studio execs, the director, the technicians, and the writers were pleased with the progress of the preliminary rehearsals. They felt that Parks had captured the moods, the characteristics of the great singer.

And now Jolson was in his element. He strutted about the set, singing his songs for the sound track. He gave it all he had. He was riding high in top form, cavorting through the singing sequences with his old-time brashness.

"My Mammy," "Toot-Toot-Tootsie," "California, Here I Come," "Rock-a-Bye Your Baby with a Dixie Melody," "Rosie, You Are

My Posy," "I Wanna Girl Just Like the Girl That Married Dear Old Dad," "April Showers"—all the old favorites, the Jolson classics, to live again through the medium of a somewhat bewildered young actor named Larry Parks.

4

The story itself was a sweetened-up version of Jolson's life and career. The thin thread of Al's real life was embellished with fancy incidents that were more or less fictionalized. Many of his experiences were omitted entirely, the characters of the people he knew and lived with were not true to the originals, and some had not even existed.

Only one wife was shown, played by Evelyn Keyes and presumed to be Ruby Keeler, and the early stages of his life were camouflaged into a pretty but impossible fairy tale.

But it was the character of the blackfaced singer upon the screen as portrayed by Larry Parks and given singing voice by Jolson himself that gave the picture its tremendous impact upon the spellbound movie audiences.

Warner Brothers had stood by and watched what was being produced at the Columbia studios, and they had shaken their combined heads in silent sympathy. Their pronouncement was, the public will never go for another Jolson picture. The Warners had considered themselves wise for steering clear of this rather precarious venture, until they were shocked out of their complacency by the effect of "Columbia's folly" when it reached the theaters.

When the new Jolson film was released in October 1946, it was a complete and immediate success.

At a studio preview Jolson, sitting next to Sid Skolsky, watched the picture. Seeing himself portrayed on the screen, Al forgot that it was Larry Parks but could see only himself, as he had been more than a quarter century ago. The performance of Parks was an ingenious one, and Jolson gripped Skolsky's arm as his emotions got the better of him. When the lights went on Sid saw the tears in Jolson's eyes, and the columnist understood.

That kid was great, said Sid. But how is he ever going to escape the Jolson personality?

Meanwhile the picture swept the country from coast to coast. Wherever it played the audiences went wild over what they saw and heard. The performances were sellouts and many were turned away. The name of Al Jolson became once more a household word. Youngsters in their teens who had heard their parents speak about Jolson and had considered him as some dim legendary figure of the past now knew him as a vibrant, thrilling personality. His voice—as it had done in the past with another generation—charmed and electrified these youngsters.

Jolson became, in the image of Larry Parks, a revered performer. His phonograph records again sold in the millions, and a new generation was singing the old Jolie classics. Newspapers and magazines published articles about the comeback of the Mammy singer, and everywhere once again, as in the past, it was Jolson leading the parade.

And no one spoke of Larry Parks—no one commended him as an excellent performer. As far as the public was concerned, Parks was a shadow in the background—it was Jolson in the center of the spotlight, loving it, forgetting to draw Parks into it as well. On his Encino ranch in that year of 1947, Al Jolson was a man reborn, a man who had come back from the realm of the has-beens.

He was mobbed by newspaper reporters, fan mag writers, and theatrical agents. He was in the glare of the limelight and he enjoyed every minute of it. He was a college hero who had just completed a run for a touchdown. Also—not to be overlooked— he was richer by more than a million dollars.

5

Jack Warner could have kicked himself. I must have been asleep, he told himself. He had surely missed the boat. By right of priority this great success should have emanated from Warner Brothers, the studio that had first put Jolson upon the talking screen.

Offers began to flow in from radio and television, from other motion picture studios, even from the austere realm of the legit theater.

But Jolson was too busy enjoying his conquest.

His wife Erle accepted the triumph, but was wary of the price.

Al's happiness meant everything to her, but she was also concerned about his health, his well-being. She had on her hands now an unduly excited husband. Honey chile, you're lookin' at a guy who's come back and knocked 'em for a loop, but honest-to-God, Sugar, I never thought it would be this big. This picture is an earthquake. That kid Larry Parks—he did a job. Shame they don't push some of this glory his way. It all seems to come in my direction.

This was true. After all, it was Larry Parks who had made Al Jolson live again to win the hearts of all America. And yet Parks had now become the forgotten man. People watched him perform in *The Jolson Story* and could see only Al Jolson before them. Larry Parks? Who was he and what did he matter?

Columbia Studios reaped a tremendous financial harvest from the picture's run. Harry Cohen had anticipated some measure of success but never to such degree. It was incredible, but the cold cash in the box office totaled an eight million gross.

The Jolson magic had survived through almost fifty years of show business. Perhaps another man would have shied away from the glare of publicity at an age when tranquility was more in order. But not Jolson. Past the sixty-years mark now, he welcomed any notoriety; he basked in the limelight; he made himself seen and heard on every occasion. He drank fully and deeply of the wine of his success, and Erle was breathless trying to keep up with him.

They attended receptions, parties, and testimonial dinners. Erle was always obliging, patient, smiling, as she stood by his side.

But her concern for his physical welfare increased with the acceleration of her husband's pace. She cautioned him, gently, to slow down, to rest.

Honey, you're talkin' to a guy who's free-wheelin' high, wide and handsome. Don't hold your Jolie back, sweetheart. When I get to the end of the ride, I'll not only slow down, I'll stop.

Yes, darling. But perhaps if we'd get away from the rush a bit, you might like it.

Sweetheart, I've waited a long time for this to happen. My comeback. Now I've got to take it all in. I don't want to miss a thing. And honey, you're in on it right along with me.

I understand, Al. But please be careful.

I've got plenty of moxie left, kiddo. Here's a kiss, be a good girl, and stop worryin'. Your Uncle Jolie can still lick his weight in tomcats.

Approached by the producers of a television network to appear on a video show, Jolson summarily refused. I'm strictly a radio man. People listen to me without seeing a face that looks like a slice of imported Swiss cheese on the television screen. No, thank you. Anyway, I'm pretty well booked up with radio.

32

1

Jolson was called for guest spots on the radio programs of Bing Crosby, Jack Benny, and Eddie Cantor. He received $40,000 a week for appearing at the Roxy Theater in New York to wildly cheering Manhattanites who considered him one of their own, a returned prodigal.

He signed a four-year contract to conduct a radio program for NBC's Kraft Music Hall at a salary of $7,500 per week. Everything opened up for Al Jolson—the world was his. He was king again.

Sometimes he stopped in his tracks and a disturbing thought struck him—there were no accolades for the kid who had made all this possible—modest, quiet Larry Parks.

2

Jolson had broken the ice about the subject of children. He knew that a woman couldn't live happily in a house with no young voices about her, no little mouths to feed and little bodies to bathe and dress.

Erle, honey, we gotta talk about kids.

Of course, Al. I know. Don't try to explain to me that perhaps we won't have any children of our own. Darling, believe it or not, I know more about you than you think.

Then it's all right if we adopt a couple of kids?

It would be heavenly, Mr. Jolson. The sooner the better.

Good. We'll visit the adoption board. I'm one of their good customers and I can guarantee getting quick service.

Oh, Al, darling, a boy and a girl?

Sugar, your message has already gone to the stork. Boy and girl comin' up.

Al and Erle followed through with the necessary legal procedures and, faster than Erle had anticipated, she became the proud mother of a baby boy and a baby girl, whom they christened Asa and Alicia. Though Alicia was not a well baby, Al and Erle were only too anxious to give the infant a home and the best medical care attainable.

3

In the spacious living room of the Jolson ranch home Al was lying on the thick-carpeted floor, and roughhousing with Asa and Alicia to the accompaniment of the infants' gleeful laughter and gurglings of delight.

Erle, sitting on the sofa, enjoyed the performance. Epstein, esconced comfortably in his favorite Morris chair, watched with a pleased expression. That was how he liked to see Al spend his time—with his kids.

But with Al playtime was soon over. He called a halt to the session and rose to his feet, dabbing his forehead with his handkerchief. Eppy, I'm so busy these days with radio work, personal appearances, recordings, I plumb forgot to tell you— Harry Cohen has approached me for another Jolson story.

Epstein sighed, sank deeper into his chair. I don't believe it. What happened to Rudy Vallee?

Al said, Columbia is all set to go ahead with the plans. Remember where *The Jolson Story* ended—in a night club scene, with the wife walking out on him? Well, we're going to continue from there to the present. Pretty good for someone supposed to be washed up, eh, Eppy?

I always said that with you miracles happen every day. Anybody looking for a miracle? Come to Al Jolson.

But Erle's face paled. She looked at Al. Darling, you won't mind if I say something?

Sugar, I'd rather listen to you talk than to one of my own records playing a Mammy song.

Al, you've been working too hard. As a nurse, I know something about these things. Your breathing last night seemed too labored, a sign you're not getting enough rest.

Now, Sugar, you're not goin' to ask me to stop, just when I'm rollin' along in high gear.

A vacation, darling. Just us and the children. You'd spend time with them, watch them grow.

Honey, that's exactly what I intend to do, as sure as my name's Jolie.

I'm so relieved, Al.

He came closer to her, took her hand in his. But, first, Sugar, there's just one more duty I got to do for that ol' man public— finish what I've started—my life story on film. This new picture will complete the whole project. After that, it's home for me.

Erle leaned back, sighing. I suppose your heart is set on doing that picture.

But I want your word, Sugar. You've got to tell me it's okay.

It's okay, Al. But I'm going to hold you to your promise that after this one you'll settle down and rest.

You have my promise. After this number it's you and the kids all the time. And honey, here's a kiss to seal the bargain.

Erle smiled. Eppy is our witness.

Epstein nodded. The story of my life. A witness—to everything.

4

While preparations were in progress for the filming of *Jolson Sings Again,* Al received a telegram from Washington informing him of the death of his father.

Al immediately cancelled all appointments and activities and phoned Erle at the ranch. She would remain with the children while he took the first plane east. In flight, high above the earth, he reviewed the past. His father had reached the age of ninety, a full long life, successful and complete. He had lived according to his own principles, just as Al himself was living his own life, following his own star.

At the funeral there was a rare reunion of the Yoelson family.

Al's mother, now seventy-nine, was, as always, glad to see him. Harry came forward and the two brothers embraced each other, tearfully.

Harry, you old son-of-a-gun. I hear you're a top insurance man.

Harry nodded. Thanks to your financial help. From a vaudeville headliner to an insurance agent. Would you call that progress?

Al said, The world changes. Like my friend Eppy would say, today we are Broadway stars—tomorrow we sell insurance.

They were silent for a moment. They were walking out of the cemetery now. Al had his arm about his mother who leaned against him, for in her eyes Al was her favorite. He still called her his "new Momma." There was a gray sky, a fitting canopy for the solemn scene. Harry and his wife, Lillian, walked directly behind Al and Mrs. Yoelson on their way to the cars.

When they were in the old home Al addressed his brother. Harry, remember the old days? We had great fun right here in Washington.

Harry smiled. That watermelon venture of ours. And you always running off to the theaters and singing from the balconies. You'd sing at the drop of a hat.

Harry, what happened to the years? We're both getting to the end of the road. Shame we can't meet more often and talk.

No objection on my part.

Harry, listen to your brother Jolie. I want you to come with me as my representative. I'm opening an office in New York to take care of details and you run it. Now with this new picture coming up I'll be head over heels in work. You can take some of that off my shoulders. I'll pay you twice as much as you're earning now. If you're not satisfied with that, then name your own price. Besides you've got to get Lillian away from that insurance business. It's running her ragged and believe me she needs a rest. She's not too well.

You're right about Lillian. She's failing fast. I may lose her. About your offer, Al, I've got security now with this insurance business of mine. Could I rely on your word that the position you offer me will be a permanent one? I'm too old to take chances now.

Harry, if you won't take my word, we'll draw up a contract and make it a binding thing. I want you with me as long as we live. From now on we'll be Asa and Harry, peddling our watermelons. Think it over.

They both laughed and Mrs. Yoelson and Lillian exchanged happy glances. The brothers might get together again before it was too late.

Al wired Erle, back in Encino, that the funeral was over and that he was flying back. He ended the message with, Here's a kiss for the kids and yours I'll deliver in person.

5

In the days that followed, Harry's wife, the patient and long-suffering Lillian who had been at her husband's side for thirty-nine years, wasted away to a shadow of her former self and finally passed on.

Harry was the picture of grief. To him it was like the sun passing behind a great cloud, leaving him in darkness.

Al understood his brother's despondency and walked off by himself, to think, to remember how it was. Lillian—an unsung heroine, having received no medals, no citations for courage. Her life had been one of sacrifice and hope for her husband. During World War II she had worked as a factory hand in an aircraft factory, trying to save her husband from total despair.

They had known some measure of success when Harry had hit the top in vaudeville, but with the demise of vaude and with age creeping up on Harry, Lillian had found herself the wife of an unemployed actor who could do nothing else to earn a living.

Harry had seen his brother go up the ladder of fame and fortune from the days of their old acts—*Jolson, Palmer, and Jolson* and *The Hebrew and the Cadet*. Harry had never been able to understand it. He could sing almost as well as Al; in addition he could dance and deliver fast comedy patter that Al himself could not do so well, and yet what was it that had catapulted Al to the loftiest heights of show business while he,

Harry, had dragged along near the bottom, in the wake of his brother's breathtaking flight?

And now with Lillian gone, Harry found himself a lonely man, yet his head was always held high. He was a proud man and he held on to his principles. He would have starved rather than come asking Al for a handout. People had often wondered why, in all those years of brilliant successes and smash hits on Broadway, Al had never taken Harry into his own flourishing show world and given him a profitable career, pushing him along to the top. But the public in general did not know about Harry's hurt pride when Al had rejected him as an agent, leaving him with a furious resentment against anyone who offered him a helping hand. He would make it on his own or else—

There were times when Al had pleaded with his brother to accept an "executive" position with him, but Harry had assured Al, I'm not an old woman to be helped across the street. Your giving me a job is really a blind, isn't it? What you're really doing is handing out some charity. Well, brother, I don't need it. I've played the big time—in the best theaters—in my day and I'll do it again.

Sure you will, kiddo, Al had agreed. But just the same, anytime you're at liberty, the doors of my theater are open.

On one occasion Al said to his brother, For heaven's sake, Harry, you treat me like I was a villain in one of those melodramas, about to foreclose the mortgage. Could I help it if the producers bellyached about my brother being my agent? It was everyone's opinion that you were in the wrong line. Even if I did make a mistake, it's all water under the dam.

I don't blame you for my condition, Al. Maybe I was too touchy about help from you, or maybe I was just plain jealous of your success. I know now I could have made it easier for Lillian. If your offer is still open to work for you, I'll be honored to accept it.

Al gripped his brother's hand.

He announced, Harry, from now on it's Jolson and Jolson.

6

In *Jolson Sings Again,* Larry Parks was again called to the colors, and like a good soldier he gave his all for the Jolson legend. It was not a new thing with him. He had steeped himself in the Jolson personality, had absorbed Al's traits and idiosyncrasies until there were times when Larry considered himself the Mammy singer reincarnated.

This time, also, it was easier for Al, who did not have to go through the entire routines, showing Larry how to be Jolson. But he was always on hand, ready with his suggestions, still offering his services as coach, besides singing his songs once more for the sound track of the film.

1

When *Jolson Sings Again* was released in 1949, it made an instant hit with the public, and remained the hottest box-office magic. This picture established Jolson without a shadow of doubt as the "Greatest Entertainer in the World." *Jolson Sings Again* took his life from the separation from Ruby Keeler through the doldrums in his career, when the public had forgotten him for new and more intriguing idols. The picture showed him during World War II on his singing trips through the war-torn lands, wherever the G.I.'s fought.

The old familiar songs assailed the audiences again, and once more they listened with that same wonder and awe, their emotions stirred even as the emotions of their parents had been stirred a generation ago.

In the wake of the production came the inevitable requests for vaude engagements, radio guest spots, and personal appearances. On a single night he appeared in five different theaters in Manhattan and Brooklyn, in each one singing his traditional numbers.

This picture proved to be one of the biggest money-makers in film history, surpassing *The Jolson Story* with a margin of five million and with plenty yet to go. Once again Larry Parks did an excellent job and, as before, his own personality, his own talents were buried in the personality of Jolson. So it was Jolson himself the public recognized and acclaimed, overlooking the hard-

working young actor who had brought the blackfaced singer back to life. Any future work Parks would do in pictures would be short-lived and ineffective. His brief film career was in the rejuvenation of Al Jolson.

And now Jolson, as so many times before, spent very little time at home. Excitement held an irresistible lure. It was an elixir for him, a fountain of youth. It made him kid around, pull practical jokes. This was the way it had to be with him. Wherever he went, whatever he did was news to the public. He was a friend to everyone. It was always "Hi, Al." "How y'doin', Al." "How's the wife, Al?" There were offers and requests for performances, to sign contracts at fabulous prices.

The money was flowing into his coffers, a golden flood. He became wealthier by the minute. He had reached the pinnacle of fame, fortune, and influence. He could ask for and get whatever he wanted. But the reward he treasured was that people liked him, that his singing pleased them.

His wife tried to grasp the extent of her husband's popularity. She tried to orient herself to the situation. Here she was, a hitherto unknown apprentice hospital technician, now the wife of the world's most feted singing star. But in calmer moments she would rationalize that all this might cost too much of the health of her husband. She had learned that in the very nature of things, one could not take without giving something in return. Everything had its toll—whether it be in money or in precious heartbeats.

When Al did come home, she could see the anguish on his face, the weariness in his walk, the dragging movement of his body. He would slump into a chair and sit, welcoming the opportunity. She knew he was a tired man, chasing that brilliantly colored rainbow of popularity. She had pleaded with him so many times to stop, to retire. She had the feeling that his former wives had gone through the same process until they had grown weary of it all.

But she would not grow weary. She loved that man, though some had ridiculed her for the difference in their ages and that he did not heed her pleas. She was his only real mainstay, his one comfort—this she knew.

Then there was Epstein, always at Al's side. Epstein, the friend. She knew that Epstein played the same tune—begging Al to end the roller-coaster ride—to chuck the whole business.

But Jolson kept on and on. He promised, yes—he always promised he'd stop—but first. . . .

Epstein and Erle were used to that now.

But first, there was always one more thing he had to do. And the promise again. Sugar, take Jolie's word for it, you're goin' to see a retired Mammy singer, sho' nuff.

In the nights there were times when his sudden spasms of wild tossing would wake her in alarm. She'd sit up in bed and watch him, and she was frightened, but fought down her panic. She'd put her arms about him and try to comfort him. And he would open his eyes and say, What's the matter, honey? Time to get up? I've got a million things to do today—

Al, dear, it's 3 A. M. You were having some sort of nightmare.

The sweat was cold upon his forehead. He grinned sheepishly. Sugar, I'm gettin' to be a nuisance in my old age. A pretty young kid like you—goin' through all this.

Al, please, don't ever talk like that again. In a moment I'm going to cry.

Now wait, Honey Chile. We'll forget about all that. Now you get back to sleep. I'm doin' the same. He yawned.

On another occasion she listened to his breathing. It had become a habit with her from hospital days. Not a normal breathing, she was sure. It was labored. She planned to have him go to a doctor, get a complete physical checkup, just to make sure.

Jolson Sings Again was going strong throughout the country. At Erle's constant urging, Jolson did try to relax, to spend more time with Asa and Alicia. He took on the role of a real father and husband, catering to the needs and moods of his family.

He lounged around and had a merry time with Erle, with the children. Erle dared to hope that, at last, Al had truly come home to stay. From now on she would not have to worry about an overworked, harassed husband.

His radio contract had ended. He could accept guest spots on other programs or reject them as he desired. Epstein was especially happy to see Al finally won over to the tranquil life of a gentleman farmer.

2

In June 1950, headlines began to appear in the newspapers, out of a clear sky, about the North Korean armies moving down below the limit of the 38th Parallel with the objective of absorbing South Korea. In defense of those Koreans who did not want Communist rule, President Truman had ordered American forces into the area, at first as a warning and precautionary measure; then the threat of fighting became real and a new war had broken out. The United Nations backed the action. More and more American troops were shipped overseas, with all the implements of battle. England, Canada, France, and the Netherlands contributed troops, as well as other United Nations members.

Soon there was a full-scale war in progress and once more the G.I.'s were in the thick of it. General Douglas MacArthur was appointed commander of the armies.

Back in Encino, Jolson read the newspaper accounts of the trouble in Korea and his eyes took on an abstract look as though his thoughts were far afield. He listened to the news on the radio. Day after day as the reports of the Korean struggle came in, he began to fidget. He paced the floor like a caged being. Erle noticed his reaction and she immediately understood. Her fears mounted. She hoped he wouldn't do anything rash. She watched him anxiously, as every morning he grew more and more restive. Finally he came out with it.

Erle, honey, I hate to say this to you, but I've got to do something for those boys.

Erle stared at him, unbelieving. Al, darling, you've already done more than enough. I'm sure everybody understands.

It's not that, Honey Chile. I can't sleep at night, thinking of those kids. I sort o' got used to them in the last war. I can still see their faces looking up at me, listening to me as if I were their godfather or something.

Al, I suppose nothing I say can hold you back?

Honey, listen to your ol' Uncle Jolie. They wouldn't let me carry a gun at my age, but I can sing. I could make those kids forget their miseries for a while with my songs. "Come on, fellows, how about some laughs? This is your old man Jolie speakin' to you, tellin' you all you ain't heard nothin' yet!" Now, do you see what I mean, Sugar?

You win, Al. But this I must tell you. Our family doctor has prescribed rest for you. I thought I'd let you know.

Doctors—all they think about is people gettin' sick. Everybody knows Jolson is an iron man. I can take it. Strong as an ox. I used to lick all the kids in the neighborhood. Nothing's too tough for old Jolie.

The following morning, at the Los Angeles Airport, Erle saw her husband off.

Please, Al, can you stand the trip?

I'll be all right. And honey, when I get back nobody's gonna budge me out of our house.

I'll be waiting.

She placed her hands on his shoulders, gazed up into his eyes. Darling, don't try to do too much.

Erle stood behind the gate of the airfield, watching the plane take off and wing its way up above the western horizon in the direction of a place called Korea.

She watched the plane until it became a speck, and the speck became part of the sky.

But she knew the plane was still there, speeding her husband to keep a rendezvous with destiny.

Appendixes

DISCOGRAPHY
1912–1950

R.C.A. Victor Records

Record Number
17037   That Haunting Melody/Rum-Tum-Tiddle*
17915   Asleep in the Deep
17075   Snap Your Fingers
17068   Brass Band Ephraim Jones
17081   Moving Man Don't Move My Baby Grand/Raggin' the Baby to Sleep*
17119   That Loving Traumerei
17318   My Yellow Jacket Girl/The Spaniard That Blighted My Life*

Columbia Records

1356   That Little German Band/Everybody Snap Your Fingers*
1374   Pullmen Porters on Parade/You Made Me Love You*
1621   Back to the Carolina You Love/On Revival Day*
1671   Sister Susie's Sewing Shirts for Soldiers/When the Grown Up Ladies Act Like Babies*
1956   Yaaka-Hoola-Hickey-Doola
1976   Where Did Robinson Crusoe Go?
2007   Down Where the Swanee River Flows
2080   Now He's Got a Beautiful Girl
2021   I Sent My Wife to the Thousand Isles
2041   You're a Dangerous Girl
2064   I'm Savin' Up the Means
2124   Someone Else May Be There While I'm Gone
2106   Don't Write Me Letters
2154   A Broken Doll

2181   Every Little While
2224   From Here to Shanghai
2169   Pray for Sunshine
2296   Tillie Titwillow
2478   I'm All Bound Round with the Mason-Dixon Line
2512   Wedding Bells
2491   There's a Lump of Sugar Down in Dixie
2519   'N Everything
2560   Rock-a-Bye Your Baby with a Dixie Melody
2542   Hello Central / Give Me No Man's Land
2657   Tell That to the Marines
2671   I Wonder Why She Kept Saying "Si, Si, Si, Si, Senor"

*Flip-side of record
2746   I'll Say She Does
2690   On the Road to Calais
2940   Some Beautiful Morning
2787   Who Played Poker with Pocahontas
2794   I've Got My Captain Working for Me Now
2836   You Ain't Heard Nothin' Yet
2835   I Gave Her That
2821   Tell Me
2861   Chloe
2884   Swanee
2898   That Wonderful Kid from Madrid
2946   In Sweet September
2995   Avalon
3361   Down by the O-HI-O
3375   Ding-a-Ring
3382   Scandinavia
3500   April Showers
3540   Give Me My Mammy
3513   Yoo Hoo
3568   Angel Child
3588   Oogie-Oogie-Wa-Wa
3626   Coo-Coo
3694   I'll Stand Beneath Your Window
3705   Toot-Toot-Tootsie
3744   Lost (A Wonderful Girl)
3779   Who Cares
3812   Wanita

3854   Coal Black Mammy
3880   Morning Will Come
3913   Stella
3933   Waiting for the Evening Mail
3968   That Big Blond Momma of Mine
3984   You've Simply Got Me Coo-Coo
43-D   Arcady
61-D   I'm Going South
79-D   Twelve O'Clock at Night

Little Wonder Records

20   Back to the Carolina You Love

Brunswick Records

2567   The One I Love Belongs to Somebody Else / Steppin' Out
2569   I'm Going South / California, Here I Come
2582   Mr. Radio Man / Home in Pasadena
2611   Feeling the Way I Do / Never Again
2595   Lazy / My Poppa Doesn't Two Time No Time
2650   Mandalay / Who Wants a Bad Little Boy
2671   I Wonder Why She Kept on Saying "Si, Si, Si, Si, Senor"
2743   All Alone / I'm Gonna Tramp Tramp Tramp
2763   Trouble's a Bubble / Hello, Tucky, Tucky Hello
3013   Miami / You Forgot to Remember
3014   I'm Sitting on Top of the World / You Flew Away from the Nest
3183   I Wish I Had My Old Gal Back Again / If I Knew I'd Find You
3196   At Peace with the World / Tonight's My Night with Baby
3222   When the Red Red Robin Comes Bob-Bob-Bobbin' Along /
        Here I Am
3719   Mother of Mine / Blue River
3775   Golden Gate / Four Walls
3867   Old Man River / Back in Your Own Backyard
3912   My Mammy / Dirty Hands, Dirty Face
4033   There's a Rainbow Round My Shoulder / Sonny Boy
4400   Little Pal / I'm in the Seventh Heaven
4401   Used to You / Why Can't You

4402   Liza / One Sweet Kiss
4721   Let Me Sing and I'm Happy / Looking at You
4722   To My Mammy / When the Little Red Roses Get the Blues for You
6500   Hallelujah I'm a Bum / You Are Too Beautiful
6501   The Cantor
6502   April Showers / Rock-a-Bye Your Baby with a Dixie Melody

Souvenir Records

101   Du Host a Liebes Punim (You Have a Lovely Face)

Opal Records

555   You Have a Lovely Face

U.S.A. V-Discs

86-B   April Showers / Rosie
763   The One I Love Belongs to Somebody Else / Swanee
773   My Mammy
780   Lazy
814   Alexander's Ragtime Band / Easter Parade / All by Myself

Audio Rarities Records

A TRIBUTE to AL JOLSON—Record Number 2285

Decca Records

10 inch 33 1/3 rpm, also released as 78 rpm albums, also released as 78 rpm singles.

JOLSON SINGS AGAIN—Decca 5006
    1. Pretty Baby
    2. I'm Looking Over a Four Leaf Clover / Baby Face
    3. Give My Regards to Broadway

4. I'm Just Wild About Harry
5. After You've Gone
6. Chinatown, My Chinatown
7. I Only Have Eyes for You
8. Is It True What They Say About Dixie?

AL JOLSON in Songs He Made Famous, Decca DLP 5026 (Volume 1)
1. April Showers
2. Swanee
3. California, Here I Come
4. Rock-a-Bye Your Baby with a Dixie Melody
5. You Made Me Love You
6. Ma Blushin' Rosie
7. Sonny Boy
8. My Mammy

AL JOLSON, Souvenir Album, Decca DLP 5029 (Volume 2)
1. Waiting for the Robert E. Lee
2. When You Were Sweet Sixteen
3. Golden Gate
4. I'm Sitting on Top of the World
5. Toot-Toot-Tootsie! (Goo' Bye)
6. Back in Your Own Back Yard
7. Carolina in the Morning
8. Liza

AL JOLSON, Decca DLP 5030 (Volume 3)
1. I Want a Girl
2. Where the Black-Eyed Susans Grow
3. When the Red Red Robin Comes Bob-Bob-Bobbin Along
4. Someone Else May Be There While I'm Gone
5. For Me and My Gal
6. When I Leave the World Behind
7. There's a Rainbow 'Round My Shoulder
8. About a Quarter to Nine

AL JOLSON, Souvenir Album, Decca DLP 5031 (Volume 4)
1. Avalon

  2. Anniversary Song
  3. All My Love
  4. Keep Smiling at Trouble
  5. If I Only Had a Match
  6. Let Me Sing and I'm Happy
  7. By The Light of the Silvery Moon
  8. I Wish I Had a Girl

AL JOLSON, Stephen Foster Songs, Decca DLP 5308
  1. Beautiful Dreamer
  2. Old Folks at Home
  3. I Dream of Jeanie with the Light Brown Hair
  4. Old Black Joe
  5. My Old Kentucky Home
  6. Massa's in de Cold, Cold Ground
  7. Oh, Susanna
  8. De Camptown Races

AL JOLSON, Souvenir Album, Decca DLP 5314 (Volume 5)
  1. God's Country
  2. Let's Go West Again
  3. Some Enchanted Evening
  4. It All Depends on You
  5. (Just One Way to Say) I Love You
  6. Paris Wakes Up and Smiles
  7. I'm Crying Just for You
  8. In Our House

AL JOLSON, Souvenir Album, Decca DLP 5315 (Volume 6)
  1. Kol Nidre
  2. Cantor On The Sabbath
  3. Hatikvoh (National Anthem of Israel)
  4. Israel
  5. That Wonderful Girl of Mine
  6. I Only Have Eyes for You
  7. My Mother's Rosary
  8. Remember Mother's Day

AL JOLSON and Bing Crosby with the Andrews Sisters, Mills
    Brothers, and Gordon Jenkins—Decca DLP 5316
      1. Alexander's Ragtime Band, with Crosby
      2. The Spaniard That Blighted My Life, with Crosby
      3. 'Way Down Yonder in New Orleans, with the Andrews Sisters
      4. The Old Piano Roll Blues, with the Andrews Sisters
      5. Down Among the Sheltering Palms, with the Mills Brothers
      6. Is It True What They Say About Dixie, with the Mills Brothers
      7. Are You Lonesome Tonight, directed by Gordon Jenkins
      8. No Sad Songs for Me, directed by Gordon Jenkins

Decca Records

12 inch 33-1/3 rpm

You Made Me Love You, DLP, 9034
      1. When You Were Sweet Sixteen
      2. Ma Blushin' Rosie
      3. Give My Regards to Broadway
      4. I Wish I Had a Girl
      5. By the Light of the Silvery Moon
      6. Chinatown, My Chinatown
      7. Alexander's Ragtime Band, with Bing Crosby
      8. The Spaniard That Blighted My Life, with Bing
         Crosby
      9. I Want a Girl
    10. Waiting for the Robert E. Lee
    11. You Made Me Love You
    12. I'm Crying Just for You
    13. When I Leave the World Behind
    14. Down Among the Sheltering Palms, with the Mills Brothers

Rock-a-Bye Your Baby, DLP, 9035
      1. My Mother's Rosary
      2. Pretty Baby
      3. Where the Black-Eyed Susans Grow
      4. For Me and My Gal

5. Someone Else May Be There While I'm Gone
6. After You've Gone
7. Rock-a-Bye Your Baby with a Dixie Melody
8. Swanee
9. Avalon
10. My Mammy
11. April Showers
12. I'm Just Wild About Harry
13. Toot-Toot-Tootsie (Goo' Bye)
14. Carolina in the Morning

Rainbow 'Round My Shoulder, DLP, 9036
1. 'Way Down Yonder in New Orleans, with the Andrews Sisters
2. Keep Smiling at Trouble
3. California, Here I Come
4. I'm Sitting on Top of the World
5. When the Red Red Robin Comes Bob-Bob-Bobbin' Along
6. It All Depends on You
7. (a) I'm Looking Over a Four-Leaf Clover, (b) Baby Face
8. Are You Lonesome Tonight, directed by Gordon Jenkins
9. Golden Gate
10. Back in Your Own Back Yard
11. Sonny Boy
12. There's a Rainbow 'Round My Shoulder
13. Liza
14. Let Me Sing and I'm Happy

You Ain't Heard Nothin' Yet, DLP, 9037
1. I Only Have Eyes for You
2. About a Quarter to Nine
3. Is It True What They Say About Dixie? with the Mills Brothers
4. Anniversary Song
5. If I Only Had a Match
6. All My Love
7. The Old Piano Roll Blues, with the Andrews Sisters
8. Let's Go West
9. Some Enchanted Evening
10. (Just One Way to Say) I Love You
11. That Wonderful Girl of Mine
12. Paris Wakes Up and Smiles

13. No Sad Songs for Me, directed by Gordon Jenkins. [This was the last song Jolson composed.]
14. God's Country

Memories, DLP, 9038
1. Cantor on the Sabbath
2. Kol Nidre
3. Israel
4. Hatikvoh
5. Remember Mother's Day
6. In Our House
7. Old Black Joe
8. My Old Kentucky Home
9. Beautiful Dreamer
10. Massa's in de Cold, Cold Ground
11. Old Folks at Home
12. I Dream of Jeanie with the Light Brown Hair
13. Oh, Susannah
14. De Camptown Races

The following album (33-1/3 rpm 12 inch) contains selections never before released. Although many of the titles are the same since these were all taken from Jolson's 1947–49 Kraft Music Hall Shows, the interpretations are different. All were done in front of a studio audience.

Among My Souvenirs—DLP, 9050
1. Among My Souvenirs
2. Roses of Picardy
3. Say It Isn't So
4. Little Pal
5. Without a Song
6. After You've Gone
7. When Day Is Done
8. I'm Always Chasing Rainbows
9. Memories
10. Always
11. That Old Gang of Mine
12. Old Man River

The Immortal Al Jolson, Decca, DLP, 9063
   1. Alexander's Ragtime Band
   2. Medley:
        (a) Ma, She's Makin' Eyes at Me
        (b) Dinah
   3. A Tree in the Meadow
   4. Don't Let It Get You Down
   5. Just One of Those Things
   6. Nearest Thing to Heaven
   7. Chicago
   8. Rock-a-Bye Your Baby with a Dixie Melody
   9. Yaaka-Hula-Hickey-Dula
  10. Easter Parade
  11. She's a Latin from Manhattan
  12. For Me and My Gal
  13. The Best Things in Life Are Free

Al Jolson Overseas, Decca, DLP, 9070
   1. At Sundown
   2. Margie
   3. Whispering
   4. Peg O' My Heart
   5. And Mimi
   6. Where Did Robinson Crusoe Go with Friday on Saturday
      Night
   7. I Wonder What's Become of Sally
   8. Chinatown, My Chinatown
   9. What'll I Do
  10. Medley:
        (a) My Melancholy Baby
        (b) My Blue Heaven
  11. A Fellow Needs a Girl
  12. Hannah in Savannah
  13. Remember Mother's Day

The World's Greatest Entertainer, Al Jolson, DLP, 9072
   1. Alabamy Bound
   2. Ma Blushin' Rosie

3. My Gal Sal
4. Medley:
    (a) Bright Eyes
    (b) Little Girl
5. I've Gotta Get Back to New York
6. When You Were Sweet Sixteen
7. Medley:
    (a) Toot-Toot-Tootsie, Goodbye
    (b) You Made Me Love You
8. The One I Love Belongs to Somebody Else
9. That Certain Party
10. She Is Ma Daisy
11. Baby Face
12. Hello 'Tucky
13. I'll Be Seeing You

Al Jolson with Oscar Levant at the piano—Decca, DLP, 9095
1. Rock-a-Bye Your Baby with a Dixie Melody
2. I Can't Give You Anything but Love
3. At the Candlelight Cafe
4. In the Good Old Summertime
5. Shine On, Harvest Moon
6. Hot Time in the Old Town Tonight
7. When Irish Eyes Are Smiling
8. Composer Bit—Introducing:
    (a) Oh, How I Miss You Tonight
    (b) I'm Always Chasing Rainbows
    (c) Till The End of Time
    (d) Anniversary Song
9. Ramona
10. Mary's a Grand Old Name
11. Maxim's
12. All Alone
13. Poor Butterfly
14. Dirty Hands, Dirty Face
15. Traumeri
16. It Ain't Necessarily So
17. Waterboy
18. The One I Love Belongs to Somebody Else

Stageography

Shubert's Winter Garden Shows

1911   La Belle Paree
1911   Vera Violetta
1912   The Whirl of Society
1913   The Honeymoon Express
1914   Dancing Around
1916   Robinson Crusoe, Jr.
1918   Sinbad
1921   Bombo
1925   Big Boy
1931   Wonderbar
1940   Hold On to Your Hats

Screenography

1927   The Jazz Singer—The First Talkie
1928   The Singing Fool
1929   Mammy
1929   Say It with Songs
1930   Big Boy
1933   Hallelujah, I'm a Bum
1935   Wonderbar
1935   Go into Your Dance (Cafe De Paree)
1936   The Singing Kid
1939   Rose of Washington Square/Swanee River
1946   The Jolson Story (Impersonated by Larry Parks—Soundtrack
            of Jolson singing)
1948   Jolson Sings Again (Impersonated by Larry Parks—Soundtrack
            of Jolson singing)

Radiography

NBC Radio Shows

APPEAL for Mississippi Valley flood victims, broadcast from Memphis,
    Tenn., April 30, 1927.

DODGE VICTORY HOUR—Jan. 4, 1928; Jolson sings four songs.

PURE OIL BAND—Jan. 4.

AL JOLSON SHOW—Nov. 18, 1932 to Feb. 24, 1933; fifteen half-hour shows, sponsored by Chevrolet.

KRAFT MUSIC HALL—Originated by Jolson, June 26, 1933; he starred in twelve one-hour shows from Aug. 3 to Oct. 19, 1933; twelve one-hour shows from Feb. 8 to April 26, 1934; six one-hour shows from July 12 to Aug. 16, 1934.

SHELL CHATEAU starring Al Jolson—twenty-six one-hour shows from April 6 to Sept. 28, 1935; thirteen one-hour shows from Jan. 4 to March 28, 1936.

NBC HOLLYWOOD STUDIO OPENING—starring Jolson as master of ceremonies, one-hour show, Dec. 7, 1935.

SCREEN ACTORS GUILD BROADCAST—from the Hollywood Bowl, June 26, 1939.

LOOKING THEM OVER AT THE BELMONT RACE TRACK—interviewed, May 16, 1941.

STAR SPANGLED THEATRE—title role in "Uncle Tom's Cabin," Aug. 10, 1941.

DESOTO HANDICAP FROM TROPICAL RACE TRACK—interviewed, March 28, 1942.

HORSE RACE FROM PIMLICO, MARYLAND—interviewed, May 9, 1942.

MELROSE TRACK MEET AT MADISON SQUARE GARDEN—interviewed, Feb. 6, 1943.

YOUR ALL-TIME HIT PARADE—guest star, July 23, 1944.

KRAFT MUSIC HALL—second series starring Al Jolson: thirty-six half-hour shows from Oct. 2, 1947 to June 10, 1948; thirty-five half-hour shows from Sept. 30, 1948 to May 26, 1949, with the exception of March 31, when preempted by speech by Winston Churchill.

GUEST APPEARANCES:

Eddie Cantor shows: June 4, 1941; March 6, 1947; Jan. 8 and June 8, 1948; Jan. 7, 1949.

Burns and Allen shows: Nov. 1, 1937; Feb. 20, 1947; Feb. 1 and March 29, 1950.

Bergen and McCarthy shows: Aug. 16, 1942; Jan. 25, 1948; Jan. 15, 1950.

Jack Benny show: May 18, 1947.

Jimmy Durante shows: Jan. 21, 1948; March 4 and Nov. 11, 1949.

Bing Crosby shows: Jan. 15, March 5, April 2, May 7, and Dec. 3, 1947; Nov. 29 and Dec. 28, 1949; Jan. 4, Feb. 15, and May 3, 1950.

Tex and Jinx Falkenberg shows: June 22 and Nov. 20, 1946; Dec. 31, 1947; Aug. 14, 1950.

Colgate Sports Newsreel: Feb. 13, 1943; Jan. 7 and Oct. 14, 1949.
Amos and Andy: Dec. 17, 1946.
Bob Hope show: April 8, 1947.
This Is Your Life: Surprise guest appearance, Nov. 23, 1948.
Elgin Two Hours of Stars: Dec. 25, 1948.
Opportunity U.S. Savings Bond Program: May 16, 1949.
Confidential Closeups: Nov. 12, 1949.

CBS Radio Shows

WARNER BROTHERS VITAPHONE HOUR—starring Jolson, March 4, 1929.
APPEAL FOR JEWISH CONSUMPTIVE HOME, Monrovia, California—
    March 18, 1934.
LOUELLA PARSONS SHOW, HOLLYWOOD HOTEL—Jolson and Ruby
    Keeler, guest stars, Nov. 23, 1934; Jolson, guest star, June 11,
    1937.
LUX RADIO THEATER—
    Burlesque, June 15, 1936, co-starring Ruby Keeler.
    The Jazz Singer, Aug. 10, 1936.
    Swanee River, April 2, 1945.
    Alexander's Ragtime Band, April 7, 1947.
    The Jazz Singer, June 2, 1947.
    The Jolson Story, Feb. 16, 1948.
    Jolson Sings Again, May 22, 1950.
LIFEBUOY AND RINSO SHOWS, sometimes called CAFE TROCADERO.
    First Season: twenty-eight half-hour shows, Dec. 22, 1936 to June 29,
        1937, also featuring Martha Raye and Parkyakarkus.
    Second Season: forty-five half-hour shows, Sept. 7, 1937 to July 12,
        1938.
    Third Season: twenty-six half-hour shows, Sept. 20, 1938 to March
        14, 1939.
    Fourth Season: thirteen half-hour shows, Sept. 19 to Dec. 12, 1939.
GEORGE GERSHWIN MEMORIAL CONCERT AT HOLLYWOOD BOWL—
    guest star, Sept. 8, 1937.
AMERICAN CAN COMPANY SPECIAL—master of ceremonies, Sept. 14,
    1937.
ALEXANDER'S RAGTIME BAND—guest on special tribute to Irving Berlin,
    Aug. 3, 1938.
SPECIAL APPEAL FOR THE MARCH OF DIMES—guest, Jan. 22, 1939.

KATE SMITH SHOW—guest, Dec. 29, 1939.

STAGE DOOR CANTEEN—Jolson was special guest star and sang ten
    songs, Dec. 24, 1942.

AL JOLSON RADIO SHOW, sponsored by Colgate, thirty-nine one-hour
    shows, Oct. 6, 1942 to June 29, 1943.

ORANGE BOWL FOOTBALL GAME—interviewed at half-time, Jan. 1,
    1943.

REPORT TO THE NATION—war bond appeal, Oct. 5, 1943.

SPECIAL USO CHRISTMAS SHOW—guest, Dec. 25, 1943.

NIGHT CLUBS FOR VICTORY—guest star, Jan. 20, 1944.

LET YOURSELF GO—guest star, June 6, 1945.

OPERATION NIGHTMARE—star, June 9, 1947.

JOAN DAVIES SHOW—guest, May 6, 1949.

JIMMY DURANTE SHOW—guest star, Nov. 11, 1949.

BERGEN AND MCCARTHY SHOW—guest star, Jan. 15, 1950.

BURNS AND ALLEN SHOW—guest star, March 29, 1950.

JACK BENNY SHOW—guest star, April 2, 1950.

BING CROSBY SHOW—last guest appearance, May 3, 1950.

LOUELLA PARSONS SHOW—special shortwave broadcast from Korea,
    Sept. 15, 1950.

BING CROSBY SHOW—Jolson was to have been a guest star on Bing's
    show on Oct. 24, 1950, but died suddenly Oct. 23.